Contents

Crispy chilli turkey noodles ....
Orzo & tomato soup 16
Pasta arrabbiata with aubergine 17
Two-minute breakfast smoothie 18
Tomato & spinach kitchari 19
Slow-cooker chicken casserole 20
Veggie yaki udon 21
Bombay potato frittata 21
Healthy pancakes 23
Low-fat roasties 23
Smoky spiced veggie rice 24
Mango sorbet 25
Vegan shepherd's pie 26
Red pepper, squash & harissa soup 28
Cabbage soup 28
Roasted roots & sage soup 29
Artichoke & aubergine rice 30
Hearty lentil one pot 31
Spiced carrot & lentil soup 32
Chana masala with pomegranate raita 33
Prosciutto, kale & butter bean stew 34
Leek, pea & watercress soup 34
Easy slow cooker chicken casserole 35
Spiced chicken, spinach & sweet potato stew 36
Chilli chicken wraps 37
Pistachio nut & spiced apple Bircher muesli 38

Broccoli pasta shells 39

Chocolate sponge with hot chocolate custard 39

Asparagus & lemon spaghetti with peas 41

Mustardy greens 41

Courgette, leek & goat's cheese soup 42

Salmon salad with sesame dressing 43

Mediterranean potato salad 44

Potato, pea & egg curry rotis 44

Easy chicken casserole 45

Warm roasted squash and Puy lentil salad 46

Tuna sweetcorn burgers 46

♣ Chicken & leek pies 47

Mushroom, spinach & potato pie 48

Harissa chicken with chickpea salad 49

Spicy vegetable chapati wraps 50

Spicy turkey & pepper bake 50

Crab & sweetcorn chowder 51

Fruitburst muffins 52

♦ Thai turkey stir-fry 53

Spicy prawn noodle salad 53

Avocado, labneh, roasted carrots & leaves 54

Lighter apple & pear pie 55

♦ Haddock & spinach cheese melt 56

Spiced cod with quinoa salad & mint chutney 57

Smashed chicken with corn slaw 58

Fruity sponge cake 59

Hearty mushroom soup 60

Poached apricots with rosewater 61

Pan-fried rib-eye steak 61
- **Moroccan-style chicken stew** **62**
- Leek, tomato & barley risotto with pan-cooked cod 63
Green minestrone with tortellini 63
- Lighter moussaka with crunchy feta & oregano 64
Easy vegan pho 65
Vegetable fried rice 66
Tomato & rice soup 67
Seared beef salad with capers & mint 67
Minty griddled chicken & peach salad 69
Artichoke, red onion & rosemary risotto 70
- Easy tomato pizzas 71
Indian winter soup 72
- Quick banana ice cream 73
- Curried turkey lettuce wraps 73
Fruity coconut creams 74
Mushroom & potato soup 74
- Sticky pork 75
- Veggie okonomiyaki 76
Thai spiced turkey patties with noodle salad 77
Prawn chow mein 78
Thai fried prawn & pineapple rice 78
Feta & clementine lunch bowl 79
Mushroom brunch 80
Tuna, avocado & quinoa salad 81
Creamy linguine with ham, lemon & basil 81
Steamed bass with pak choi 82
- Sausage & butternut squash shells 83

- Rhubarb & strawberry meringue pots 84
- Miso mushroom & tofu noodle soup 85
- Mexican egg roll 85
- Puy lentils with spinach & sour cherries 86
- Tuna sweet potato jackets 87
- New potato & tamarind salad 87
- Sesame salmon, purple sprouting broccoli & sweet potato mash 88
- Creamy smoked salmon, leek & potato soup 89
- Open leek & sweet potato pie 90
- Apple & sultana porridge 91
- Chipotle chicken tacos with pineapple salsa 91
- Peach crumble 92
- Coriander cod with carrot pilaf 93
- Ginger & lime chicken with sweet potato mash 94
- Easy lentil curry 94
- Curried aubergine & potato pie 95
- Spinach & barley risotto 96
- Braised baby leeks 97
- Turkey & avocado toast 98
- Herb & garlic baked cod with romesco sauce & spinach 98
- Chicken with crispy Parma ham 99
- Five-spice beef & sugar snap noodles 100
- Lemony salmon & lettuce wraps 101
- Chicken & avocado sandwich topper 101
- Raspberry chia jam 102
- Thai-style fish broth with greens 102
- Pepper & lemon spaghetti with basil & pine nuts 103
- Pasta with tuna & tomato sauce 104

Oaty fish & prawn gratins 105

- Skinny chicken Caesar salad 106

Chocolate chia pudding 106

Leek, mushroom & goat's cheese strudels 107

Cabbage with caraway 108

Lime prawn cocktail pitta salad 108

- Ham, mushroom & spinach frittata 109

Crunchy detox salad 110

- Peach Melba smoothie 110

- Ham hock & cabbage hash 111

- Chicken & mushroom pancake topping 112

- Crisp chicken burgers with lemon mayo 112

- Courgette lasagne 113

Pea & feta pearl barley stew 114

Veggie olive wraps with mustard vinaigrette 115

Cucumber, pea & lettuce soup 116

Mexican rice & bean salad 116

Thin-stemmed broccoli with hoisin sauce & fried shallots 117

Rich paprika seafood bowl 118

One-pan prawn & tomato curry 118

Easy Thai beef salad 119

Penne with broccoli, lemon & anchovies 120

Walnut & almond muesli with grated apple 121

Lemony prawn pasta 121

Minced beef cobbler 122

- Tasty cottage pie with parsnip mash 123

Turkey & spring onion wraps 124

Lighter chicken tacos 124

Chicken & broccoli potato-topped pie 126

Chinese chicken noodle soup with peanut sauce 128

Crab & lemon spaghetti with peas 129

Apple pie samosas 129

Banana pancakes 130

Green eggs 131

Roast pork with couscous & ginger yogurt 132

Lamb & squash biryani with cucumber raita 132

Roasted red pepper & tomato soup with ricotta 133

Creamy yogurt porridge 134

Noodles with turkey, green beans & hoisin 135

Ginger & soy sea bass parcels 136

Vegetarian bean pot with herby breadcrumbs 137

Savoy cabbage with shallots & fennel seeds 138

Healthy salad Niçoise 138

Mumbai potato wraps with minted yogurt relish 139

Banana & cinnamon pancakes with blueberry compote 140

15-minute chicken pasta 141

Easy turkey paella 142

Teriyaki prawns & broccoli noodles 142

Spicy mince & lettuce cups 143

Black-eyed bean mole with salsa 144

Avocado hummus & crudités 145

Breakfast super-shake 145

Avocado & strawberry ices 146

Salmon pasta salad with lemon & capers 146

Thai shredded chicken & runner bean salad 147

Squash & chorizo stew 148

Miso steak	149
Beef bulgogi stir-fry	149
Beetroot & butternut stew	150
Thai cucumber slaw	151
● BBQ salad pizza	152
Courgetti bolognese	153
Lighter aubergine Parmigiana	154
Yogurt parfaits with crushed strawberries & amaretti	155
Slow-cooker ham with sticky ginger glaze	156
Wild salmon with coconut chutney & green pilau	157
Bean, ham & egg salad	158
Lemony mushroom pilaf	158
● Ultimate toad-in-the-hole with caramelised onion gravy	159
Turkey burgers with beetroot relish	161
Berry bake with passion fruit drizzle	162
Prawn & pak choi stir-fry	162
Mushroom & chickpea burgers	163
Asian pulled chicken salad	164
Curtido	165
Goat's cheese, tomato & olive triangles	165
Pork & rosemary lasagne	166
Turkey & coriander burgers with guacamole	167
Curried spinach, eggs & chickpeas	168
Spicy chickpeas	169
Sweet potato falafels with coleslaw	169
Zesty haddock with crushed potatoes & peas	170
Wild salmon veggie bowl	171
Linguine with avocado, tomato & lime	172

Stuffed cherry peppers	172
Garden veg pasta	173
White fish with spicy beans and chorizo	173
Salmon noodle soup	174
• Swedish meatballs	175
Speedy red pepper chana masala	176
• Individual summer puddings	177
Creamy seafood stew	178
Steamed trout with mint & dill dressing	179
Poached beef & noodles (Gyudon)	180
Rice noodle & turkey salad with lime-chilli dressing	180
Egg & soldiers	181
Hearty lamb & barley soup	182
Haddock & leek au gratin with sweetcorn mash	183
Lemon chicken with fruity olive couscous	183
Moroccan pomegranate & roast veg salad	184
Steamed fish with ginger & spring onion	185
Italian borlotti bean, pumpkin & farro soup	186
• Strawberry cheesecakes	187
Spiced chickpea soup	187
Moroccan roast lamb with roasted roots & coriander	188
Asparagus & new potato frittata	189
Cashew curry	190
Veggie kofta pittas with pick & mix sides	191
Little spicy veggie pies	193
• Best Yorkshire puddings	194
Coleslaw with tahini yogurt dressing	195
Harissa-crumbed fish with lentils & peppers	195

Turkey minestrone	196
Hake & seafood cataplana	197
Lamb with buckwheat noodles & tomato dressing	198
Paneer jalfrezi with cumin rice	199
• Spicy tuna & cottage cheese jacket	200
• Tomato, onion & cucumber raita	200
Low 'n' slow rib steak with Cuban mojo salsa	201
Herbed pork fillet with roast vegetables	202
Charred broccoli, lemon & walnut pasta	203
==Chicken, chickpea & lemon casserole==	204
Chicken gumbo	205
Smoky chickpeas on toast	205
Frazzled chorizo & rocket linguine	206
Pasta with chilli tomatoes & spinach	207
Prawn sweet chilli noodle salad	208
Pickled red onion & radish	208
• Baked asparagus risotto	209
Creamy chicken & asparagus braise	210
Prawn jambalaya	210
Asparagus & broad bean lasagne	211
• Mediterranean turkey-stuffed peppers	212
Super-quick sesame ramen	213
Ginger, sesame and chilli prawn & broccoli stir-fry	214
• Slow cooker shepherd's pie	215
Vietnamese chicken noodle soup	216
Cod with cucumber, avocado & mango salsa salad	217
Easy soup maker lentil soup	218
Singapore noodles with prawns	218

Ginger chicken & green bean noodles 219
Spicy meatballs with chilli black beans 220
Golden goose fat potatoes & parsnips 221
Soup maker tomato soup 222
Slow cooker lasagne 223
Turkey meatloaf 224
All-in-one chicken with wilted spinach 225
Green chowder with prawns 226
Easy chicken stew 226
Healthy bolognese 227
Fennel spaghetti 228
Carrot & ginger soup 229
Thai prawn & ginger noodles 230
Squash & spinach fusilli with pecans 231
Lighter chicken cacciatore 231
Cod puttanesca with spinach & spaghetti 232
Sesame chicken & prawn skewers 233
Charred spring onions & teriyaki tofu 234
Hearty pasta soup 235
Slow cooker mushroom risotto 236
Spicy meatball tagine with bulgur & chickpeas 236
Herb & garlic pork with summer ratatouille 238
Peri-peri chicken pilaf 239
Chicken & sweetcorn soup 240
Yaki udon 241
Basic lentils 242
Baked piri-piri tilapia with crushed potatoes 242
Parma pork with potato salad 243

Red lentil, chickpea & chilli soup 244

Low-sugar lime & basil green juice 245

Rustic vegetable soup 246

Garlicky mushroom penne 247

Miso aubergines 248

Balsamic beef with beetroot & rocket 249

Chicken & pearl barley risotto 250

Low-sugar granola 251

Chunky butternut mulligatawny 251

Creamy leek & bean soup 252

Healthy stuffing balls 253

Raspberry tea ice lollies 254

Moroccan harira 254

Healthy gravy 255

Ham & piccalilli salad 256

Lamb dopiaza with broccoli rice 256

White velvet soup with smoky almonds 258

Vegan bolognese 259

Samosa pie 260

Red pepper & bean tikka masala 261

Spicy chicken & bean stew 261

Lentil & cauliflower curry 262

Mushroom baked eggs with squished tomatoes 263

Crispy cod fingers with wedges & dill slaw 264

Sunshine smoothie 265

Caramelised onion & goat's cheese pizza 265

Beef goulash soup 267

Prawn jalfrezi 268

Vegan chocolate banana ice cream 269

Lighter South Indian fish curry 269

Mexican chicken stew 270

Healthy banana bread 271

Broccoli and kale green soup 272

Easy creamy coleslaw 273

Spicy spaghetti with garlic mushrooms 274

Chakalaka (Soweto chilli) 274

Cheat's chicken ramen 276

Summer carrot, tarragon & white bean soup 276

Curried fishcake bites 277

Singapore chilli crab 278

Lentil fritters 279

Stir-fried pork with ginger & honey 280

Prawn tikka masala 281

Celery soup 282

Beetroot & onion seed soup 282

Lighter spaghetti & meatballs 283

Braised red cabbage 284

Bean & barley soup 285

Curried cod 286

Spice-crusted aubergines & peppers with pilaf 286

Creamy tomato soup 287

Curried lentil, parsnip & apple soup 288

Berry Bircher 289

Spinach & chickpea curry 290

Sweet potato & sprout hash with poached eggs 290

Spiced mushroom & lentil hotpot 291

Mexican bean soup with crispy feta tortillas	292
Rosemary chicken with oven-roasted ratatouille	293
Moroccan chicken with sweet potato mash	294
Butternut & cinnamon oats	294
● Pizza sauce	295
Ultimate veggie burger with pickled carrot slaw	296
Gnocchi with roasted red pepper sauce	297
Speedy Mediterranean gnocchi	298
Creamy tomato, courgette & prawn pasta	298
Spelt & wild mushroom risotto	299
Chickpea & coriander burgers	300
Korean clam broth - Jogaetang	301
Cajun prawn pizza	302
Spicy turkey sweet potatoes	303
● Creamy mashed potatoes	304
● Tomato & thyme cod	304
Peppered pinto beans	305
● Baked fish with tomatoes, basil & crispy crumbs	306
Thai-style steamed fish	306
Meatball & tomato soup	307
Better-than-baked beans with spicy wedges	308
● Ham & potato hash with baked beans & healthy 'fried' eggs	309
Indian butternut squash curry	310
● Curried chicken pie	311
Instant berry banana slush	312
Apple & clementine Bircher	312
Wild garlic & nettle soup	313
Cranberry & raspberry smoothie	314

Indian-spiced shepherd's pie 314
●Sticky lemon chicken 315
Chickpea soup with chunky gremolata 316
✷ ● Bagels for brunch 317
Instant frozen berry yogurt 318
Inside-out chicken Kiev 318
Creamy cod chowder stew 319
Singapore noodles 320
Chipotle chicken & slaw 321
Super-quick fish curry 321
Pitta pocket 322
Jerk cod & creamed corn 322
Ruby cranberry sauce 323
Supergreen soup with yogurt & pine nuts 324
Butternut soup with crispy sage & apple croutons 325
●Healthy carrot soup 326
Chinese-style pork fillet with fried rice 326
Courgette & quinoa-stuffed peppers 327
Carrot biryani 328
Spicy fish stew 329
Crushed pea & mint dip with carrot sticks 330
Prawn & rice noodle stir-fry 330
● Slow cooker spiced apples with barley 331
Breakfast burrito 331
Pea & new potato curry 332
● Low-fat Spanish omelette 333
Low-fat turkey bolognese 334
Low-fat chicken biryani 335

Low-fat moussaka 336

Mushroom stroganoff 337

20-minute seafood pasta 338

● Low-fat cherry cheesecake 339

Chilli prawn linguine 340

Spinach, sweet potato & lentil dhal 342

West Indian spiced aubergine curry 343

● Rice pudding 344

Burnt aubergine veggie chilli 345

Spiced lentil & butternut squash soup 346

Lentil soup 347

Tandoori chicken 347

Mexican penne with avocado 348

Double bean & roasted pepper chilli 349

● Slow-cooker chicken curry 350

Vegetarian bolognese 351

Quinoa chilli with avocado & coriander 352

Crispy chilli turkey noodles

Prep: 5 mins **Cook:** 15 mins

Serves 4

Ingredients

- 2 tbsp sesame oil
- 500g turkey mince
- 5cm piece ginger , grated
- 1 large garlic clove , crushed
- 3 tbsp honey
- 3 tbsp soy sauce
- 1 tbsp hot sriracha chilli sauce
- 350g dried udon noodles
- 2 limes , juiced, plus wedges to serve (optional)
- 2 large carrots , peeled and cut into matchsticks
- 4 spring onions , shredded
- 1 small bunch coriander , sliced (optional)

Method

STEP 1

Heat 1 tbsp oil in a large non-stick frying pan over a high heat. Once hot, add the turkey mince to the pan and fry for 10-12 mins until golden brown and crispy, breaking up the meat with a wooden spoon as you go. Add the ginger and garlic to the pan and cook for 1 min. Stir in the honey, soy and chilli sauce and cook for 2 mins.

STEP 2

Meanwhile, bring a large pan of water to the boil, add the noodles and cook following pack instructions. Drain and toss the noodles with the remaining 1 tbsp oil and all the lime juice, then divide between bowls. Top with the crispy turkey mince, carrot, onion and coriander. Serve with extra lime wedges for squeezing over, if you like.

Orzo & tomato soup

Prep: 5 mins **Cook:** 25 mins

Serves 4

Ingredients

- 2 tbsp olive oil
- 1 onion, chopped
- 2 celery sticks, chopped
- 2 garlic cloves, crushed
- 1 tbsp tomato purée
- 400g can chopped tomatoes
- 400g can chickpeas
- 150g orzo pasta
- 700ml vegetable stock
- 2 tbsp basil pesto
- crusty bread, to serve

Method

STEP 1

Heat 1 tbsp olive oil in a large saucepan. Add the onion and celery and fry for 10-15 mins, or until starting to soften, then add the garlic and cook for 1 min more. Stir in all the other ingredients, except for the pesto and remaining oil, and bring to the boil.

STEP 2

Reduce the heat and leave to simmer for 6-8 mins, or until the orzo is tender. Season to taste, then ladle into bowls.

STEP 3

Stir the remaining oil with the pesto, then drizzle over the soup. Serve with chunks of crusty bread.

Pasta arrabbiata with aubergine

Prep: 8 mins **Cook:** 35 mins

Serves 2

Ingredients

- 1 tbsp cold-pressed rapeseed oil
- 1 large onion , finely chopped (160g)
- 2 large garlic cloves , finely grated
- 1 tsp chilli flakes
- 1 tsp smoked paprika
- 400g can chopped tomatoes
- 1 tsp vegetable bouillon powder
- 1 aubergine , chopped
- 150g wholemeal penne or fusilli
- large handful of basil , plus extra to serve
- 25g parmesan or vegetarian Italian-style hard cheese, finely grated

Method

STEP 1

Heat the oil in a large non-stick pan, add the onions, cover and cook for 5 mins. Remove the lid and cook for 5 mins more, stirring frequently until softened. Add the garlic, chilli flakes and paprika, stir briefly, then tip in the tomatoes and a can of water. Stir in the bouillon and aubergine, then bring to a simmer, cover and cook for 20 mins.

STEP 2

Cook the penne in a pan of boiling water for 12 mins until al dente. Drain, reserving 60ml of the cooking water. Add the cooked penne to the sauce, and toss well with the basil and a little of the reserved water, if needed. Spoon into two shallow bowls, and serve topped with the cheese and some extra basil, if you like.

Two-minute breakfast smoothie

Prep: 2 mins No cook

Serves 2

Ingredients

- 1 banana
- 1 tbsp porridge oats
- 80g soft fruit (whatever you have – strawberries, blueberries, and mango all work well)
- 150ml milk
- 1 tsp honey
- 1 tsp vanilla extract

Method

STEP 1

Put all the ingredients in a blender and whizz for 1 min until smooth.

STEP 2

Pour the banana oat smoothie into two glasses to serve.

Tomato & spinach kitchari

Prep: 10 mins **Cook:** 40 mins

Serves 4

Ingredients

- 130g basmati rice
- 200g split red lentils
- 3 tbsp olive oil
- 1 onion , finely sliced
- 1 thumb-sized piece ginger , finely grated
- 2 garlic cloves , crushed
- 2 tsp turmeric
- 2 tsp ground coriander
- 2 tsp cumin seeds
- 1-2 tsp medium chilli powder
- 1.2l vegetable stock
- 150g cherry tomatoes
- 200g spinach
- 1 red chilli , finely chopped
- chapatis , to serve (optional)

Method

STEP 1

Tip the rice and lentils into a sieve and rinse thoroughly under cold, running water. Set aside.

STEP 2

Heat 1 tbsp of the oil in a large saucepan or casserole. Add the onion along with a pinch of salt and fry over a medium-high heat for 10 mins or until golden. Stir through the ginger, garlic, turmeric, ground coriander, half the cumin seeds and the chilli powder and fry for 1 min. Add the rice and lentils to the pan and pour in the stock, bring to a simmer then cover, turn down and cook for 25 mins, stirring now and then, until the lentils have turned creamy. Add the tomatoes and spinach and cook for 5 mins.

STEP 3

Heat the remaining oil in a small frying pan and add the remaining cumin seeds, cooking for 1 min. Spoon the lentils into four bowls, drizzle over the cumin oil and top with the chilli. Serve with warm chapatis, if you like.

Slow-cooker chicken casserole

Prep: 10 mins **Cook:** 4 hrs and 15 mins - 7 hrs and 15 mins

Serves 2 adults + 2 children

Ingredients

- knob of butter
- ½ tbsp rapeseed or olive oil
- 1 large onion, finely chopped
- 1 ½ tbsp flour
- 650g boneless, skinless chicken thigh fillets
- 3 garlic cloves, crushed
- 400g baby new potatoes, halved
- 2 sticks celery, diced
- 2 carrots, diced
- 250g mushrooms, quartered
- 15g dried porcini mushroom, soaked in 50ml boiling water
- 500ml stock made with 2 very low salt chicken stock cubes (we used Kallo)
- 2 tsp Dijon mustard, plus extra to serve
- 2 bay leaves

Method

STEP 1

Heat a knob of butter and ½ tbsp rapeseed or olive oil in a large frying pan, cook 1 finely chopped large onion for 8-10 mins until softened and starting to caramelise.

STEP 2

Meanwhile, put 1 ½ tbsp flour and a little salt and pepper in a bowl and toss 650g boneless, skinless chicken thigh fillets in it.

STEP 3

Add 3 crushed garlic cloves and the chicken to the pan and cook for 4-5 mins more until the chicken is starting to brown.

STEP 4

Transfer to your slow cooker, along with 400g halved baby new potatoes, 2 diced celery sticks, 2 diced carrots, 250g quartered mushrooms, 15g dried and soaked porcini mushrooms with the 50ml soaking liquid, 500ml chicken stock, 2 tsp Dijon mustard and 2 bay leaves.

STEP 5

Give it a good stir. Cook on Low for 7 hours or High for 4 hours.

STEP 6

Remove the bay leaves and serve with a little Dijon mustard on the side.

Veggie yaki udon

Prep: 10 mins **Cook:** 15 mins

Serves 2

Ingredients

- 1½ tbsp sesame oil
- 1 red onion , cut into thin wedges
- 160g mangetout
- 70g baby corn , halved
- 2 baby pak choi , quartered
- 3 spring onions , sliced
- 1 large garlic clove , crushed
- ½ tbsp mild curry powder
- 4 tsp low-salt soy sauce
- 300g ready-to-cook udon noodles
- 1 tbsp pickled sushi ginger , chopped, plus 2 tbsp of the brine

Method

STEP 1

Heat the oil in a non-stick frying pan or wok over a high heat. Add the onion and fry for 5 mins. Stir in the mangetout, corn, pak choi and spring onions and cook for 5 mins more. Add the garlic, curry powder and soy sauce, and cook for another minute.

STEP 2

Add the udon noodles along with the ginger and reserved brine, and stir in 2-3 tbsp hot water until the noodles are heated through. Divide between bowls and serve.

Bombay potato frittata

Prep: 15 mins **Cook:** 35 mins

Serves 2

Ingredients

- 4 new potatoes, sliced into 5mm rounds
- 100g baby spinach, chopped
- 1 tbsp rapeseed oil
- 1 onion, halved and sliced
- 1 large garlic clove, finely grated
- ½ tsp ground coriander
- ½ tsp ground cumin
- ¼ tsp black mustard seeds
- ¼ tsp turmeric
- 3 tomatoes, roughly chopped
- 2 large eggs
- ½ green chilli, deseeded and finely chopped
- 1 small bunch of coriander, finely chopped
- 1 tbsp mango chutney
- 3 tbsp fat-free Greek yogurt

Method

STEP 1

Cook the potatoes in a pan of boiling water for 6 mins, or until tender. Drain and leave to steam-dry. Meanwhile, put the spinach in a heatproof bowl with 1 tbsp water. Cover and microwave for 3 mins on high, or until wilted.

STEP 2

Heat the rapeseed oil in a medium non-stick frying pan. Add the onion and cook over a medium heat for 10 mins until golden and sticky. Stir in the garlic, ground coriander, ground cumin, mustard seeds and turmeric, and cook for 1 min more. Add the tomatoes and wilted spinach and cook for another 3 mins, then add the potatoes.

STEP 3

Heat the grill to medium. Lightly beat the eggs with the chilli and most of the fresh coriander and pour over the potato mixture. Grill for 4-5 mins, or until golden and just set, with a very slight wobble in the middle.

STEP 4

Leave to cool, then slice into wedges. Mix the mango chutney, yogurt and remaining fresh coriander together. Serve with the frittata wedges.

Healthy pancakes

Prep: 15 mins **Cook:** 30 mins

Makes 10-12

Ingredients

- 50g self-raising flour
- 50g wholemeal or wholegrain flour
- 2 small eggs, separated
- 150ml skimmed milk
- berries and low-fat yogurt or fromage frais to serve

Method

STEP 1

Sift the flours into a bowl or wide jug and tip any bits in the sieve back into the bowl. Add the egg yolks and a splash of milk then stir to a thick paste. Add the remaining milk a little at a time so you don't make lumps in the batter.

STEP 2

Whisk the egg whites until they stand up in stiff peaks, then fold them carefully into the batter – try not to squash out all the air.

STEP 3

Heat a non-stick pan over a medium heat and pour in enough batter to make a pancake about 10 cm across. Cook for just under a minute until bubbles begin to pop on the surface and the edges are looking a little dry. Carefully turn the pancake over. If it is a bit wet on top, it may squirt out a little batter as you do so. In that case, leave it on the other side a little longer. Keep warm while you make the remaining pancakes Serve with your favourite healthy toppings.

Low-fat roasties

Prep: 10 mins **Cook:** 1 hr

Serves 2

Ingredients

- 800g roasting potatoes, quartered
- 1 garlic clove, sliced
- 200ml vegetable stock (from a cube is fine)
- 2 tbsp olive oil

Method

STEP 1

Heat oven to 200C/fan 180C/gas 6. Put the potatoes and garlic in a roasting tin. Pour over the stock, then brush the tops of the potatoes with half the olive oil. Season, then cook for 50 mins. Brush with the remaining oil and cook 10-15 mins more until the stock is absorbed and the potatoes have browned and cooked through.

Smoky spiced veggie rice

Prep: 15 mins **Cook:** 1 hr

Serves 6

Ingredients

- 25g cashews
- 4 tbsp olive oil
- 1 corn cob
- 250g rainbow baby carrots, halved lengthways
- 2 red onions, finely chopped
- 2 celery sticks, finely chopped
- 2 large red peppers, finely sliced
- 3 garlic cloves, crushed
- 2 tbsp Cajun seasoning
- 1½ tbsp smoked paprika
- 1 tsp chipotle paste
- 2 tbsp tomato purée
- 200g heirloom cherry tomatoes, halved
- 400g can kidney beans, drained and rinsed
- 400g can cherry tomatoes
- 300g long-grain rice, washed
- 400ml vegetable or vegan stock
- 1 tbsp red wine vinegar (vegan varieties are readily available)
- 2 tbsp caster sugar
- 2 spring onions, finely sliced

Method

STEP 1

Dry-fry the cashews in a large saucepan or casserole dish over a medium heat until golden brown. Remove from the heat, leave to cool, then roughly chop. Heat 1 tbsp oil in the same pan over a high heat, then fry the corn on each side for 20 seconds to char. Remove from the pan, set aside, then tip in the carrots and fry for 5 mins. Remove from the pan and set aside.

STEP 2

Heat the rest of the oil in the same pan over a medium heat and fry the onions and celery for 10 mins until soft and slightly coloured. Tip in the peppers and garlic, then fry for another 5 mins before adding the Cajun seasoning, smoked paprika, chipotle paste and tomato purée. Fry for 1 min until the spices are fragrant, then add the cherry tomatoes and fry for another 2 mins.

STEP 3

Stir in the kidney beans, canned tomatoes, rice, stock, vinegar and sugar, then stir until everything is combined. Bring to the boil, then cover with a lid and simmer with a lid on for 35-40 mins on a medium-low heat, stirring halfway through, until the rice is cooked and liquid absorbed.

STEP 4

Slice the corn off the cob and mix it through the rice along with the carrots. Season and garnish with the spring onions and cashews.

Mango sorbet

Prep: 15 mins plus freezing

Serves 8

Ingredients

- 3 large, ripe mangoes
- 200g caster sugar
- 1 lime , juiced

Method

STEP 1

Peel the mangoes with a vegetable peeler, cut as much of the flesh away from the stone as you can, put it in a food processor or blender.

STEP 2

Add the sugar, lime juice and 200ml water. Blend for a few minutes, until the mango is very smooth and the sugar has dissolved – rub a little of the mixture between your fingers, if it still feels gritty, blend for a little longer. Pour into a container and put in the freezer for a few hours.

STEP 3

Scrape the sorbet back into the blender (if it's very solid, leave at room temperature for 5-10 mins first). Whizz until you have a slushy mixture, then pour back into the tin and freeze for another hour or so.

STEP 4

Repeat step 3. Freeze until solid (another hour or two). Will keep covered in the freezer for three months.

Vegan shepherd's pie

Prep: 30 mins **Cook:** 1 hr and 20 mins

Serves 8 (makes eight individual or two large pies)

Ingredients

- 1.2kg floury potatoes, such as Maris Piper or King Edward
- 50ml vegetable oil
- 30g dried porcini mushrooms, soaked in hot water for 15 mins, then drained (reserve the liquid)
- 2 large leeks, chopped
- 2 small onions, chopped
- 4 medium carrots (about 300g), cut into small cubes
- 1 vegetable stock cube (make sure it's vegan - we used Kallo)
- 3 garlic cloves, crushed
- 2 tbsp tomato purée
- 2 tsp smoked paprika
- 1 small butternut squash, peeled and cut into small cubes
- ½ small pack marjoram or oregano, leaves picked and roughly chopped
- ½ small pack thyme, leaves picked
- ½ small pack sage, leaves picked and roughly chopped
- 4 celery sticks, chopped
- 400g can chickpeas

- 300g frozen peas
- 300g frozen spinach
- 20ml olive oil
- small pack flat-leaf parsley, chopped
- tomato ketchup, to serve (optional)

Method

STEP 1

Put the unpeeled potatoes in a large saucepan, cover with water, bring to the boil and simmer for 40 mins until the skins start to split. Drain and leave to cool a little.

STEP 2

Meanwhile, heat the vegetable oil in a large heavy-based sauté pan or flameproof casserole dish. Add the mushrooms, leeks, onions, carrots and the stock cube and cook gently for 5 mins, stirring every so often. If it starts to stick, reduce the heat and stir more frequently, scraping the bits from the bottom. The veg should be soft but not mushy.

STEP 3

Add the garlic, tomato purée, paprika, squash and herbs. Stir and turn the heat up a bit, cook for 3 mins, add the celery, then stir and cook for a few more mins.

STEP 4

Tip in the chickpeas along with the water in the can and reserved mushroom stock. Add the peas and spinach and stir well. Cook for 5 mins, stirring occasionally, then season, turn off and set aside. There should still be plenty of liquid and the veg should be bright and a little firm.

STEP 5

Peel the potatoes and discard the skin. Mash 200g with a fork and stir into the veg. Break the rest of the potatoes into chunks, mix with the olive oil and parsley and season.

STEP 6

Divide the filling into the pie dishes and top with the potatotes. Heat oven to 190C/170C fan/gas 5 and bake the pies for 40-45 mins, until the top is golden and the filling is heated through. If making individual pies, check after 20 mins. Best served with tomato ketchup – as all great shepherd's pies are.

Red pepper, squash & harissa soup

Prep: 15 mins **Cook:** 1 hr

Serves 6

Ingredients

- 1 small butternut squash (about 600-700g), peeled and cut into chunks
- 2 red pepper , roughly chopped
- 2 red onion , roughly chopped
- 3 tbsp rapeseed oil
- 3 garlic cloves in their skins
- 1 tbsp ground coriander
- 2 tsp ground cumin
- 1.2l chicken or vegetable stock
- 2 tbsp harissa paste
- 50ml double cream

Method

STEP 1

Heat oven to 180C/160C fan/gas 4. Put all the veg on a large baking tray and toss together with rapeseed oil, garlic cloves in their skins, ground coriander, ground cumin and some seasoning. Roast for 45 mins, moving the veg around in the tray after 30 mins, until soft and starting to caramelise. Squeeze the garlic cloves out of their skins. Tip everything into a large pan. Add the chicken or vegetable stock, harissa paste and double cream. Bring to a simmer and bubble for a few mins. Blitz the soup in a blender, check the seasoning and add more liquid if you need to. Serve swirled with extra cream and harissa.

Cabbage soup

Prep: 20 mins **Cook:** 50 mins

Serves 6

Ingredients

- 2 tbsp olive oil
- 1 large onion , finely chopped
- 2 celery sticks , finely chopped
- 1 large carrot , finely chopped
- 70g smoked pancetta , diced (optional)
- 1 large Savoy cabbage , shredded
- 2 fat garlic cloves , crushed
- 1 heaped tsp sweet smoked paprika
- 1 tbsp finely chopped rosemary
- 1 x 400g can chopped tomatoes

- 1.7l hot vegetable stock
- 1 x 400g can chickpeas , drained and rinsed
- shaved parmesan (or vegetarian alternative), to serve (optional)
- crusty bread , to serve (optional)

Method

STEP 1

Heat the oil in a casserole pot over a low heat. Add the onion, celery and carrot, along with a generous pinch of salt, and fry gently for 15 mins, or until the veg begins to soften. If you're using pancetta, add it to the pan, turn up the heat and fry for a few mins more until turning golden brown. Tip in the cabbage and fry for 5 mins, then stir through the garlic, paprika and rosemary and cook for 1 min more.

STEP 2

Tip the chopped tomatoes and stock into the pan. Bring to a simmer, then cook, uncovered, for 30 mins, adding the chickpeas for the final 10 mins. Season generously with salt and black pepper.

STEP 3

Ladle the soup into six deep bowls. Serve with the shaved parmesan and crusty bread, if you like.

Roasted roots & sage soup

Prep: 15 mins **Cook:** 45 mins

Serves 2

Ingredients

- 1 parsnip , peeled and chopped
- 2 carrots , peeled and chopped
- 300g turnip , swede or celeriac, chopped
- 4 garlic cloves , skin left on
- 1 tbsp rapeseed oil , plus ½ tsp
- 1 tsp maple syrup
- ¼ small bunch of sage , leaves picked, 4 whole, the rest finely chopped
- 750ml vegetable stock
- grating of nutmeg
- 1½ tbsp fat-free yogurt

Method

STEP 1

Heat the oven to 200C/180C fan/gas 6. Toss the root vegetables and garlic with 1 tbsp oil and season. Tip onto a baking tray and roast for 30 mins until tender. Toss with the maple syrup and the chopped sage, then roast for another 10 mins until golden and glazed. Brush the whole sage leaves with ½ tsp oil and add to the baking tray in the last 3-4 mins to crisp up, then remove and set aside.

STEP 2

Scrape the vegetables into a pan, squeeze the garlic out of the skins, discarding the papery shells, and add with the stock, then blend with a stick blender until very smooth and creamy. Bring to a simmer and season with salt, pepper and nutmeg.

STEP 3

Divide between bowls. Serve with a swirl of yogurt and the crispy sage leaves.

Artichoke & aubergine rice

Prep: 15 mins **Cook:** 50 mins

Serves 6

Ingredients

- 60ml olive oil
- 2 aubergines , cut into chunks
- 1 large onion , finely chopped
- 2 garlic cloves , crushed
- small pack parsley , leaves picked, stalks finely chopped
- 2 tsp smoked paprika
- 2 tsp turmeric
- 400g paella rice
- 1 ½l Kallo vegetable stock
- 2 x 175g packs chargrilled artichokes
- 2 lemons 1 juiced, 1 cut into wedges to serve

Method

STEP 1

Heat 2 tbsp of the oil in a large non-stick frying pan or paella pan. Fry the aubergines until nicely coloured on all sides (add another tbsp of oil if the aubergine begins catching too much), then remove and set aside. Add another tbsp of oil to the pan and lightly fry the onion for 2-3 mins or until softened. Add the garlic and parsley stalks, cook for a few mins more, then stir in the spices and rice until everything is well coated. Heat for 2 mins, add half the stock and cook, uncovered, over a medium heat for 20 mins, stirring occasionally to prevent it from sticking.

STEP 2

Nestle the aubergine and artichokes into the mixture, pour over the rest of the stock and cook for 20 mins more or until the rice is cooked through. Chop the parsley leaves, stir through with the lemon juice and season well. Bring the whole pan to the table and spoon into bowls, with the lemon wedges on the side.

Hearty lentil one pot

Prep: 10 mins **Cook:** 1 hr

Serves 4

Ingredients

- 40g dried porcini mushrooms, roughly chopped
- 200g dried brown lentils
- 1 ½ tbsp chopped rosemary
- 3 tbsp rapeseed oil
- 2 large onions, roughly chopped
- 150g chestnut baby button mushrooms
- 4 garlic cloves, finely grated
- 2 tbsp vegetable bouillon powder
- 2 large carrots (350g), cut into chunks
- 3 celery sticks (165g), chopped
- 500g potatoes, cut into chunks
- 200g cavolo nero, shredded

Method

STEP 1

Cover the mushrooms in boiling water and leave to soak for 10 mins. Boil the lentils in a pan with plenty of water for 10 mins. Drain and rinse, then tip into a pan with the dried mushrooms and soaking water (don't add the last bit of the liquid as it can contain some grit), rosemary and 2 litres water. Season, cover and simmer for 20 mins.

STEP 2

Meanwhile, heat the oil in a large pan and fry the onions for 5 mins. Stir in the fresh mushrooms and garlic and fry for 5 mins more. Stir in the lentil mixture and bouillon powder, then add the carrots, celery and potatoes. Cover and cook for 20 mins, stirring often, until the veg and lentils are tender, topping up the water level if needed.

STEP 3

Remove any tough stalks from the cavolo nero, then add to the pan and cover and cook for 5 mins more. If you're following our Healthy Diet Plan, serve half in bowls, then chill the rest to eat another day. Will keep in the fridge for two to three days. Reheat in a pan until hot.

Spiced carrot & lentil soup

Prep: 10 mins **Cook:** 15 mins

Serves 4

Ingredients

- 2 tsp cumin seeds
- pinch chilli flakes
- 2 tbsp olive oil
- 600g carrots, washed and coarsely grated (no need to peel)
- 140g split red lentils
- 1l hot vegetable stock (from a cube is fine)
- 125ml milk (to make it dairy-free, see 'try' below)
- plain yogurt and naan bread, to serve

Method

STEP 1

Heat a large saucepan and dry-fry 2 tsp cumin seeds and a pinch of chilli flakes for 1 min, or until they start to jump around the pan and release their aromas.

STEP 2

Scoop out about half with a spoon and set aside. Add 2 tbsp olive oil, 600g coarsely grated carrots, 140g split red lentils, 1l hot vegetable stock and 125ml milk to the pan and bring to the boil.

STEP 3

Simmer for 15 mins until the lentils have swollen and softened.

STEP 4

Whizz the soup with a stick blender or in a food processor until smooth (or leave it chunky if you prefer).

STEP 5

Season to taste and finish with a dollop of plain yogurt and a sprinkling of the reserved toasted spices. Serve with warmed naan breads.

Chana masala with pomegranate raita

Prep: 10 mins **Cook:** 35 mins

Serves 2

Ingredients

- 1 tbsp rapeseed oil
- 2 onions , halved and thinly sliced
- 1 tbsp chopped ginger
- 2 large garlic cloves , finely grated or crushed
- 1 green chilli , halved, deseeded and thinly sliced
- ½ tsp cumin seeds
- ½ tsp mustard seeds
- ½ tsp garam masala
- ½ tsp turmeric
- 1 tsp ground coriander
- 400g can chickpeas , undrained
- 4 small tomatoes (about 160g), cut into wedges
- 2 tsp vegetable bouillon powder
- cooked wholegrain rice , to serve (optional)

For the pomegranate raita

- 150ml plain bio yogurt
- 25g pomegranate seeds
- 2 tbsp finely chopped coriander , plus extra leaves to serve

Method

STEP 1

Heat the oil in a large non-stick pan, then cook the onions, ginger, garlic and chilli for 15-20 mins.

STEP 2

Add the spices, chickpeas, the liquid from the can, ¾ can cold water, the tomatoes and bouillon. Cover and simmer for 10 mins.

STEP 3

Meanwhile, mix the ingredients for the raita in a small bowl, reserving a few coriander leaves. Roughly mash some of the curry to thicken it. Spoon into bowls with rice, if you like. Scatter over the reserved coriander and serve with the raita on the side.

Prosciutto, kale & butter bean stew

Prep: 5 mins **Cook:** 20 mins

Serves 4

Ingredients

- 80g pack prosciutto , torn into pieces
- 2 tbsp olive oil
- 1 fennel bulb , sliced
- 2 garlic clove , crushed
- 1 tsp chilli flakes
- 4 thyme sprigs
- 150ml white wine or chicken stock
- 2 x 400g cans butter beans
- 400g can cherry tomatoes
- 200g bag sliced kale

Method

STEP 1

Fry the prosciutto in a dry saucepan over a high heat until crisp, then remove half with a slotted spoon and set aside. Turn the heat down to low, pour in the oil and tip in the fennel with a pinch of salt. Cook for 5 mins until softened, then throw in the garlic, chilli flakes and thyme and cook for a further 2 mins, then pour in the wine or stock and bring to a simmer.

STEP 2

Tip both cans of butter beans into the stew, along with their liquid, then add the tomatoes, season well and bring everything to a simmer. Cook, undisturbed, for 5 mins, then stir through the kale. Once wilted, ladle the stew into bowls, removing the thyme sprigs and topping each portion with the remaining prosciutto.

Leek, pea & watercress soup

Prep: 10 mins **Cook:** 22 mins

Serves 4

Ingredients

- 1 tbsp olive oil , plus a drizzle to serve
- 2 leeks , finely sliced
- 4 small garlic cloves , crushed
- 650-800ml hot veg stock
- 80g watercress
- 400g frozen peas
- 1 small lemon , zested and juiced
- small bunch of parsley , finely chopped
- dairy-free crème fraîche and crusty bread, to serve (optional)

Method

STEP 1

Heat the oil in a large saucepan over a medium heat. Add the leeks and garlic and fry for 7-10 mins or until softened and translucent.

STEP 2

Pour in the hot stock and simmer for 5-10 mins. Stir through the watercress, reserving a few leaves for garnish, then the peas, and cook for 5 mins until wilted. Use a hand blender or processor and whizz until smooth. Stir through the lemon juice and zest, then season to taste. Stir through half the parsley. Ladle into bowls and top with the remaining parsley, reserved watercress and a drizzle of olive oil. Swirl through some crème fraîche, then serve with crusty bread, if you like.

Easy slow cooker chicken casserole

Prep: 10 mins **Cook:** 4 hrs - 8 hrs

Serves 4

Ingredients

- 1 leek, roughly chopped
- 1 carrot, roughly chopped
- 1 onion, roughly chopped
- 350g new potatoes, roughly chopped
- 6 skinless, boneless chicken thighs, chopped
- 500ml chicken stock
- 4 tbsp vegetable gravy granules

Method

STEP 1

Put the veg and chicken in a slow cooker. Pour the stock over and around the chicken thighs, then mix in the gravy granules to thicken it up (the sauce will be quite thick – use less gravy if you prefer a runnier casserole).

he slow cooker to low and leave to cook for at least 4 hrs, or up to 8 hrs – try putting ore you go to work, so that it's ready when you get home. Season well, then serve.

Spiced chicken, spinach & sweet potato stew

Prep: 15 mins **Cook:** 40 mins

Serves 4

Ingredients

- 3 sweet potatoes, cut into chunks
- 190g bag spinach
- 1 tbsp sunflower oil
- 8 chicken thighs, skinless and boneless
- 500ml chicken stock
- For the spice paste
- 2 onions, chopped
- 1 red chilli, chopped
- 1 tsp paprika
- thumb-sized piece ginger, grated
- 400g can tomatoes
- 2 preserved lemons, deseeded and chopped

To serve

- pumpkin seeds, toasted
- 2-3 preserved lemons, deseeded and chopped
- 4 naan bread, warmed

Method

STEP 1

Put the sweet potato in a large, deep saucepan over a high heat. Cover with boiling water and boil for 10 mins. Meanwhile, put all the paste ingredients in a food processor and blend until very finely chopped. Set aside until needed.

STEP 2

Put the spinach in a large colander in the sink and pour the sweet potatoes and their cooking water over it to drain the potatoes and wilt the spinach at the same time. Leave to steam-dry.

STEP 3

Return the saucepan to the heat (no need to wash it first), then add the oil, followed by the spice paste. Fry the paste for about 5 mins until thickened, then add the chicken. Fry for 8-10 mins until the chicken starts to colour. Pour over the stock, bring to the boil and leave to simmer for 10 mins, stirring occasionally.

STEP 4

Check the chicken is cooked by cutting into one of the thighs and making sure it's white throughout with no signs of pink. Season with black pepper, then add the sweet potato. Leave to simmer for a further 5 mins. Meanwhile, roughly chop the spinach and add to the stew. At this point you can leave the stew to cool and freeze for up to 3 months, if you like.

STEP 5

Scatter over the pumpkin seeds and preserved lemons, and serve with warm naan bread on the side.

Chilli chicken wraps

Prep: 10 mins **Cook:** 25 mins

Serves 4

Ingredients

- 2 tbsp vegetable oil
- 6 boneless, skinless chicken thighs, cut into bite-sized pieces
- 1 large onion, thinly sliced into half-moons
- 2 garlic cloves, finely chopped
- 3cm piece ginger, peeled and finely chopped
- ½ tsp ground cumin
- ½ tsp garam masala
- 1 tbsp tomato purée
- 1 red chilli, thinly sliced into rings
- juice ½ lemon
- 4 rotis, warmed
- ½ small red onion, chopped
- 4 tbsp mango chutney or lime pickle
- 4 handfuls mint or coriander
- 4 tbsp yogurt

Method

STEP 1

Heat the oil in a large frying pan over a medium heat. Add the chicken, brown on all sides, then remove. Add the onion, garlic, ginger and a pinch of salt. Cook for 5 mins or until softened.

STEP 2

Increase the heat to high. Return the chicken to the pan with the spices, tomato purée, chilli and lemon juice. Season well and cook for 10 mins or until the chicken is tender.

STEP 3

Divide the chicken, red onion, chutney, herbs and yogurt between the four warm rotis. Roll up and serve with plenty of napkins

Pistachio nut & spiced apple Bircher muesli

Prep: 10 mins plus overnight soaking, no cook

Serves 2

Ingredients

For the base ingredients

- 50g jumbo porridge oat
- 50ml apple juice
- large pinch cinnamon
- large pinch nutmeg
- 1 medium apple , cored and grated
- 2 tbsp low-fat natural yogurt

For the topping

- 25g chopped pistachio
- 3 tbsp pomegranate seeds or mixed berries

Method

STEP 1

Mix all the base ingredients, except the yogurt, with 150ml water and leave to soak for at least 20 mins or overnight, if possible. Once the oats have softened, stir through the yogurt, then divide the mixture between 2 bowls. Sprinkle half of the topping over each bowl and serve.

Broccoli pasta shells

Prep: 5 mins **Cook:** 15 mins

Serves 4

Ingredients

- 1 head of broccoli, chopped into florets
- 1 garlic clove, unpeeled
- 2 tbsp olive oil
- 250g pasta shells
- ½ small pack parsley
- ½ small pack basil
- 30g toasted pine nuts
- ½ lemon, zested and juiced
- 30g parmesan (or vegetarian alternative), plus extra to serve

Method

STEP 1

Heat the oven to 200C/180C fan/gas 6. Toss the broccoli and garlic in 1 tbsp of the olive oil on a roasting tray and roast in the oven for 10-12 mins, until softened.

STEP 2

Tip the pasta shells into a pan of boiling, salted water. Cook according to packet instructions and drain. Tip the parsley, basil, pine nuts, lemon juice and parmesan into a blender. Once the broccoli is done, set aside a few of the smaller pieces. Squeeze the garlic from its skin, add to the blender along with the rest of the broccoli, pulse to a pesto and season well.

STEP 3

Toss the pasta with the pesto. Add the reserved broccoli florets, split between two bowls and top with a little extra parmesan, the lemon zest and a good grinding of black pepper, if you like.

Chocolate sponge with hot chocolate custard

Prep: 30 mins **Cook:** 40 mins plus soaking

Serves 12

Ingredients

- 300g stoned date , chopped
- 6 large eggs , separated
- 350g light muscovado sugar
- 200g wholemeal flour
- 2 tsp baking powder
- 100g cocoa

For the custard

- 5 tbsp custard powder
- 5 tbsp light muscovado sugar
- 50g cocoa powder
- 1.2l skimmed milk

Method

STEP 1

Cover the dates with boiling water and set aside to soften for 30 mins.

STEP 2

Heat oven to 160C/140C fan/gas 3 and line a 20 x 30cm baking tin with baking parchment. Drain the dates, reserving the liquid, then whizz the dates to a purée with 100ml of the soaking liquid.

STEP 3

Beat the egg whites in a large bowl with an electric whisk until stiff peaks hold on the end of your whisk. Add half the sugar and beat until thick and glossy.

STEP 4

In another bowl, beat the yolks and remaining sugar until pale. Whisk in the mashed date mixture, then fold into the egg white mixture until well combined. Mix the flour, baking powder and cocoa with a pinch of salt. Sprinkle over the wet mixture and very gently fold in until well combined. Gently scrape into the tin and spread to the edges. Bake for 35-40 mins until a skewer poked in comes out clean.

STEP 5

Meanwhile, mix the custard powder, sugar and cocoa together in a saucepan. Stir in dribbles of milk until you get a smooth paste. Gradually add more milk until it's all incorporated with no lumps. Put over a medium heat and warm, stirring constantly, until thick and just bubbling.

STEP 6

Cut the warm cake into slabs and pour over the hot chocolate custard to serve.

Asparagus & lemon spaghetti with peas

Prep: 7 mins **Cook:** 12 mins

Serves 2

Ingredients

- 150g wholemeal spaghetti
- 160g asparagus, ends trimmed and cut into lengths
- 2 tbsp rapeseed oil
- 2 leeks (220g), cut into lengths, then thin strips
- 1 red chilli, deseeded and finely chopped
- 1 garlic clove, finely grated
- 160g frozen peas
- 1 lemon, zested and juiced, plus wedges to serve

Method

STEP 1

Boil the spaghetti for 12 mins until al dente, adding the asparagus for the last 3 mins. Meanwhile, heat the oil in a large non-stick frying pan, add the leeks and chilli and cook for 5 mins. Stir in the garlic, peas and lemon zest and juice and cook for a few mins more.

STEP 2

Drain and add the pasta to the pan with ¼ mug of the pasta water and toss everything together until well mixed. Spoon into shallow bowls and serve with lemon wedges for squeezing over, if you like.

Mustardy greens

Prep: 10 mins **Cook:** 5 mins

Serves 4

Ingredients

- 300g spring green

- 300g frozen pea
- 25g butter
- 1 tbsp wholegrain mustard
- 2 tbsp Dijon mustard

Method

STEP 1

Heat 250ml water in a large pan. Add the greens and peas, cover with a lid and boil for 4 mins. Drain into a colander, put the pan back on the heat, and add the butter and mustards. When the butter has melted, add the veg back to the pan, season well and toss everything together. Serve straight away.

Courgette, leek & goat's cheese soup

Prep: 8 mins **Cook:** 17 mins

Serves 4

Ingredients

- 1 tbsp rapeseed oil
- 400g leeks, well washed and sliced
- 450g courgettes, sliced
- 3 tsp vegetable bouillon powder, made up to 1 litre with boiling water
- 400g spinach
- 150g tub soft vegetarian goat's cheese
- 15g basil, plus a few leaves to serve
- 8 tsp omega seed mix (see tip)
- 4 x 25g portions wholegrain rye bread

Method

STEP 1

Heat the oil in a large pan and fry the leeks for a few mins to soften. Add the courgettes, then cover the pan and cook for 5 mins more. Pour in the stock, cover and cook for about 7 mins.

STEP 2

Add the spinach, then cover the pan and cook for 5 mins so that it wilts. Take off the heat and blitz until really smooth with a hand blender. Add the goat's cheese and basil, then blitz again.

STEP 3

If you're making this recipe as part of our two-person Summer Healthy Diet Plan, spoon half the soup into two bowls or large flasks, then cool and chill the remainder for another day. Reheat in a pan or microwave to serve. If serving in bowls, scatter with some extra basil leaves and the seeds, and eat with the rye bread.

Salmon salad with sesame dressing

Prep: 7 mins **Cook:** 16 mins

Serves 2

Ingredients

For the salad

- 250g new potatoes, sliced
- 160g French beans, trimmed
- 2 wild salmon fillets
- 80g salad leaves
- 4 small clementines, 3 sliced, 1 juiced
- handful of basil, chopped
- handful of coriander, chopped

For the dressing

- 2 tsp sesame oil
- 2 tsp tamari
- ½ lemon, juiced
- 1 red chilli, deseeded and chopped
- 2 tbsp finely chopped onion (1/4 small onion)

Method

STEP 1

Steam the potatoes and beans in a steamer basket set over a pan of boiling water for 8 mins. Arrange the salmon fillets on top and steam for a further 6-8 mins, or until the salmon flakes easily when tested with a fork.

STEP 2

Meanwhile, mix the dressing ingredients together along with the clementine juice. If eating straightaway, divide the salad leaves between two plates and top with the warm potatoes and beans and the clementine slices. Arrange the salmon fillets on top, scatter over the herbs and spoon over the dressing. If taking to work, prepare the potatoes, beans and salmon the night before, then pack into a rigid airtight container with the salad leaves kept separate. Put the salad elements together and dress just before eating to prevent the leaves from wilting.

Mediterranean potato salad

Prep: 10 mins **Cook:** 25 mins

Serves 4

Ingredients

- 1 tbsp olive oil
- 1 small onion , thinly sliced
- 1 garlic clove , crushed
- 1 tsp oregano , fresh or dried
- ½ x 400g can cherry tomatoes
- 100g roasted red pepper , from a jar, sliced
- 300g new potato , halved if large
- 25g black olive , sliced
- handful basil leaves , torn

Method

STEP 1

Heat the oil in a saucepan, add the onion and cook for 5-10 mins until soft. Add the garlic and oregano and cook for 1 min. Add the tomatoes and peppers, season well and simmer gently for 10 mins.

STEP 2

Meanwhile, cook the potatoes in a pan of boiling salted water for 10-15 mins until tender. Drain well, mix with the sauce and serve warm, sprinkled with olives and basil.

Potato, pea & egg curry rotis

Prep: 5 mins **Cook:** 25 mins

Serves 4

Ingredients

- 1 tbsp oil
- 2 tbsp mild curry paste
- 400g can chopped tomatoes
- 2 potatoes , cut into small chunks
- 200g peas
- 3 eggs , hard-boiled
- pack rotis , warmed through
- 150g tub natural yogurt , to serve

Method

STEP 1

Heat the oil in a saucepan and briefly fry the curry paste. Tip in the tomatoes and half a can of water and bring to a simmer. Add the potatoes and cook for 20 mins, or until the potato is tender. Stir in the peas and cook for 3 mins.

STEP 2

Halve the eggs and place them on top of the curry, then warm everything through. Serve with the rotis and yogurt on the side.

Easy chicken casserole

Prep: 20 mins **Cook:** 1 hr

Serves 4

Ingredients

- 2 tbsp sunflower oil
- 400g boneless, skinless chicken thigh , trimmed and cut into chunks
- 1 onion , finely chopped
- 3 carrots , finely chopped
- 3 celery sticks, finely chopped
- 2 thyme sprigs or ½ tsp dried
- 1 bay leaf , fresh or dried
- 600ml vegetable or chicken stock
- 2 x 400g / 14oz cans haricot beans , drained
- chopped parsley , to serve

Method

STEP 1

Heat the oil in a large pan, add the chicken, then fry until lightly browned. Add the veg, then fry for a few mins more. Stir in the herbs and stock. Bring to the boil. Stir well, reduce the heat, then cover and cook for 40 mins, until the chicken is tender.

STEP 2

Stir the beans into the pan, then simmer for 5 mins. Stir in the parsley and serve with crusty bread.

Warm roasted squash and Puy lentil salad

Prep: 10 mins **Cook:** 30 mins

Serves 4

Ingredients

- 1kg butternut squash, chunkily diced
- 1 ½ tbsp olive oil
- 1 garlic clove, crushed
- 2 tsp thyme leaves
- 1 tbsp balsamic vinegar
- 1 tsp wholegrain mustard
- x cans Puy lentils in water
- ½ red onion sliced
- 100g bag spinach
- 150g cherry tomatoes, halved
- 40g Cheshire cheese
- 1-2 tbsp toasted pumpkin seeds

Method

STEP 1

Heat oven to 200C/180C fan/gas 4. Toss the butternut squash with 1 tbsp olive oil, garlic clove, thyme leaves and seasoning. Roast for 25-30 mins or until tender.

STEP 2

Mix together the balsamic vinegar, ½ tbsp olive oil, the wholegrain mustard and 1-2 tbsp water. Drain the Puy lentils in water and toss with the dressing, red onion, spinach and cherry tomatoes.

STEP 3

Divide the lentils between four plates. Top with the squash, then crumble over Cheshire cheese and pumpkin seeds.

Tuna sweetcorn burgers

Prep: 5 mins **Cook:** 10 mins

Serves 4

Ingredients

- 85g white bread, torn into pieces
- 198g can sweetcorn, drained

- 2 x cans tuna in water, drained well
- 25g grated cheddar
- 3 spring onions, finely chopped
- 1 egg, beaten
- 2 tbsp vegetable oil
- wholegrain bread rolls, lettuce, salsa, to serve

Method

STEP 1

Whizz the bread in a food processor to crumbs, tip into a bowl, then whizz half the sweetcorn until finely chopped. Add the chopped corn, remaining whole corn, tuna, cheese, spring onions and some seasoning into the bowl with the bread and mix well. Add the egg, bit by bit (you may not need it all), until the mixture is sticky enough to be shaped into four even-size burgers.

STEP 2

Heat the oil in a non-stick pan, then cook the burgers for 5 mins on each side until golden and hot through the middle. Stuff into wholemeal buns with your favourite lettuce and a good dollop of salsa.

Chicken & leek pies

Prep: 15 mins **Cook:** 40 mins

Serves 2

Ingredients

- 1 large sweet potato, cut into chunky chips
- 4 tsp olive oil
- 2 chicken breasts, chopped into bite-size chunks
- 1 leek, finely sliced
- 1 carrot, chopped
- 225ml low-sodium chicken stock
- 2 tsp wholegrain mustard
- 85g light soft cheese
- 2 tbsp chopped tarragon leaves
- 2 sheets filo pastry

Method

STEP 1

Heat oven to 200C/180C fan/gas 6. In a roasting tray toss the sweet potatoes with 2 tsp of the oil and some seasoning. Cook for 30-40 mins, until golden and crisp. Heat 1 tsp oil in a medium frying pan. Fry the chicken until browned, remove from the pan and set aside. Add the leek and a splash of water, and gently fry until soft, about 7 mins. Add the carrot and cook for 3 mins more. Pour in the stock and boil until reduced by half, then add the mustard and soft cheese, stirring well to combine. Return the chicken to the pan, add the tarragon and some seasoning.

STEP 2

Divide the mixture between 2 small ovenproof dishes. Take the filo sheets and scrunch them up. Top each pie with a sheet and brush with remaining 1 tsp oil. Cook the pies in the oven with the chips for 15 mins, until the pastry is golden.

Mushroom, spinach & potato pie

Prep: 15 mins **Cook:** 45 mins

Serves 4

Ingredients

- 400g baby spinach
- 1 tbsp olive oil
- 500g mushroom , such as chestnut, shiitake and button
- 2 garlic cloves , crushed
- 250ml vegetable stock (made from half a low sodium vegetable stock cube)
- 300g cooked new potatoes , cut into bite-sized pieces
- 1 tbsp grain mustard
- 1 tsp freshly grated nutmeg
- 2 heaped tbsp light crème fraîche
- 3 sheets filo pastry
- 300g each green beans and broccoli, steamed

Method

STEP 1

Heat oven to 200C/180C fan/gas 6. Wilt spinach in a colander by pouring a kettleful of hot water over it.

STEP 2

Heat half the oil in a large non-stick pan and fry mushrooms on a high heat until golden. Add garlic and cook for 1 min, then tip in stock, mustard, nutmeg and potatoes. Bubble for a few mins until reduced. Season, then remove from the heat; add crème fraîche and spinach. Pour into a pie dish and allow to cool for a few mins.

STEP 3

Brush filo with remaining oil, quarter sheets then loosely scrunch up and lay on top of pie filling. Bake for 20-25 mins until golden. Serve with vegetables.

Harissa chicken with chickpea salad

Prep: 15 mins **Cook:** 8 mins

Serves 2

Ingredients

- 250g punnet cherry tomatoes, halved
- ½ small red onion, chopped
- 400g can chickpeas, drained
- small bunch parsley, roughly chopped
- juice 1 lemon
- 2 skinless chicken breasts, halved lengthways through the middle
- 1 tbsp harissa
- fat-free natural yogurt and wholemeal pitta bread, to serve

Method

STEP 1

Mix the tomatoes, onion and chickpeas together, stir through the parsley and lemon juice and season.

STEP 2

Coat the chicken with the harissa. Heat a griddle or frying pan or barbecue. Cook the chicken for 3-4 mins each side until lightly charred and cooked through.

STEP 3

Divide the salad between 2 plates, top with the harissa chicken and serve with a dollop of yogurt and warmed pitta bread.

Spicy vegetable chapati wraps

Prep: 10 mins **Cook:** 20 mins Ready in 20-30 minutes

Serves 2

Ingredients

- 150g sweet potato , peeled and roughly cubed
- 200g can peeled plum tomatoes
- 200g can chickpeas , drained
- ½ tsp dried chilli flakes
- 1 tbsp mild curry paste
- 50g baby spinach leaves
- 1 tbsp chopped, fresh coriander
- 2 plain chapatis (Indian flatbreads)
- 2 tbsp fat-free Greek or natural yogurt

Method

STEP 1

Cook the sweet potatoes in a pan of boiling water for 10-12 minutes until tender. Meanwhile, put the tomatoes, chickpeas, chilli flakes and curry paste in another pan and simmer gently for about 5 minutes.

STEP 2

Preheat the grill. Drain the sweet potatoes and add to the tomato mixture. Stir in the spinach and cook for a minute until just starting to wilt. Stir in the coriander, season to taste and keep warm.

STEP 3

Sprinkle the chapatis with a little water and grill for 20-30 seconds each side. Spoon on the filling, top with yogurt and fold in half to serve.

Spicy turkey & pepper bake

Prep: 15 mins **Cook:** 45 mins

Serves 4

Ingredients

- 1kg potatoes , chopped
- 25g butter

- 300g frozen pepper
- 1 onion , chopped
- 500g pack turkey mince
- 1 red chilli , deseeded and chopped
- 1 tbsp smoked paprika
- 200ml hot chicken stock

Method

STEP 1

Heat oven to 200C/180C fan/gas 6. Cook the potatoes in a large pan of salted water for 12-15 mins or until tender. Drain well, then return to the pan and allow to steam for 3 mins. Add some seasoning and the butter, then roughly mash with a fork and set aside until later.

STEP 2

Meanwhile, cook the peppers and onion in a large pan for 5 mins – the water in the peppers should stop them sticking. Stir in the turkey mince, chilli and paprika and cook until browned. Pour in the stock, then bubble for 10 mins until thickened. Transfer the turkey mince into an ovenproof dish, top with the mash and cook for 30 mins or until golden and bubbling.

Crab & sweetcorn chowder

Prep: 5 mins **Cook:** 30 mins

Serves 4

Ingredients

- 1 onion , finely chopped
- 1 leek , green and white parts separated and sliced
- 2 carrots , chopped
- 850ml-1 litre/1.5 pints - 1.75 pints low-sodium chicken or vegetable stock
- 1 large potato , diced
- 175g/ 6oz frozen sweetcorn
- 170g can white crabmeat , drained
- 4 tbsp light crème fraîche
- 1 tsp chopped chives

Method

STEP 1

Put the onion, white part of the leek and carrots in a large pan and pour on a few tbsp of the stock. Cook over a medium heat for about 10 mins, stirring regularly until soft. Add a splash more stock if the vegetables start to stick.

STEP 2

Add the potato, green leek and most of the stock, and simmer for 10-15 mins, until the potato is tender. Tip in the sweetcorn and crab meat, then cook for a further 1-2 mins. Remove from the heat and stir in the crème fraîche and some seasoning. Add the rest of the stock if the soup is too thick. Sprinkle with the chives and serve with brown bread, if you like.

Fruitburst muffins

Prep: 20 mins - 25 mins **Cook:** 20 mins - 25 mins Takes 40-50 minutes

12 muffins

Ingredients

- 225g plain flour
- 2 tsp baking powder
- 2 large eggs
- 50g butter, melted
- 175ml skimmed milk
- 100ml clear honey
- 140g fresh blueberry
- 85g dried cranberry
- 140g seedless raisin
- 140g dried apricot, chopped
- 1 tsp grated orange zest
- 1 tsp ground cinnamon

Method

STEP 1

Preheat the oven to 200C/gas 6/ fan 180C and very lightly butter a 12-hole muffin tin. Sift the flour and baking powder into a bowl. In another bowl, lightly beat the eggs, then stir in the melted butter, milk and honey. Add to the flour with the remaining ingredients. Combine quickly without overworking (it's fine if there are some lumps left – you want it gloopy rather than fluid). Spoon the mixture into the muffin tin. Bake for 20-25 minutes until well risen and pale golden on top.

STEP 2

Leave in the tin for a few minutes before turning out. When cool, they'll keep in an airtight tin for two days. (Can be frozen for up to 1 month.)

Thai turkey stir-fry

Prep: 10 mins **Cook:** 15 mins

Serves 4

Ingredients

- 300g rice noodles
- 1 tsp sunflower oil
- 400g turkey breast steak , cut into thin strips and any fat removed
- 340g green beans , trimmed and halved
- 1 red onion , sliced
- 2 garlic cloves , sliced
- juice 1 lime , plus extra wedges for serving
- 1 tsp chilli powder
- 1 red chilli , finely chopped
- 1 tbsp fish sauce
- handful mint , roughly chopped
- handful coriander , roughly chopped

Method

STEP 1

Cook the rice noodles following pack instructions. Heat the oil in a non-stick pan and fry the turkey over a high heat for 2 mins. Add the beans, onion and garlic, and cook for a further 5 mins.

STEP 2

Stir in the lime juice, chilli powder, fresh chilli and fish sauce, then cook for 3 mins more. Stir in the noodles and herbs, then toss everything together before serving.

Spicy prawn noodle salad

Prep: 15 mins **Cook:** 5 mins

Serves 4

Ingredients

- 200g glass noodles (available from thai-food-online.co.uk) or rice vermicelli
- 1 tbsp vegetable oil
- 3 spring onions , sliced
- 2 lemongrass stalks , sliced
- 300g raw jumbo king prawns
- small handful mint

- small handful coriander
- small handful Thai basil
- ½ cucumber, cut into matchsticks

For the dressing

- 1 red bird's-eye chilli, roughly chopped
- 2 garlic cloves
- 2 limes, juiced
- 2 tbsp fish sauce
- 1 tsp soft brown sugar or palm sugar

Method

STEP 1

Cook the noodles following pack instructions. Drain, rinse with cold water and set aside.

STEP 2

Heat the oil in a frying pan over a medium heat and cook the spring onions and lemongrass for 2 mins or until softened. Add the prawns and cook for 3 mins or until they have turned pink. Tip everything into a large bowl and allow to cool while you make the dressing.

STEP 3

Put all the dressing ingredients in a mini chopper and blitz until very finely chopped. Taste and add a little more sugar (to sweeten) and fish sauce (to make saltier), if you like. Tip the noodles into the bowl with the prawns, then add the rest of the ingredients and dressing, and toss really well before serving.

Avocado, labneh, roasted carrots & leaves

Prep: 20 mins **Cook:** 30 mins plus overnight chilling

Serves 2

Ingredients

- 200g full-fat bio yoghurt
- grated zest 1 lime, plus 1 tbsp juice, cut into wedges, to serve
- 1/2 small pack coriander leaves, finely chopped
- 300g carrots, cut into batons
- 1 tbsp cold-pressed rapeseed oil
- 1/2 tsp ground cumin
- 1 ripe but firm avocado
- 50g bag mixed salad leaves
- 1 tbsp mixed seeds (such as sunflower, pumpkin, sesame and linseed)

Method

STEP 1

To make the labneh, mix the yoghurt, lime and coriander together in a bowl. Line another small bowl with a square of muslin. Spoon the yogurt mixture into the bowl, pull up the ends of the muslin and tie the yoghurt into a ball. Tie the ends of the muslin onto a wooden spoon and suspend over a bowl or jug. Place in the fridge overnight to strain.

STEP 2

Heat oven to 200C/180C fan/gas 6. Toss the carrots with 1 tsp of the oil, 2 tsp of the lime juice, the cumin and lots of ground black pepper. Tip onto a foil-lined baking tray and roast for 20 mins. Turn the carrots and return to the oven for a further 10 mins or until tender and lightly browned. Set aside.

STEP 3

Cut the avocado in half and remove the stone. Scoop out the flesh from each half in one piece with a serving spoon. Slice on a chopping board, then toss with the remaining lime juice.

STEP 4

Untie the labneh and spread it over two plates, top with the salad leaves, carrots and avocado. Drizzle over the remaining oil, sprinkle with the seeds and serve with lime wedges.

Lighter apple & pear pie

Prep: 20 mins **Cook:** 40 mins - 45 mins

Serves 6

Ingredients

- 6 eating apples (we used Braeburn)
- 4 ripe pears
- zest and juice 1 lemon
- 3 tbsp agave syrup
- 1 tsp mixed spice
- 1 tbsp cornflour
- 4 filo pastry sheets
- 4 tsp rapeseed oil
- 25g flaked almond

To serve

- custard (made with custard powder and skimmed milk), fat-free Greek yogurt or low-fat frozen vanilla yogurt

Method

STEP 1

Peel, core, and chop the apples and pears into large pieces, and throw into a big saucepan with the lemon juice, agave syrup, mixed spice and 200ml water. Bring to a simmer with the lid on, then take off the lid and cook, stirring, for about 5 mins until the apple is softening. Use a slotted spoon to scoop out three-quarters of the fruit chunks and put into a pie dish.

STEP 2

Cover and cook the remaining fruit for another 4-5 mins until soft, then mash with a potato masher. Mix 1 tbsp of this with the cornflour to a smooth paste, then add back to the pan and bring back to a simmer, stirring, to thicken the sauce. Pour over the fruit in the pie dish and stir together. Heat oven to 180C/160C fan/gas 4.

STEP 3

Lay out your sheets of filo and brush all over with oil – 1 tsp should be enough for 1 sheet. Scatter over the almonds and press to stick to the pastry, then crumple up each sheet as you lift it on top of the fruit. Bake for 20-25 mins until the pastry is browned and crisp. Serve straight away.

Haddock & spinach cheese melt

Prep: 5 mins **Cook:** 25 mins

Serves 2

Ingredients

- 200g baby spinach
- 85g low-fat soft cheese
- 2 x 140g/5oz pieces skinless haddock
- 1 large tomato , sliced
- 2 tbsp grated parmesan

Method

STEP 1

Heat oven to 200C/180C fan/gas 6. Pile the spinach into a large pan over a medium heat, turning it over and over until wilted. Remove from the heat and drain off the excess liquid.

STEP 2

Mix spinach with the soft cheese, then place in the bottom of a small baking dish and sit haddock pieces on top. Lay sliced tomatoes on top of the fish and sprinkle with the Parmesan. Bake for 15-20 mins (depending on thickness of the haddock), or until the fish flakes easily.

Spiced cod with quinoa salad & mint chutney

Prep: 5 mins **Cook:** 25 mins

Serves 2

Ingredients

- 40g quinoa (or 85g pre-cooked quinoa)
- 3 tbsp chopped mint
- 3 tbsp chopped coriander
- 150g pot 0% natural yogurt
- 1 garlic clove
- ¼ tsp turmeric
- pinch of cumin seeds
- 2 x 150g chunky fillets skinless white fish , such as sustainable cod
- ¼ cucumber , finely diced
- 1 small red onion , finely chopped
- 4 tomatoes , chopped
- good squeeze of lemon juice

Method

STEP 1

Tip the quinoa (if not pre-cooked) into a pan, cover with water and boil, covered, for 25 mins, checking the water level to make sure it doesn't boil dry. Drain well.

STEP 2

Meanwhile, put 2 tbsp each of the mint and coriander in a bowl. Add the yogurt and garlic, and blitz with a hand blender until smooth. Stir 2 tbsp of the herby yogurt with the turmeric and cumin, then add the fish and turn in the mixture to completely coat.

STEP 3

Turn the grill to High. Arrange the fish in a shallow heatproof dish and grill for 8-10 mins, depending on thickness, until it flakes. Toss the quinoa with the cucumber, onion, tomatoes, lemon juice and remaining herbs. Spoon onto a plate, add the fish and spoon round the mint chutney, or add it at the table.

Smashed chicken with corn slaw

Prep: 10 mins **Cook:** 5 mins

Serves 4

Ingredients

For the chicken

- 4 skinless chicken breast fillets
- 1 lime , zested and juiced
- 2 tbsp bio yogurt
- 1 tsp fresh thyme leaves
- ¼ tsp turmeric
- 2 tbsp finely chopped coriander
- 1 garlic clove , finely grated
- 1 tsp rapeseed oil

For the slaw

- 1 small avocado
- 1 lime , zested and juiced
- 2 tbsp bio yogurt
- 2 tbsp finely chopped coriander
- 160g corn , cut from 2 cobs
- 1 red pepper , deseeded and chopped
- 1 red onion , halved and finely sliced
- 320g white cabbage , finely sliced
- 150g new potatoes , boiled, to serve

Method

STEP 1

Cut the chicken breasts in half, then put them between two sheets of baking parchment and bash with a rolling pin to flatten. Mix the lime zest and juice with the yogurt, thyme, turmeric, coriander and garlic in a large bowl. Add the chicken and stir until well coated. Leave to marinate while you make the slaw.

STEP 2

Mash the avocado with the lime juice and zest, 2 tbsp yogurt and the coriander. Stir in the corn, red pepper, onion and cabbage.

STEP 3

Heat a large non-stick frying pan or griddle pan, then cook the chicken in batches for mins each side – they'll cook quickly as they're thin. Serve the hot chicken with the new potatoes. If you're cooking for two, chill half the chicken and slaw for lunch day (eat within two days).

Fruity sponge cake

Prep: 10 mins **Cook:** 20 mins

Serves 8

Ingredients

- butter or oil, for greasing
- 50g plain flour
- 3 tbsp cornflour
- 1 tsp baking powder
- 4 eggs, separated
- 175g caster sugar

For the filling

- 295g can mandarin segment, drained
- 200g tub low-fat fromage frais
- icing sugar, for dusting

Method

STEP 1

Heat oven to 180C/fan 160C/gas 4. Grease then line the base and sides of 2 x 20cm sandwich tins with greaseproof paper. Sieve the flours and baking powder together.

STEP 2

Use electric hand beaters to whisk the egg whites until stiff, then briefly whisk in the sugar. Beat the egg yolks quickly, then whisk into the whites. Fold in the dry ingredients using a large metal spoon, then spoon the mixture into the tins and level the tops. Bake for 18-20 mins until risen, light golden and a skewer inserted into the middle comes out clean. Cool in the tins for 10 mins, then gently remove and leave to cool completely.

STEP 3

Mix the mandarins and fromage frais together. Peel away the greaseproof paper, sandwich the cakes with the mandarin mix, then dust with the icing sugar to serve. Best eaten on the day it's made.

Hearty mushroom soup

Prep:30 mins **Cook:**30 mins

Serves 4 - 6

Ingredients

- 25g pack porcini mushrooms
- 2 tbsp olive oil
- 1 medium onion , finely diced
- 2 large carrots , diced
- 2 garlic cloves , finely chopped
- 1 tbsp chopped rosemary , or 1 tsp dried
- 500g fresh mushroom , such as chestnut, finely chopped
- 1.2l vegetable stock (from a cube is fine)
- 5 tbsp marsala or dry sherry
- 2 tbsp tomato purée
- 100g pearl barley
- grated fresh parmesan , to serve (optional)

Method

STEP 1

Put the porcini in a bowl with 250ml boiling water and leave to soak for 25 mins. Heat the oil in a pan and add the onion, carrot, garlic, rosemary and seasoning. Fry for 5 mins on a medium heat until softened. Drain the porcini, saving the liquid, and finely chop. Tip into the pan with the fresh mushrooms. Fry for another 5 mins, then add the stock, marsala or sherry, tomato purée, barley and strained porcini liquid.

STEP 2

Cook for 30 mins or until barley is soft, adding more liquid if it becomes too thick. Serve in bowls with parmesan sprinkled over, if desired.

Poached apricots with rosewater

Prep: 5 mins **Cook:** 15 mins Plus cooling

Serves 2

Ingredients

- 50g golden caster sugar
- 400g ripe apricot, halved and stoned
- few drops rosewater
- Greek yogurt, to serve
- handful pistachios, roughly chopped, to serve

Method

STEP 1

Put the sugar into a medium pan with 150ml water. Heat gently until the sugar dissolves, then add the apricots and simmer for 15 mins until soft. Take off the heat, splash in the rosewater and leave to cool. Spoon into glasses to serve, topped with a few dollops of the yogurt and a scattering of nuts.

Pan-fried rib-eye steak

Prep: 5 mins **Cook:** 10 mins

Serves 2

Ingredients

- 2 rib-eye steaks, each about 200g and 2cm thick
- 1 tbsp sunflower oil
- 1 tbsp/25g butter
- 1 garlic clove, left whole but bashed once
- thyme, optional

Method

STEP 1

Up to 8 hrs before cooking, pat the steaks dry with kitchen paper and season with salt and pepper. Heat the oil over a high flame in a heavy-based frying pan that will comfortably fit both steaks. When the oil is shimmering, turn the heat down to medium-high and add the butter. Once it's sizzling, carefully lay the steaks in the pan, tucking the garlic and herbs in at the sides.

STEP 2

Stand over the steaks with a pair of tongs, searing and turning them every 30 seconds to 1 min so they get a nice brown crust. As a rough guide, each steak will take 4 mins in total for rare, 5-6 mins in total for medium and 8-10 mins for well done. If you have a digital cooking thermometer, the temperatures you're looking for in middle of the steak are 50C for rare, 60C for medium and 70C for well done. Leave the steaks to rest for at least 5 mins. While the steaks are resting, you can make a classic red wine sauce to go with them.

Moroccan-style chicken stew

Prep: 10 mins **Cook:** 20 mins

Serves 4

Ingredients

- 1 tbsp olive oil
- 1 onion , chopped
- 1 garlic clove , crushed
- 1 tbsp ras-el-hanout or Moroccan spice mix
- 4 skinless chicken breasts , sliced
- 300ml reduced-salt chicken stock
- 400g can chickpeas , drained
- 12 dried apricots , sliced
- small bunch coriander , chopped

Method

STEP 1

Heat the oil in a large shallow pan, then cook the onion for 3 mins. Add the garlic and spices and cook for a further min. Tip in the chicken and cook for 3 mins, then pour in the chicken stock, chickpeas and apricots. Simmer for 5 mins or until the chicken is cooked through. Stir through the coriander and serve immediately with couscous and a green salad, if you like.

Leek, tomato & barley risotto with pan-cooked cod

Prep: 10 mins **Cook:** 20 mins

Serves 2

Ingredients

- 2 tsp rapeseed oil
- 1 large leek (315g), thinly sliced
- 2 garlic cloves , chopped
- 400g can barley (don't drain)
- 2 tsp vegetable bouillon
- 1 tsp finely chopped sage
- 1 tbsp thyme leaves , plus a few extra to serve
- 160g cherry tomatoes
- 50g finely grated parmesan
- 2 skin-on cod fillets or firm white fish fillets

Method

STEP 1

Heat 1 tsp oil in a non-stick pan and fry the leek and garlic for 5-10 mins, stirring frequently until softened, adding a splash of water to help it cook if you need to.

STEP 2

Tip in the barley with its liquid, then stir in the bouillon, sage and thyme. Simmer, stirring frequently for 3-4 mins. Add the tomatoes and cook about 4-5 mins more until they soften and start to split, adding a drop more water if necessary. Stir in the parmesan.

STEP 3

Meanwhile, heat the remaining oil in a non-stick pan and fry the cod, skin side down, for 4-5 mins. Flip the fillets over to cook briefly on the other side. Spoon the risotto into two bowls. Serve the cod on top with a few thyme leaves, if you like.

Green minestrone with tortellini

Prep: 5 mins **Cook:** 25 mins

Serves 4

Ingredients

- 2 tbsp olive or rapeseed oil
- 1 onion , chopped
- 1 small leek , chopped
- 1 celery stick , chopped
- 3 garlic cloves , crushed
- 2 bay leaves
- 1l good-quality chicken or vegetable stock
- 100g shredded spring veg or cabbage
- 50g frozen peas
- 1 lemon , zested
- 250g tortellini

Method

STEP 1

Heat the olive or rapeseed oil in a large pan. Add the onion, leek and celery stick. Cook for 8-10 mins until softened, then stir in the garlic and bay leaves. Pour in the chicken or vegetable stock, then cover and simmer for 10 mins. Add the spring veg or cabbage, peas, lemon zest and tortellini (spinach tortellini works well). Cover and cook for another 3 mins, season well and ladle into bowls.

Lighter moussaka with crunchy feta & oregano

Prep: 10 mins **Cook:** 50 mins

Serves 4

Ingredients

- 300g extra-lean lamb mince
- 1 tsp olive oil
- 2 courgettes , finely chopped
- 1 large aubergine , finely chopped
- 140g red lentil
- 2 tsp dried oregano
- 680g jar passata with garlic & herbs
- 1 low-sodium lamb or beef stock cube
- 200g low-fat Greek yogurt
- 75g light feta cheese
- 2 tbsp breadcrumb
- salad and flatbreads , to serve (optional)

Method

STEP 1

Heat a dry non-stick pan and add the lamb, breaking it up with a fork. Cook until brown, then tip the meat into a bowl. Heat the oil in the pan and fry the courgettes and aubergines until golden, about 6-8 mins.

STEP 2

Return the meat to the pan and add the lentils, half the oregano and the passata. Crumble in the stock cube. Fill the passata jar to about half full with water (about 340ml), swirl and add to the pan. Simmer for 25-30 mins until the lentils are tender, adding more water if you need to. Season to taste.

STEP 3

Heat the grill to high. Mash together the rest of the oregano with the yogurt, feta and some seasoning. Pour the lamb mixture into 1 large or 4 individual ovenproof dishes, spoon over the topping, scatter on the crumbs, then grill for 3-4 mins until bubbling. Serve with salad and flatbreads, if you like.

Easy vegan pho

Prep: 10 mins **Cook:** 20 mins

Serves 2

Ingredients

- 100g rice noodles
- 1 tsp Marmite
- 1 tsp vegetable oil
- 50g chestnut mushrooms, sliced
- 1 leek, sliced
- 2 tbsp soy sauce

To serve

- 1 red chilli, sliced (deseeded if you don't like it too hot)
- ½ bunch mint, leaves picked and stalk discarded
- handful salted peanuts
- sriracha, to serve

Method

STEP 1

Tip the noodles into a bowl and cover with boiling water. Leave to stand for 10 mins, then drain, rinse in cold water and set aside.

STEP 2

In a jug, mix the Marmite with 500ml boiling water. Set aside while you cook the vegetables.

STEP 3

Heat the oil in a saucepan, then add the mushrooms and leek. Cook for 10-15 mins until softened and beginning to colour, then add the soy sauce and Marmite and water mixture and stir. Bring to the boil for 5 mins.

STEP 4

Divide the noodles between two deep bowls, then ladle over the hot broth. Top with the chilli slices, mint leaves and peanuts, and serve with some sriracha on the side.

Vegetable fried rice

Prep: 2 mins **Cook:** 8 mins

Serves 2

Ingredients

- 1 bag stir-fry vegetables
- a pouch of cooked rice
- 2 eggs
- 2 tbsp teriyaki sauce

Method

STEP 1

In a wok, stir-fry the vegetables for 1-2 mins until softening, then add the rice and warm through. Crack in the eggs and stir through with the teriyaki sauce.

Tomato & rice soup

Prep: 10 mins **Cook:** 35 mins

Serves 4

Ingredients

- 2 tsp olive oil
- 1 onion , finely chopped
- 1 carrot , finely chopped
- 1 celery stick, finely chopped
- 1 tbsp golden caster sugar
- 2 tbsp vinegar (white, red or balsamic)
- 1 tbsp tomato purée
- 400g can chopped tomato or passata
- 1l vegetable stock made with 2 cubes
- 140g rice (long-grain, basmati, wild, brown or a mixture)
- ¼ small pack parsley , leaves only, chopped, and a few drops of pesto, to serve (optional)

Method

STEP 1

Heat the oil in a large saucepan and add the onion, carrot and celery, then cook gently until softened. Add the sugar and vinegar, cook for 1 min, then stir through the tomato purée. Add the chopped tomatoes or passata, the vegetable stock, and any brown rice, if using, then cover and simmer for 10 mins. If you are using wild rice, add this and simmer for 10 mins more. Finally, add any white rice you're using, and simmer for a final 10 mins until the rice is tender.

STEP 2

Just before serving, sprinkle over some chopped parsley and season to taste. Divide into bowls and add a swirl of pesto to each, if you like.

Seared beef salad with capers & mint

Prep: 10 mins **Cook:** 12 mins

Serves 2

Ingredients

- 150g new potatoes , thickly sliced

- 160g fine green beans, trimmed and halved
- 160g frozen peas
- rapeseed oil, for brushing
- 200g lean fillet steak, trimmed of any fat
- 160g romaine lettuce, roughly torn into pieces

For the dressing

- 1 tbsp extra virgin olive oil
- 2 tsp cider vinegar
- ½ tsp English mustard powder
- 2 tbsp chopped mint
- 3 tbsp chopped basil
- 1 garlic clove, finely grated
- 1 tbsp capers

Method

STEP 1

Cook the potatoes in a pan of simmering water for 5 mins. Add the beans and cook 5 mins more, then tip in the peas and cook for 2 mins until all the vegetables are just tender. Drain.

STEP 2

Meanwhile, measure all the dressing ingredients in a large bowl and season with black pepper. Stir and crush the herbs and capers with the back of a spoon to intensify their flavours.

STEP 3

Brush a little oil over the steak and grind over some black pepper. Heat a non-stick frying pan over a high heat and cook the steak for 4 mins on one side and 2-3 mins on the other, depending on the thickness and how rare you like it. Transfer to a plate to rest while you carry on with the rest of the salad.

STEP 4

Mix the warm vegetables into the dressing until well coated, then add the lettuce and toss again. Pile onto plates. Slice the steak and turn in any dressing left in the bowl, add to the salad and serve while still warm.

Minty griddled chicken & peach salad

Prep: 10 mins **Cook:** 15 mins

Serves 2

Ingredients

- 1 lime , zested and juiced
- 1 tbsp rapeseed oil
- 2 tbsp mint , finely chopped, plus a few leaves to serve
- 1 garlic clove , finely grated
- 2 skinless chicken breast fillets (300g)
- 160g fine beans , trimmed and halved
- 2 peaches (200g), each cut into 8 thick wedges
- 1 red onion , cut into wedges
- 1 large Little Gem lettuce (165g), roughly shredded
- ½ x 60g pack rocket
- 1 small avocado , stoned and sliced
- 240g cooked new potatoes

Method

STEP 1

Mix the lime zest and juice, oil and mint, then put half in a bowl with the garlic. Thickly slice the chicken at a slight angle, add to the garlic mixture and toss together with plenty of black pepper.

STEP 2

Cook the beans in a pan of water for 3-4 mins until just tender. Meanwhile, griddle the chicken and onion for a few mins each side until cooked and tender. Transfer to a plate, then quickly griddle the peaches. If you don't have a griddle pan, use a non-stick frying pan with a drop of oil.

STEP 3

Toss the warm beans and onion in the remaining mint mixture, and pile onto a platter or into individual shallow bowls with the lettuce and rocket. Top with the avocado, peaches and chicken and scatter over the mint. Serve with the potatoes while still warm.

Artichoke, red onion & rosemary risotto

Prep: 15 mins **Cook:** 35 mins

Serves 4

Ingredients

- 1 tbsp olive oil
- 2 red onions , sliced into thin wedges
- 2 red peppers , cut into chunks
- 2 tbsp rosemary needles
- 140g arborio risotto rice
- 150ml white wine
- 850ml low-salt vegetable stock
- 400g tin artichoke heart in water, drained and halved
- 2 tbsp grated parmesan or vegetarian alternative
- 2 tbsp toasted pine nuts

Method

STEP 1

Heat the oil in a large frying pan or wok. Cook the onions gently for 6-7 mins until softened and browning. Add the peppers and rosemary and cook for a further 5 mins. Add rice and stir well.

STEP 2

Pour in the wine and of the stock. Bring to the boil then reduce the heat and simmer gently, stirring occasionally until almost all the liquid is absorbed.

STEP 3

Stir in another of the stock and simmer again, until it's all absorbed. Add the final with the artichokes and simmer again until rice is tender.

STEP 4

Season and stir in the Parmesan and ½ the pine nuts. Scatter over the remainder and serve.

Easy tomato pizzas

Prep: 10 mins **Cook:** 12 mins

Makes 8 small pizzas

Ingredients

For the dough

- 450g strong white bread flour , plus more to dust
- 7g sachet fast-action yeast
- 2 tbsp extra-virgin olive oil , plus extra to serve
- 350ml warm water

For the topping

- about 5 tbsp roast tomato sauce (see tip below), or stir together 100ml passata and a crushed garlic clove
- 8 tomatoes (green, orange, red, yellow - all different shapes and sizes)
- your choice of toppings: goat's cheese (with rind), grated Parmesan or Parmesan shavings, handful rocket, prosciutto

Method

STEP 1

For the dough, put the flour, yeast and 2 tsp salt into a large bowl and mix. Make a well. Mix the oil and water in a jug, then tip into the bowl. Use a wooden spoon to work the liquid into the flour – it will seem pretty wet. Set the bowl aside for 15 mins. Leaving the dough like this will save you from lengthy kneading later.

STEP 2

Turn the dough onto a well-floured surface, flour your hands, then knead it very gently for about 2 mins until it is fairly even, soft and bouncy. Return the dough to the bowl, cover with oiled cling film, then let it rise in a warm place (or in the fridge overnight) until doubled in size.

STEP 3

When ready to cook, heat oven to 240C/220C fan/gas 9 or as hot as it will go, then put a baking sheet in on a high shelf. Dust another sheet with flour. Split the dough into 8, then roll 3 balls thinly into rough circles. Lift onto the floured sheet. Smear over a thin layer of the sauce, scatter over a few slices of tomato, season, then add sliced goat's or grated Parmesan cheese if you want to. Slide the sheet on top of the heated sheet. Bake for 12 mins or until golden and crisp and the tomatoes are starting to caramelise around the edges. Top with any fresh toppings, then drizzle with more olive oil to serve.

Indian winter soup

Prep: 15 mins **Cook:** 30 mins

Serves 4 - 6

Ingredients

- 100g pearl barley
- 2 tbsp vegetable oil
- ½ tsp brown mustard seeds
- 1 tsp cumin seeds
- 2 green chillies, deseeded and finely chopped
- 1 bay leaf
- 2 cloves
- 1 small cinnamon stick
- ½ tsp ground turmeric
- 1 large onion, chopped
- 2 garlic cloves, finely chopped
- 1 parsnip, cut into chunks
- 200g butternut squash, cut into chunks
- 200g sweet potato, cut into chunks
- 1 tsp paprika
- 1 tsp ground coriander
- 225g red lentils
- 2 tomatoes, chopped
- small bunch coriander, chopped
- 1 tsp grated ginger
- 1 tsp lemon juice

Method

STEP 1

Rinse the pearl barley and cook following pack instructions. When it is tender, drain and set aside. Meanwhile, heat the oil in a deep, heavy-bottomed pan. Fry the mustard seeds, cumin seeds, chillies, bay leaf, cloves, cinnamon and turmeric until fragrant and the seeds start to crackle. Tip in the onion and garlic, then cook for 5-8 mins until soft. Stir in the parsnip, butternut and sweet potato and mix thoroughly, making sure the vegetables are fully coated with the oil and spices. Sprinkle in the paprika, ground coriander and seasoning, and stir again.

STEP 2

Add the lentils, pearl barley, tomatoes and 1.7 litres water. Bring to the boil then turn down and simmer until the vegetables are tender. When the lentils are almost cooked, stir in the chopped coriander, ginger and lemon juice.

Quick banana ice cream

Prep: 5 mins Plus freezing

Serves 4

Ingredients

- 4 ripe bananas, cut into chunks
- 3-4 tbsp milk
- 2 tbsp toasted flaked almonds
- 2 tbsp ready-made toffee or chocolate sauce

Method

STEP 1

Pop the banana chunks on a flat tray and cover well. Freeze for at least 1 hr, or until frozen through. When ready to eat throw the banana into a food processor and whizz until smooth with enough of the milk to achieve a creamy texture. Scoop into 4 bowls or glasses, then top with the sauce and nuts.

Curried turkey lettuce wraps

Prep: 5 mins **Serves 2**

Ingredients

- 100g natural yogurt
- 1 tsp curry powder
- 1 tsp tomato purée
- 2 tbsp raisins
- 100g cooked skinless turkey or chicken breast meat
- 8 Little Gem lettuces leaves
- 2 tsp sunflower seeds
- coriander leaves

Method

STEP 1

Mix the natural yogurt with the curry powder, tomato purée and raisins. Stir in the cooked turkey or chicken, then spoon onto the lettuce leaves. Scatter over the sunflower seeds and the coriander leaves.

Fruity coconut creams

Prep: 10 mins No cook

Serves 4

Ingredients

- 1 x 50g/2oz sachet coconut cream
- 500g 0% Greek yogurt or tub quark
- 85g icing sugar, sieved
- few drops vanilla extract
- 2 kiwi fruit
- 400g can pineapple chunks

Method

STEP 1

Dissolve the coconut cream in 50ml boiling water, then leave to cool. Spoon the quark or yogurt into a mixing bowl, then stir in the icing sugar and vanilla. Combine with the coconut mix, then spoon into individual glasses. Chill until ready to serve.

STEP 2

Peel and chop the kiwi fruit into small pieces. Drain the pineapple, then chop the chunks into small pieces. Mix the fruit together, then spoon over the top of the coconut creams to serve.

Mushroom & potato soup

Prep: 15 mins **Cook:** 30 mins

Serves 4

Ingredients

- 1 tbsp rapeseed oil
- 2 large onions, halved and thinly sliced
- 20g dried porcini mushrooms
- 3 tsp vegetable bouillon powder
- 300g chestnut mushrooms, chopped
- 3 garlic cloves, finely grated

- 300g potato, finely diced
- 2 tsp fresh thyme
- 4 carrots, finely diced
- 2 tbsp chopped parsley
- 8 tbsp yogurt
- 55g walnut pieces

Method

STEP 1

Heat the oil in a large pan. Tip in the onions and fry for 10 mins until golden. Meanwhile, pour 1.2 litres boiling water over the dried mushrooms and stir in the bouillon.

STEP 2

Add the fresh mushrooms and garlic to the pan with the potatoes, thyme and carrots, and continue to fry until the mushrooms soften and start to brown.

STEP 3

Pour in the dried mushrooms and stock, cover the pan and leave to simmer for 20 mins. Stir in the parsley and plenty of pepper. Ladle into bowls and serve each portion topped with 2 tbsp yogurt and a quarter of the walnuts. The rest can be chilled and reheated the next day.

Sticky pork

Prep: 5 mins **Cook:** 30 mins

Serves 4

Ingredients

- 500g piece pork fillet

For the marinade

- 4 tbsp soy sauce
- 1 tbsp clear honey
- finely grated zest and juice 1 orange
- large knob of root ginger, finely grated

Method

STEP 1

Tip all the marinade ingredients into a shallow dish and stir to combine. Coat the pork in the marinade and, if you have time, leave for 1 hr or even better overnight. Heat oven to 200C/fan 180C/gas 6.

STEP 2

Heat an ovenproof pan and take the pork out of the marinade. Brown on all sides, then baste over the rest of the marinade and roast the pork for 20 mins until cooked all the way through, basting with its juices every 5 mins or so. Serve the pork sliced with rice and your favourite steamed greens.

Veggie okonomiyaki

Prep: 15 mins **Cook:** 10 mins

Serves 2

Ingredients

- 3 large eggs
- 50g plain flour
- 50ml milk
- 4 spring onions , trimmed and sliced
- 1 pak choi , sliced
- 200g Savoy cabbage , shredded
- 1 red chilli , deseeded and finely chopped, plus extra to serve
- ½ tbsp low-salt soy sauce
- ½ tbsp rapeseed oil
- 1 heaped tbsp low-fat mayonnaise
- ½ lime , juiced
- sushi ginger , to serve (optional)
- wasabi , to serve (optional)

Method

STEP 1

Whisk together the eggs, flour and milk until smooth. Add half the spring onions, the pak choi, cabbage, chilli and soy sauce. Heat the oil in a small frying pan and pour in the batter. Cook, covered, over a medium heat for 7-8 mins. Flip the okonomiyaki into a second frying pan, then return it to the heat and cook for a further 7-8 mins until a skewer inserted into it comes out clean.

STEP 2

Mix the mayonnaise and lime juice together in a small bowl. Transfer the okonomiyaki to a plate, then drizzle over the lime mayo and top with the extra chilli and spring onion and the sushi ginger, if using. Serve with the wasabi on the side, if you like.

Thai spiced turkey patties with noodle salad

Prep: 15 mins **Cook:** 10 mins

Serves 4

Ingredients

- 400g turkey breast or fillet, roughly chopped
- 1 lemongrass stalk, finely chopped
- 2 garlic cloves , crushed
- zest and juice 1 lime
- 3 tbsp low-sodium soy sauce
- small bunch coriander , chopped
- 1 red chilli , deseeded and chopped
- 2 nests medium wheat noodles
- 300g pack mixed peppers stir-fry vegetables
- sweet chilli sauce , to serve (optional)

Method

STEP 1

Heat the grill to Medium. Put the turkey in a food processor and pulse until minced. Add the lemongrass, garlic and lime zest, and half the soy sauce, coriander and chilli, then pulse again until combined. Tip the mix into a bowl and add some black pepper. Shape into 8 patties, then transfer to a non-stick baking tray and grill for 3-4 mins each side, until cooked through.

STEP 2

Meanwhile, soak the noodles following pack instructions, then drain and add the vegetables, the remaining soy sauce and the lime juice. Toss well, divide between plates and sprinkle with the remaining coriander and chilli. Serve with the turkey patties and some sweet chilli sauce for dipping, if you like.

Prawn chow mein

Prep: 5 mins **Cook:** 20 mins

Serves 4

Ingredients

- 3 nests medium egg noodles
- 140g broccoli , chopped into small florets
- 140g baby corn , halved

For the sauce

- 3 tbsp tomato ketchup
- 2 tbsp oyster sauce

- 1 tbsp olive oil
- 1 red pepper , sliced
- 300g prawns

Method

STEP 1

Cook the noodles, broccoli and corn in boiling water for 3-4 mins, or until tender. Drain and set aside. Heat the oil in a large frying pan or wok and fry the pepper for 3 mins, until starting to soften.

STEP 2

Tip in the noodles and vegetables along with the prawns and toss together. Add the sauce ingredients and heat everything through for 2-3 mins, until piping hot.

Thai fried prawn & pineapple rice

Prep: 10 mins **Cook:** 15 mins

Serves 4

Ingredients

- 2 tsp sunflower oil
- bunch spring onions , greens and whites separated, both sliced

- 1 green pepper , deseeded and chopped into small chunks

- 140g pineapple, chopped into bite-sized chunks
- 3 tbsp Thai green curry paste
- 4 tsp light soy sauce, plus extra to serve
- 300g cooked basmati rice (brown, white or a mix - about 140g uncooked rice)
- 2 large eggs, beaten
- 140g frozen peas
- 225g can bamboo shoots, drained
- 250g frozen prawns, cooked or raw
- 2-3 limes, 1 juiced, the rest cut into wedges to serve
- handful coriander leaves (optional)

Method

STEP 1

Heat the oil in a wok or non-stick frying pan and fry the spring onion whites for 2 mins until softened. Stir in the pepper for 1 min, followed by the pineapple for 1 min more, then stir in the green curry paste and soy sauce.

STEP 2

Add the rice, stir-frying until piping hot, then push the rice to one side of the pan and scramble the eggs on the other side. Stir the peas, bamboo shoots and prawns into the rice and eggs, then heat through for 2 mins until the prawns are hot and the peas tender. Finally, stir in the spring onion greens, lime juice and coriander, if using. Spoon into bowls and serve with extra lime wedges and soy sauce.

Feta & clementine lunch bowl

Prep: 15 mins **Cook:** 15 mins

Serves 2

Ingredients

- 1 red onion, halved and thinly sliced
- 1 lemon, zested and juiced
- 2 clementines, 1 zested, flesh sliced
- 2 garlic cloves, chopped
- 400g can green lentils, drained
- 1 tbsp balsamic vinegar
- 1 ½ tbsp rapeseed oil
- 1 red pepper, quartered and sliced
- 60g feta, crumbled
- small handful mint, chopped
- 4 walnut halves, chopped

Method

STEP 1

Mix the onion with the lemon juice, lemon and clementine zest and garlic.

STEP 2

Tip the lentils into two bowls or lunchboxes and drizzle over the balsamic and 1 tbsp oil. Heat the remaining oil in a large non-stick wok, add the pepper and stir-fry for 3 mins. Tip in half the onion and cook until tender. Pile on top of the lentils, then mix the clementines, remaining onions, feta, mint and walnut pieces.

Mushroom brunch

Prep: 5 mins **Cook:** 12 mins - 15 mins

Serves 4

Ingredients

- 250g mushrooms
- 1 garlic clove
- 1 tbsp olive oil
- 160g bag kale
- 4 eggs

Method

STEP 1

Slice the mushrooms and crush the garlic clove. Heat the olive oil in a large non-stick frying pan, then fry the garlic over a low heat for 1 min. Add the mushrooms and cook until soft. Then, add the kale. If the kale won't all fit in the pan, add half and stir until wilted, then add the rest. Once all the kale is wilted, season.

STEP 2

Now crack in the eggs and keep them cooking gently for 2-3 mins. Then, cover with the lid to for a further 2-3 mins or until the eggs are cooked to your liking. Serve with bread.

Tuna, avocado & quinoa salad

Prep: 5 mins **Cook:** 20 mins

Serves 2

Ingredients

- 100g quinoa
- 3 tbsp extra virgin olive oil
- juice 1 lemon
- ½ tbsp white wine vinegar
- 120g can tuna, drained
- 1 avocado, stoned, peeled and cut into chunks
- 200g cherry tomatoes on the vine, halved
- 50g feta, crumbled
- 50g baby spinach
- 2 tbsp mixed seeds, toasted

Method

STEP 1

Rinse the quinoa under cold water. Tip into a saucepan, cover with water and bring to the boil. Reduce the heat and simmer for 15 mins until the grains have swollen but still have some bite. Drain, then transfer to a bowl to cool slightly.

STEP 2

Meanwhile, in a jug, combine the oil, lemon juice and vinegar with some seasoning.

STEP 3

Once the quinoa has cooled, mix with the dressing and all the remaining ingredients and season. Divide between plates or lunchboxes.

Creamy linguine with ham, lemon & basil

Prep: 10 mins **Cook:** 15 mins

Serves 6

Ingredients

- 400g linguine or spaghetti
- 90g pack prosciutto

- 1 tbsp olive oil
- juice 1 lemon
- 2 egg yolks
- 3 tbsp crème fraîche
- large handful basil leaves
- large handful grated parmesan, plus extra to serve, if you like

Method

STEP 1

Cook the linguine. Meanwhile, tear the ham into small pieces and fry in the olive oil until golden and crisp.

STEP 2

Drain the pasta, reserving a little of the cooking water, then return to the pan. Tip in the cooked ham. Mix together the lemon juice, egg yolks and crème fraîche, then add this to the pan along with the basil and Parmesan. Mix in with tongs, adding a little of the cooking water, if needed, to make a creamy sauce that coats the pasta. Serve with extra Parmesan grated over the top, if you like.

Steamed bass with pak choi

Prep: 10 mins **Cook:** 5 mins

Serves 2

Ingredients

- small piece of ginger, peeled and sliced
- 2 garlic cloves, finely sliced
- 3 spring onions, finely sliced
- 2 tbsp soy sauce
- 1 tbsp sesame oil
- splash of sherry (optional)
- 2 x fillets sea bass
- 2 heads pak choi, quartered

Method

STEP 1

In a small bowl, mix all of the ingredients, except the fish and the pak choi, together to make a soy mix. Line one tier of a two-tiered bamboo steamer loosely with foil. Lay the fish, skin side up, on the foil and spoon over the soy mix. Place the fish over simmering water and throw the pak choi into the second tier and cover it with a lid. Alternatively, add the pak choi to the fish layer after 2 mins of cooking – the closer the tier is to the steam, the hotter it is.

STEP 2

Leave everything to steam for 6-8 mins until the pak choi has wilted and the fish is cooked. Divide the greens between two plates, then carefully lift out the fish. Lift the foil up and drizzle the tasty juices back over the fish.

Sausage & butternut squash shells

Prep: 15 mins **Cook:** 35 mins

Serves 4

Ingredients

- 1 medium butternut squash, peeled and cut into medium chunks
- 1 ½ tbsp olive oil
- 2 garlic cloves, crushed
- 1 fennel bulb, thinly sliced (keep the green fronds to serve)
- 4 spring onions, thinly sliced
- 2 tsp chilli flakes
- 1 tsp fennel seeds
- 300g large pasta shells
- 3 pork sausages

Method

STEP 1

Put the squash in a microwaveable bowl with a splash of water. Cover with cling film and cook on high for 10 mins until soft. Tip into a blender.

STEP 2

Meanwhile, put a frying pan over a medium heat and pour in 1 tbsp olive oil. Add the garlic, sliced fennel, spring onions, half the chilli flakes, half the fennel seeds and a splash of water. Cook, stirring occasionally, for 5 mins until softened. Scrape into the blender with squash. Blitz to a smooth sauce, adding enough water to get to a creamy consistency. Season to taste.

STEP 3

Bring a pan of water to the boil and cook the pasta for 1 min less than the pack instructions. Put the frying pan back on the heat (don't bother washing it first – it's all flavour). Pour in the remaining oil, squeeze the sausagemeat from the skins into the pan and add the remaining chilli and remaining fennel seeds. Fry until browned and crisp, breaking down the sausagemeat with a spoon.

STEP 4

Drain the pasta and return to its pan on the heat. Pour in the butternut sauce and give everything a good mix to warm the sauce through. Divide between bowls and top with the crispy sausage mix and fennel fronds.

Rhubarb & strawberry meringue pots

Prep: 15 mins **Cook:** 1 hr

Serves 4

Ingredients

- 450g rhubarb, cut into 4cm/1½in chunks
- 100g golden caster sugar
- grated zest of 1 orange
- 1 tbsp strawberry conserve
- 2 eggs, separated

Method

STEP 1

Preheat the oven to 180C/ Gas 4/fan oven 160C. Put the rhubarb in an ovenproof dish, sprinkle over 50g/2oz of the sugar and the orange zest and stir together. Cover and bake in the oven for 35-40 minutes until tender. (Alternatively, you can cook the rhubarb with the sugar and zest in the microwave for 10 minutes on full power, stirring halfway through the cooking time, until just tender.)

STEP 2

Remove the rhubarb from the oven and allow to cool slightly. Stir in the conserve then the egg yolks. Divide the rhubarb mixture between four 175ml/6fl oz ramekins. Put on a baking sheet and cook in the oven for 10 minutes until lightly thickened.

STEP 3

While the rhubarb is cooking, whisk the egg whites until stiff. Sprinkle over half of the remaining sugar and whisk again. Gently fold in the rest of the sugar. Pile the meringue on top of the rhubarb to cover it completely and swirl the top. Return to the oven for 10 minutes until the meringue is puffy and golden. Serve immediately.

Miso mushroom & tofu noodle soup

Prep: 10 mins **Cook:** 15 mins

Serves 1

Ingredients

- 1 tbsp rapeseed oil
- 70g mixed mushrooms , sliced
- 50g smoked tofu , cut into small cubes
- ½ tbsp brown rice miso paste
- 50g dried buckwheat or egg noodles
- 2 spring onions , shredded

Method

STEP 1

Heat half the oil in a frying pan over a medium heat. Add the mushrooms and fry for 5-6 mins, or until golden. Transfer to a bowl using a slotted spoon and set aside. Add the remaining oil to the pan and fry the tofu for 3-4 mins, or until evenly golden.

STEP 2

Mix the miso paste with 325ml boiling water in a jug. Cook the noodles following pack instructions, then drain and transfer to a bowl. Top with the mushrooms and tofu, then pour over the miso broth. Scatter over the spring onions just before serving.

Mexican egg roll

Prep: 5 mins **Cook:** 10 mins

Serves 2

Ingredients

- 1 large egg
- a little rapeseed oil for frying

- 2 tbsp tomato salsa
- about 1 tbsp fresh coriander

Method

STEP 1

Beat the egg with 1 tbsp water. Heat the oil in a medium non-stick pan. Add the egg and swirl round the base of the pan, as though you are making a pancake, and cook until set. There is no need to turn it.

STEP 2

Carefully tip the pancake onto a board, spread with the salsa, sprinkle with the coriander, then roll it up. It can be eaten warm or cold – you can keep it for 2 days in the fridge.

Puy lentils with spinach & sour cherries

Prep: 5 mins **Cook:** 20 mins

Serves 4

Ingredients

- 2 tsp olive oil
- 4 shallots , finely chopped
- 250g pouch ready-to-eat puy lentils
- 300ml reduced-salt vegetable or chicken stock
- 140g dried sour cherries
- 400g spinach
- small pack parsley , leaves picked and chopped

Method

STEP 1

Heat the oil in a medium saucepan. Add the shallots and cook on a medium heat for 10 mins until softened. Add the Puy lentils, stock and sour cherries, and simmer for 10 mins. Remove from the heat and stir through the spinach and parsley.

Tuna sweet potato jackets

Prep: 10 mins **Cook:** 20 mins

Serves 4

Ingredients

- 4 small sweet potatoes (about 200g each)
- 185g can tuna in spring water, drained
- ½ red onion , finely sliced
- 1 small red chilli , deseeded and chopped
- juice 1 lime
- 6 tbsp Greek yogurt
- handful coriander leaves

Method

STEP 1

Scrub the sweet potatoes and prick all over with a fork. Place on a microwaveable plate and cook on High for 18-20 mins, or until tender. Split in half and place each one, cut-side up, on a serving plate.

STEP 2

Flake the drained tuna with a fork and divide between the sweet potatoes. Top with the red onion and chilli, then squeeze over the lime juice. Top with a dollop of yogurt and scatter over the coriander, to serve.

New potato & tamarind salad

Prep: 15 mins **Cook:** 25 mins

Serves 6

Ingredients

- 1 ½ tbsp tamarind pulp or paste
- 50g golden muscovado sugar
- 1 tbsp ground cumin
- thumb-sized piece ginger , chopped
- 1.2kg new potato
- 3 tbsp natural low-fat yogurt
- 4 tbsp chopped coriander

Method

STEP 1

To make the dressing, put the tamarind pulp in a small pan, pour over 75ml boiling water and add the sugar, cumin and ginger. Simmer, without a lid, until the dressing thickens and becomes syrupy, about 10-15 mins. It should have a pleasant tang – add extra sugar if needed.

STEP 2

While the tamarind is cooking, bring a large pan of salted water to the boil and add the potatoes. Return to the boil and cook for 15 mins until tender. Drain, then cool slightly before halving them. Transfer to a big mixing bowl and spoon over the dressing, gently stirring to make sure the potatoes are well coated. Drizzle over the yogurt, scatter over the coriander, and serve warm or at room temperature.

Sesame salmon, purple sprouting broccoli & sweet potato mash

Prep: 10 mins **Cook:** 15 mins

Serves 2

Ingredients

- 1 ½ tbsp sesame oil
- 1 tbsp low-salt soy sauce
- thumb-sized piece ginger, grated
- 1 garlic clove, crushed
- 1 tsp honey
- 2 sweet potatoes, scrubbed and cut into wedges
- 1 lime, cut into wedges
- 2 boneless skinless salmon fillets
- 250g purple sprouting broccoli
- 1 tbsp sesame seeds
- 1 red chilli, thinly sliced (deseeded if you don't like it too hot)

Method

STEP 1

Heat oven to 200C/180 fan/ gas 6 and line a baking tray with parchment. Mix together 1/2 tbsp sesame oil, the soy, ginger, garlic and honey. Put the sweet potato wedges, skin and all, into a glass bowl with the lime wedges. Cover with cling film and microwave on high for 12-14 mins until completely soft.

STEP 2

Meanwhile, spread the broccoli and salmon out on the baking tray. Spoon over the marinade and season. Roast in the oven for 10-12 mins, then sprinkle over the sesame seeds.

STEP 3

Remove the lime wedges and roughly mash the sweet potato using a fork. Mix in the remaining sesame oil, the chilli and some seasoning. Divide between plates, along with the salmon and broccoli.

Creamy smoked salmon, leek & potato soup

Prep: 15 mins **Cook:** 25 mins

Serves 8

Ingredients

- large knob of butter
- 2 large leeks, halved and finely sliced
- 1 bay leaf
- 1kg floury potatoes, diced
- 1l chicken or vegetable stock
- 100ml double cream
- 200g smoked salmon, cut into strips
- small bunch chives, snipped

Method

STEP 1

Heat the butter in a large saucepan and add the leeks and bay leaf. Cook over a low heat for 8-10 mins or until the leek is really soft, then stir through the potatoes until coated in the butter. Pour over the stock and cream and bring to the simmer, then gently bubble for 10-15 mins until the potatoes are really tender. If freezing at this stage, slightly under-cook the potatoes, then defrost and bring back to a simmer to finish cooking them and continue the recipe.

STEP 2

Add two-thirds of the smoked salmon, stir through and season. Serve the soup in deep bowls with the remaining smoked salmon and snipped chives on the top.

Open leek & sweet potato pie

Prep: 20 mins **Cook:** 40 mins

Serves 6

Ingredients

- 3 tbsp olive oil , plus extra for brushing
- 2 large leeks , washed and sliced
- 2 sweet potatoes , peeled and roughly chopped into 2cm cubes
- 1 tsp coriander seeds
- 1 tsp chilli flakes
- 2 fat garlic cloves , crushed
- 150g ricotta
- 2 large eggs
- 1 lemon , zested
- 100g robust leafy greens such as cavalo nero or kale, finely shredded, tough core removed
- 1 small pack dill , chopped
- 1 pack filo pastry (around 12 sheets)
- 80g goat's cheese
- 1 tsp nigella seeds (optional)
- peppery salad , to serve

Method

STEP 1

Heat the oil in a large ovenproof frying pan. Add the leeks and a pinch of salt, then cook over a medium heat for a couple of mins until beginning to wilt. Tip in the sweet potato, cover the pan then cook, stirring occasionally, for 15 mins until the potato is mostly softened. Stir in the coriander seeds, chilli flakes, garlic and season. Give everything a gentle stir – you want the potato to remain intact as much as possible – then remove the pan from the heat and set aside to cool slightly.

STEP 2

In a large bowl, whisk together the ricotta, eggs and lemon zest with some seasoning. Stir in the greens and dill, then scrape in the sweet potato filling, (set aside the frying pan afterwards) and fold everything together. Heat oven to 220C/200C fan/gas 7.

STEP 3

Lay your first sheet of filo in the frying pan you used for the sweet potato (no need to wash it first). Brush the top with a little oil, then continue to layer the filo, setting each sheet at a different angle and oiling in between the layers until all edges of the pan are covered. Spoon the filling on top of the pastry, dot over the goat's cheese, then crumple the pastry in over the filling, leaving the centre of the pie exposed. Brush the top with a little more oil and scatter over the nigella seeds, if using.

STEP 4

Turn the hob back on and cook the pie over a medium-low heat for 3 mins to ensure the base is crisp, then transfer to the oven and bake for 12-15 mins until the pastry is crisp and golden. Let the pie cool in the pan for 10 mins before slicing.

Apple & sultana porridge

Prep: 10 mins **Cook:** 5 mins

Serves 4

Ingredients

- 100g porridge oat
- 500ml skimmed milk
- 4 apples , cored and diced
- 100g sultana
- 1 tbsp brown sugar , to serve

Method

STEP 1

Put the oats and milk in a small pan and cook, stirring, for 3 mins until almost creamy. Stir in the apples and sultanas, then cook for 2 mins more or until the porridge is thick and creamy and the apples just tender. Ladle into bowls, sprinkle with sugar and eat immediately.

Chipotle chicken tacos with pineapple salsa

Prep: 10 mins **Cook:** 10 mins

Serves 4

Ingredients

- 500g skinless boneless chicken thighs
- 1 tbsp vegetable oil
- 1 medium onion , chopped
- 2 tsp sweet smoked paprika

- 2 tsp ground cumin
- 2 tbsp cider vinegar
- 1 tbsp chipotle paste
- 200ml passata
- 2 tbsp soft brown sugar
- ½ small pineapple, cored, peeled and chopped
- ½ small pack coriander, chopped
- corn or flour tortillas
- hot sauce (I like Tabasco Chipotle), to serve

Method

STEP 1

In a food processor, roughly blitz the chicken thighs into chunky mince. Alternatively, chop into bite-sized pieces.

STEP 2

Heat the oil in a large saucepan. Add half the onion and the chicken mince. Season well and cook for about 5 mins on a high heat to brown, breaking up the meat with a spoon. Add the spices, vinegar, chipotle paste, passata and sugar. Cook for another 5 mins, then remove from the heat.

STEP 3

In a small bowl, mix the remaining onion, the pineapple and coriander. Serve the chicken and the pineapple salsa with warm tortillas and hot sauce.

Peach crumble

Prep: 10 mins **Cook:** 35 mins

Serves 6

Ingredients

- 3 x 410g cans peach slices in juice
- zest 1 lemon, plus juice ½
- 1 tbsp agave syrup
- 140g plain flour
- 50g porridge oat
- 25g cold butter, grated

Method

STEP 1

Heat oven to 200C/180C fan/gas 6. Drain the peaches, but reserve the juice. Tip the peaches into a deep baking dish, roughly 20 x 30cm. Scatter over the lemon zest and juice and 1 tbsp of the agave, then toss everything together.

STEP 2

In a bowl, combine the flour, oats, butter, remaining agave and 4 tbsp of the reserved peach juice. Mix together, first with a spoon, then with your fingers, until you have a rough crumbly mixture. Scatter over the peaches, then bake for 35 mins until golden and crunchy on top.

Coriander cod with carrot pilaf

Prep: 8 mins **Cook:** 15 mins

Serves 4

Ingredients

- 2 tbsp olive oil
- 4 skinless cod fillets, about 175g/6oz each
- 2 tbsp chopped coriander
- zest and juice 1 lemon
- 1 onion , chopped
- 2 tsp cumin seeds
- 2 large carrots , grated
- 200g basmati rice
- 600ml vegetable stock

Method

STEP 1

Heat the grill pan to high, then line with double thickness foil and curl up the edges to catch the juices. Brush lightly with oil and put the cod on top. Sprinkle over the coriander, lemon zest and juice and drizzle with a little more of the oil. Season with salt and pepper, then grill for 10-12 mins until the fish flakes easily.

STEP 2

Meanwhile, heat the remaining oil in a pan. Add the onion and cumin and fry for a few mins. Add the carrots and stir well, then stir in the rice until glistening. Add the stock and bring to the boil. Cover and cook gently for about 10 mins until the rice is tender and the stock absorbed. Spoon the rice onto 4 warm plates, top with cod and pour over the pan juices.

Ginger & lime chicken with sweet potato mash

Prep: 15 mins **Cook:** 20 mins Plus 10 mins marinating

Serves 2

Ingredients

- zest and juice 1 lime
- 1 tbsp maple syrup or clear honey
- thumb-size piece fresh root ginger , cut into matchsticks, plus 1 tsp grated root ginger
- 2 skinless, boneless chicken breasts
- 450g/1lb sweet potatoes , roughly chopped
- 1 tbsp olive oil

Method

STEP 1

Mix half the lime zest and all the juice with the maple syrup and grated ginger. Slash each chicken breast 3-4 times with a sharp knife, then coat well with the marinade. Set aside for 10 mins. Heat the grill and line the grill tray with foil.

STEP 2

Cook the sweet potatoes in salted boiling water for 10-12 mins until tender. Drain and mash well, adding the rest of the lime zest, plus some seasoning. Meanwhile, grill the chicken breasts for 10-15 mins, until cooked through and slightly caramelised.

STEP 3

Heat the oil in a small frying pan. When it's really hot, add the ginger matchsticks and fry for 1 min until the ginger is crisp. Lift out the matchsticks with a slotted spoon, then stir the mash into the gingerinfused oil. Divide the mash between 2 plates, top each with a chicken breast, scatter with the crisp ginger and serve with some sugar snap peas.

Easy lentil curry

Prep: 5 mins **Cook:** 45 mins

Serves 4

Ingredients

- 2 tbsp sunflower oil
- 2 medium onions, cut into rough wedges
- 4 tbsp curry paste
- 850ml vegetable stock
- 750g stewpack frozen vegetables
- 100g red lentil
- 200g basmati rice
- turmeric
- handful of raisins and roughly chopped parsley
- poppadums and mango chutney, to serve

Method

STEP 1

Heat the oil in a large pan. Add the onions and cook over a high heat for about 8 minutes or until they are golden brown. Stir in the curry paste and cook for a minute. Slowly pour in a little of the stock so it sizzles, scraping any bits from the bottom of the pan. Gradually pour in the rest of the stock.

STEP 2

Stir the frozen vegetables, cover and simmer for 5 minutes. Add the lentils and simmer for a further 15-20 minutes or until the vegetables and lentils are cooked.

STEP 3

While the curry is simmering, cook the rice according to the packet instructions, adding the turmeric to the cooking water. Drain well.

STEP 4

Season the curry with salt, toss in a handful of raisins and chopped parsley, then serve with the rice, poppadums and chutney.

Curried aubergine & potato pie

Prep: 10 mins **Cook:** 1 hr - 1 hr and 10 mins

Serves 4

Ingredients

- 1kg potato, peeled and cut into 3cm chunks
- 1 tbsp olive oil
- 1 large onion, chopped

- 2 large garlic cloves , crushed
- 2 medium aubergines , cut into 3cm chunks
- 1 tbsp medium curry powder
- 400g can chopped tomato
- 2 tbsp tomato purée
- 410g can green lentil , drained

Method

STEP 1

Preheat the oven to fan 200C/conventional 220C/gas 7. Cook the potatoes in lightly salted simmering water for 15-20 minutes until just tender – don't let the water boil or the potatoes will break up.

STEP 2

Meanwhile, heat the oil in a large frying pan and gently fry the onion and garlic until starting to go golden – about 4-5 minutes. Remove 2 tbsp of onion mixture and set aside.

STEP 3

Add the aubergines to the pan. Cook gently, stirring now and then, for 6-8 minutes, until softened. Stir in the curry powder. Cook for 30 seconds then add the tomatoes, tomato purée and lentils. Cook for 1-2 minutes, then transfer to a 2 litre dish. Drain the potatoes, pile on top of the aubergine mixture and sprinkle over the reserved onion mixture. (At this stage it can be frozen for up to one month.)

STEP 4

Bake for 30-35 minutes until nicely browned on top. Serve with broccoli or a salad.

Spinach & barley risotto

Prep: 10 mins **Cook:** 15 mins

Serves 2

Ingredients

- 2 tsp rapeseed oil
- 1 large leek (315g), thinly sliced
- 2 garlic cloves , chopped
- 2 x 400g can barley , undrained
- 1 tbsp vegetable bouillon powder
- 1 tsp finely chopped sage

- 1 tbsp thyme leaves
- 160g cherry tomatoes , halved
- 160g spinach
- 50g finely grated vegetarian Italian-style hard cheese

Method

STEP 1

Heat the oil in a non-stick pan and fry the leek and garlic for 5-10 mins, stirring frequently, until softened, adding a splash of water if it sticks.

STEP 2

Tip in the cans of barley and their liquid, then stir in the bouillon powder, sage and thyme. Simmer, stirring frequently, for 4-5 mins. Add the tomatoes and spinach and cook for 2-3 mins more until the spinach is wilted, adding a splash more water if needed. Stir in most of the cheese, then serve with the remaining cheese scattered over.

Braised baby leeks

Prep: 5 mins **Cook:** 20 mins

Serves 2

Ingredients

- 280g baby leeks
- knob of butter
- 500ml chicken stock
- handful thyme sprigs , plus extra leaves to serve

Method

STEP 1

Wash and trim the ends and roots of the baby leeks. Heat a knob of butter in a large frying pan, and add the leeks. Roll them around to coat them in the butter.

STEP 2

Add the chicken stock, bring to the boil, then turn down to a simmer and add the thyme. Cook for 20 mins or until tender. Serve with a sprinkling of thyme leaves.

Turkey & avocado toast

Prep: 10 mins **Cook:** 5 mins

Serves 2

Ingredients

- 1 avocado
- juice ½ lime
- 2-3 small slices ciabatta bread
- 100g turkey slices

Method

STEP 1

Halve and stone the avocado then scrape out the flesh into a bowl. Squeeze in the lime, season, then mash roughly with a fork. Toast the ciabatta, spread with mashed avocado, top with turkey and finish with ground black pepper.

Herb & garlic baked cod with romesco sauce & spinach

Prep: 10 mins **Cook:** 20 mins

Serves 2

Ingredients

- 2 x 140g skinless cod loin or pollock fillets
- 1 tbsp rapeseed oil, plus 2 tsp
- 1 tsp fresh thyme leaves
- 1 large garlic clove, finely grated
- ½ lemon, zested and juiced
- 1 large red pepper, sliced
- 2 leeks, well washed and thinly sliced
- 2 tbsp flaked almonds
- 1 tbsp tomato purée
- ¼ tsp vegetable bouillon powder
- 1 tsp apple cider vinegar
- 100g baby spinach, wilted in a pan or the microwave

Method

STEP 1

Heat oven to 220C/200C fan/ gas 7 and put the fish fillets in a shallow ovenproof dish so they fit quite snugly in a single layer. Mix 1 tbsp rapeseed oil with the thyme and garlic, spoon over the fish, then grate over the lemon zest. Bake for 10-12 mins until the fish is moist and flakes easily when tested.

STEP 2

Meanwhile, heat the remaining oil in a non-stick pan and fry the pepper and leeks for 5 mins until softened. Add the almonds and cook for 5 mins more. Tip in the tomato purée, 5 tbsp water, the bouillion powder and vinegar, and cook briefly to warm the mixture through.

STEP 3

Add the juice of up to half a lemon and blitz with a stick blender until it makes a thick, pesto-like sauce. Serve with the fish and the wilted spinach.

Chicken with crispy Parma ham

Prep: 10 mins **Cook:** 20 mins

Serves 4

Ingredients

- 450g new potato , halved if large
- 225g runner bean , trimmed and sliced
- 4 skinless chicken breasts
- 1 tbsp olive oil
- 4 slices Parma ham
- 1 garlic clove , crushed
- juice 1 lemon

Method

STEP 1

Cook the new potatoes in boiling salted water for 10-15 mins, until just tender, adding the green beans for the final 2 mins. Meanwhile, put each chicken breast between two sheets of cling film and bash them with a rolling pin until they're about 1cm thick. Season.

STEP 2

Heat a large frying pan and add the Parma ham. Cook for 2 mins, until crisp. Drain on kitchen paper. Add the oil to the pan and add two of the chicken breasts. Cook for 3 mins each side, transfer to a plate and keep warm. Cook the other two breasts in the same way.

STEP 3

Remove the pan from the heat and add the garlic and lemon juice. Toss in the drained beans and potatoes and crumble in the Parma ham. Divide the chicken and veg between four plates.

Five-spice beef & sugar snap noodles

Prep: 10 mins **Cook:** 15 mins

Serves 4

Ingredients

- 250g lean minced beef
- 3 nests medium egg noodles
- thumb-sized piece ginger, finely grated
- 3 garlic cloves, finely grated
- 1 heaped tsp five-spice powder
- ¼ tsp chilli powder
- 225g pack mangetout or sugar snap peas
- 400ml beef stock
- 3 tbsp light soy sauce, or more to taste
- sesame oil, to serve
- red chilli, deseeded and shredded to serve (optional)

Method

STEP 1

Heat a large non-stick frying pan or wok, then fry the beef for 10 mins until very well browned. Don't add any oil. Meanwhile, boil the noodles following pack instructions, then drain.

STEP 2

Add the ginger, garlic, five-spice, chilli powder and mangetout to the browned mince, then fry for a few mins more until fragrant and the pods are bright green. Splash in the stock, add the noodles, then season with the soy sauce. Pile into bowls (use tongs, it's easier), sprinkling with the sesame oil and red chilli if using.

Lemony salmon & lettuce wraps

Prep: 10 mins no cook

Serves 2

Ingredients

- 400g can cannellini beans, rinsed and drained
- 213g can wild red salmon, drained, skin and bones removed if you like
- ½ lemon, zested and juiced
- 1 spring onion, finely chopped
- 1 tbsp Greek yogurt
- 1 tbsp dill, chopped
- 8 large romaine lettuce leaves

Method

STEP 1

Mix together all the ingredients except the lettuce in a bowl.

STEP 2

Trim the chunky part of the stalk at the base of each lettuce leaf so they are easier to roll up, then place the leaves in pairs on top of each other, head to toe. Spoon on the salmon mixture, then roll up and keep in place with strips of baking parchment, which make the wraps easier to hold and eat. Pack into a container to keep the wraps from getting crushed and, if possible, chill to keep the lettuce crisp.

Chicken & avocado sandwich topper

Prep: 5 mins No cook

Serves 1

Ingredients

- 2 tsp low-fat mayonnaise
- slices cooked chicken
- ½ small avocado, diced
- squeeze of lemon
- chopped red onion
- coriander leaves
- halved cherry tomatoes
- slice wholemeal seeded bread or rye, or wholegrain pitta, to serve

Method

STEP 1

Top bread or fill pitta with mayonnaise and chicken then add avocado, lemon, red onion, coriander and cherry tomatoes.

Raspberry chia jam

Prep: 5 mins **Cook:** 15 mins Plus cooling

Makes 1 jar (about 400g)

Ingredients

- 500g raspberries
- 1 tsp vanilla bean paste
- 3 tbsp honey
- 3 tbsp chia seeds

Method

STEP 1

Put the raspberries in a pan with the vanilla and honey, then cook over a low heat for 5 mins or until the berries have broken down.

STEP 2

Stir through the chia and cook for 10 mins. Set aside to cool completely (it will thicken significantly as it cools). Spoon into a bowl or sterilised jar. Great on toast, swirled through porridge or in yogurt. Will keep in the fridge for up to one week.

Thai-style fish broth with greens

Prep: 10 mins **Cook:** 15 mins

Serves 2

Ingredients

- 100g brown rice noodle
- 500ml chicken or fish stock

- 1 tbsp Thai red curry paste
- 4 dried or fresh kaffir lime leaves
- 1 tbsp fish sauce
- 200g skinless sustainable white fish, such as pollock
- 100g raw king prawn
- 2 pak choi, leaves separated
- handful coriander leaves

Method

STEP 1

Cook the noodles following pack instructions. Refresh in cold water and drain well.

STEP 2

Put the stock in a large saucepan and stir in the curry paste, lime leaves, fish sauce and 250ml cold water. Bring to a simmer and cook for 5 mins.

STEP 3

Cut the fish into roughly 3cm cubes and add to the pan. Return to a simmer, then cook for 2 mins uncovered.

STEP 4

Stir in the noodles, prawns and pak choi, and simmer for 2-3 mins or until the fish and prawns are just cooked. Serve in bowls scattered with coriander.

Pepper & lemon spaghetti with basil & pine nuts

Prep: 7 mins **Cook:** 25 mins

Serves 2

Ingredients

- 1 tbsp rapeseed oil
- 1 red pepper, deseeded and diced
- 150g wholemeal spaghetti
- 2 courgettes (250g), grated
- 2 garlic cloves, finely grated
- 1 lemon, zested and juiced
- 15g basil, finely chopped
- 25g pine nuts, toasted
- 2 tbsp finely grated parmesan or vegetarian alternative (optional)

Method

STEP 1

Heat the oil in a large non-stick frying pan. Add the pepper and cook for 5 mins. Meanwhile, cook the pasta for 10-12 mins until tender.

STEP 2

Add the courgette and garlic to the pepper and cook, stirring very frequently, for 10-15 mins until the courgette is really soft.

STEP 3

Stir in the lemon zest and juice, basil and spaghetti (reserve some pasta water) and toss together, adding a little of the pasta water until nicely coated. Add the pine nuts, then spoon into bowls and serve topped with the parmesan, if using.

Pasta with tuna & tomato sauce

Total time 35 mins Ready in 30-35 minutes

Serves 4

Ingredients

- 2 tbsp olive oil
- 1 onion, chopped
- 2 garlic cloves, finely chopped
- 400g can chopped tomatoes with herbs
- ½ tsp chilli powder
- 1 tsp sugar
- 500g pkt pasta bows
- 100g can tuna, drained
- handful of basil leaves, optional

Method

STEP 1

Heat the oil in a pan, throw in the onion and cook for a couple of minutes. Stir in the garlic, tomatoes, chilli and sugar. Season with salt and pepper and bring to the boil. Give it a good stir, then reduce the heat and simmer for 5 minutes.

STEP 2

Meanwhile, bring a large pan of salted water to the boil. Add the pasta and cook according to packet instructions. Flake the tuna into the sauce and heat through. Drain the pasta, return to the pan and stir in the sauce and basil leaves if you have any. Serve with a generous grinding of pepper.

Oaty fish & prawn gratins

Prep: 12 mins **Cook:** 28 mins

Serves 2

Ingredients

- 340g bag baby spinach , roughly chopped
- 400g can chopped tomato with garlic and herbs
- 225g sustainable white fish fillets, chopped into large chunks
- small bunch basil , shredded
- 100g cooked and peeled prawn
- 2 tbsp finely grated parmesan
- 2 tbsp breadcrumb
- 2 tbsp oats
- 170g broccoli , boiled or steamed, to serve

Method

STEP 1

Put the spinach in a large colander and pour over boiling water. Once cool enough to handle, squeeze out any excess water, then season.

STEP 2

Tip the tomatoes into a frying pan with some seasoning and simmer for 5 mins to thicken. Add the fish and heat for 1-2 mins – it doesn't need to be fully cooked at this point. Stir in the basil.

STEP 3

Heat oven to 220C/200C fan/gas 7. Divide the spinach, fish, prawns and tomato sauce between 2 gratin dishes. Mix the Parmesan, breadcrumbs and oats together and sprinkle over the top. Bake for 20 mins until golden and bubbling. Serve with cooked broccoli.

Skinny chicken Caesar salad

Prep: 30 mins **Cook:** 10 mins - 12 mins

Serves 4

Ingredients

- 4 skinless chicken breasts
- 2 tsp olive oil
- juice 1 lemon
- 1 large Romaine or Cos lettuce , chopped into large pieces
- 1 punnet salad cress
- 4 hard-boiled eggs , peeled and quartered
- 25g parmesan , finely grated
- 50g anchovy fillets, half chopped, half left whole
- 170g pot fat-free Greek yogurt

Method

STEP 1

Put the chicken breasts in a large bowl with the olive oil and 1 tbsp lemon juice, then season. Heat the grill to high. Put the chicken breasts on a foil-lined tray and cook under the grill for 10-12 mins until golden and cooked through, turning once during cooking. Transfer to a plate or board and slice.

STEP 2

Arrange the lettuce, cress and eggs on a platter or serving plates and top with the cooked chicken. Mix together the Parmesan, chopped anchovies, yogurt and remaining lemon juice, season to taste and pour over the salad. Arrange the whole anchovy fillets on top of each salad.

Chocolate chia pudding

Prep: 5 mins No cook, plus 4 hours chilling

Serves 4

Ingredients

- 60g chia seeds
- 400ml unsweetened almond milk or hazelnut milk

- 3 tbsp cacao powder
- 2 tbsp maple syrup
- ½ tsp vanilla extract
- cacao nibs, mixed
- frozen berries, to serve

Method

STEP 1

Put all the ingredients in a large bowl with a generous pinch of sea salt and whisk to combine. Cover with cling film then leave to thicken in the fridge for at least 4 hours, or overnight.

STEP 2

Spoon the pudding into four glasses, then top with the frozen berries and cacao nibs.

Leek, mushroom & goat's cheese strudels

Prep: 20 mins **Cook:** 40 mins

Serves 4

Ingredients

- 500g leeks, thinly sliced
- 150ml low-sodium vegetable stock
- 175g chestnut mushroom, sliced
- 4 large sheets filo pastry
- 1 tbsp olive oil
- 85g soft-rinded goat's cheese or vegetarian alternative
- 1 tsp poppy seeds

Method

STEP 1

Heat oven to 200C/180C fan/gas 6. Put the leeks and stock into a large pan, then cover and cook for 5-8 mins until starting to soften. Add the mushrooms, cover again and cook for 3 mins, then remove the lid and continue to cook until the juices have evaporated. Tip the veg onto a large plate to cool slightly.

STEP 2

For each strudel, lightly brush half of each filo sheet with some olive oil. Fold the un-brushed side over to make a smaller sheet, 2 layers thick. Brush the edges with a little more oil, then spoon a quarter of the veg along one edge. Crumble over a quarter of the cheese, fold over the pastry edges, then roll up to seal in the filling.

STEP 3

Put the strudels on a baking tray, brush with any remaining oil and scatter over the poppy seeds. Bake for 25 mins until crisp and golden brown.

Cabbage with caraway

Prep: 10 mins **Cook:** 10 mins

Serves 4

Ingredients

- 1 Savoy cabbage , cored and shredded
- 1 tbsp olive oil
- 1 onion , thinly sliced
- 2-3 tsp caraway seeds

Method

STEP 1

Cook the cabbage in boiling water for 3 mins until tender, then drain. Heat the oil in a frying pan. Add the onion and cook for 2-3 mins until starting to soften and turn golden. Sprinkle over the caraway seeds and cook for a further 2 mins until fragrant. Stir in the cabbage and heat through.

Lime prawn cocktail pitta salad

Prep: 10 mins **Cook:** 15 mins

Serves 2

Ingredients

- ½ wholemeal pitta
- ½ tbsp rapeseed oil
- 1 tsp Tabasco
- 1 tsp low-sugar, low-salt ketchup

- 1 tbsp low-fat mayonnaise
- 1 tbsp fat-free natural yogurt
- ½ lime, zested and juiced, plus wedges to serve
- 60g cooked king prawns
- 1 Little Gem lettuce, leaves separated
- ¼ small cucumber, peeled into ribbons
- 4 cherry tomatoes, halved

Method

STEP 1

Heat the oven to 200C/180C fan/gas 6. Slice the pitta into triangles, put on a baking sheet and drizzle over the oil. Bake for 10-15 mins until golden and crisp.

STEP 2

Mix together the Tabasco, ketchup, mayo, yogurt and lime zest and juice. Toss the prawns in the dressing.

STEP 3

Layer the lettuce, cucumber, tomatoes and dressed prawns in a lunchbox or jar. Season, top with the pitta chips and serve with lime wedges.

Ham, mushroom & spinach frittata

Prep: 4 mins **Cook:** 9 mins

Serves 2

Ingredients

- 1 tsp oil
- 80g chestnut mushrooms, sliced
- 50g ham, diced
- 80g bag spinach
- 4 medium eggs, beaten
- 1 tbsp grated cheddar

Method

STEP 1

Heat the grill to its highest setting. Heat the oil in an ovenproof frying pan over a medium-high heat. Tip in the mushrooms and fry for 2 mins until mostly softened. Stir in the ham and spinach, and cook for 1 min more until the spinach has wilted. Season well with black pepper and a pinch of salt.

STEP 2

Reduce the heat and pour over the eggs. Cook undisturbed for 3 mins until the eggs are mostly set. Sprinkle over the cheese and put under the grill for 2 mins. Serve hot or cold.

Crunchy detox salad

Prep: 15 mins - 20 mins **Cook:** 1 min

Serves 4

Ingredients

- 250g broccoli , cut into small florets
- 100g ready-to-eat dried apricots , cut into strips
- 300g red cabbage , finely shredded
- 400g can chickpeas , rinsed and drained
- 50g sunflower seeds
- 1 small red onion , finely sliced
- 2cm piece ginger , grated
- juice 1 small orange
- 1 tbsp balsamic vinegar
- 2 tsp olive oil

Method

STEP 1

Blanch the broccoli in a pan of boiling water for 1 min. Drain and quickly cool under cold running water, then pat dry with kitchen paper. Put in a bowl with the apricots, broccoli, red cabbage, chickpeas and sunflower seeds.

STEP 2

Put the onion and ginger in a bowl with the orange juice, vinegar and oil. Mix well. Leave for 5 mins to soften the onion, then add to the salad and thoroughly toss everything together.

Peach Melba smoothie

Prep: 5 mins No cook

Serves 2

Ingredients

- 410g can peach halves

- 100g frozen raspberry , plus a few for garnish
- 100ml orange juice
- 150ml fresh custard , plus a spoonful for garnish

Method

STEP 1

Drain and rinse peaches and place in a blender with raspberries. Add orange juice and fresh custard and whizz together.

STEP 2

Pour over ice, garnish with another spoonful of custard and a few raspberries. Best served chilled.

Ham hock & cabbage hash

Prep: 15 mins **Cook:** 35 mins

Serves 5

Ingredients

- 1kg potato , unpeeled and cut into cubes
- 25g butter
- ½ Savoy cabbage , shredded
- 1 onion , thinly sliced
- 100ml low-sodium vegetable stock
- 175g ham hock, shredded
- baked beans and your favourite sauce, to serve

Method

STEP 1

Cook the potatoes in a large pan of salted water until tender, drain, then allow to steam dry for about 3 mins.

STEP 2

Meanwhile, melt half the butter in a large non-stick frying pan, then throw in the cabbage and onion and fry for 2 mins. Add the stock and cook for 5 mins more until the veg is starting to soften. Stir in the ham and potatoes and push down in the pan to flatten slightly. Cook for 8 mins until the base is golden and crisp.

STEP 3

Heat the grill. Dot the remaining butter on top of the hash, then flash under the grill until golden and crisp. Serve with baked beans and brown sauce or ketchup, if you like.

Chicken & mushroom pancake topping

Prep: 5 mins **Cook:** 15 mins

Serves 4

Ingredients

- a large knob of butter
- 250g chopped chestnut mushrooms
- 1 crushed garlic clove
- 2 tbsp flour
- 250ml milk
- 2 tsp Dijon mustard
- 2 tbsp mushroom ketchup
- 2 cooked chicken breasts
- a handful chopped parsley

Method

STEP 1

Melt the butter in a pan, add the mushrooms and cook until softened, about 8 mins. Add the garlic and cook for 1 min more, then stir in the flour, milk, mustard and ketchup. Stir for a few mins until you have a thick sauce, then season well.

STEP 2

Shred the chicken and add to the sauce along with the parsley. Top four warm pancakes (see our easy pancakes recipe) with the chicken & mushroom mix and serve.

Crisp chicken burgers with lemon mayo

Prep: 10 mins **Cook:** 10 mins

Serves 4

Ingredients

- 4 chicken breasts
- 3 slices white bread , toasted

- 1 egg
- 1 tsp Dijon mustard
- zest 1 lemon , juice from ½
- 4 tbsp reduced-fat mayonnaise
- 4 ciabatta buns, warm or toasted

Method

STEP 1

Heat grill to high. Put the chicken breasts between 2 pieces of cling film and bash with a rolling pin until they're about half their original thickness. Whizz the toast in a food processor to rough breadcrumbs, then tip out onto a plate.

STEP 2

Beat the egg and mustard together in a bowl and season. Dip the chicken into the egg, let the excess drip back into the bowl, then press into the toasty breadcrumbs. Put under the grill on a flat baking sheet and grill for about 10 mins, turning once, until golden and crisp on both sides and the chicken is cooked through.

STEP 3

Beat the lemon zest, juice and lots of black pepper into the mayonnaise. Spread some of the mayo onto the bottom halves of the buns, top with a chicken breast and salad of your choice and serve.

Courgette lasagne

Prep: 20 mins **Cook:** 1 hr and 25 mins

Serves 6

Ingredients

- 8 plum tomatoes , halved
- 2 garlic cloves , lightly bashed
- 1 tbsp olive oil
- 1 rosemary sprig
- ½ tbsp golden caster sugar
- 2 leeks , sliced into rings
- 20g unsalted butter
- 100g baby spinach
- 500g courgettes , grated
- 10 lasagne sheets
- 250g tub of ricotta
- 125g mozzarella , torn
- 50g parmesan (or vegetarian alternative), grated

Method

STEP 1

Heat oven to 200C/180C fan/gas 6. Put the tomatoes on a baking tray with the garlic, oil, rosemary and a good pinch of seasoning. Bake for 25-30 mins until soft, then discard the rosemary and peel off the garlic skin. Put the tomatoes, garlic and sugar in a blender and blitz a few times until you have a chunky sauce.

STEP 2

Meanwhile, put the leeks in a pan over a low heat, add the butter, season and cook for 7-10 mins or until soft. Add the spinach and courgettes, and cook, covered, for 2 mins until wilted and soft. Set aside.

STEP 3

In a lasagne dish, layer up the ingredients using the tomato sauce first, then some pasta, followed by the ricotta and vegetables. Keep layering until you've used up everything. Finish with a final layer of the vegetables, the mozzarella and the Parmesan. Bake in the oven for 40-45 mins until the sauce has reduced and the top is golden brown.

Pea & feta pearl barley stew

Prep: 10 mins **Cook:** 45 mins

Serves 4

Ingredients

- 2 tbsp olive oil
- 2 medium onions , chopped
- 2 garlic cloves , chopped
- zest and juice 2 lemons
- 200g pearl barley , rinsed under cold water
- 700ml vegetable stock
- 200g feta , cut into cubes
- ½ small pack mint , leaves shredded, plus a few whole leaves to serve
- 400g frozen peas , defrosted at room temperature

Method

STEP 1

Heat 1 tbsp oil in a pan or flameproof casserole dish over a medium heat. Add the onion and cook for 3 mins, then add the garlic and lemon zest and fry for another 1 min. Add the pearl barley and the stock. Season, bring to the boil, then simmer for 30 mins, stirring occasionally.

STEP 2

Meanwhile, put the feta in a bowl with the remaining olive oil, half the lemon juice, most of the mint and a good grinding of black pepper. Leave to marinate while the barley cooks.

STEP 3

Remove the lid from the barley and cook for 5 mins more. Increase the heat then add the peas, half the feta and all the feta juices. Cook for 3 mins, then check the seasoning. Divide between four bowls and top with the remaining feta and mint.

Veggie olive wraps with mustard vinaigrette

Prep: 10 mins no cook

Serves 1

Ingredients

- 1 carrot , shredded or coarsely grated
- 80g wedge red cabbage , finely shredded
- 2 spring onions , thinly sliced
- 1 courgette , shredded or coarsely grated
- handful basil leaves
- 5 green olives , pitted and halved
- ½ tsp English mustard powder
- 2 tsp extra virgin rapeseed oil
- 1 tbsp cider vinegar
- 1 large seeded tortilla

Method

STEP 1

Mix all the ingredients except for the tortilla and toss well.

STEP 2

Put the tortilla on a sheet of foil and pile the filling along one side of the wrap – it will almost look like too much mixture, but once you start to roll it firmly it will compact. Roll the tortilla from the filling side, folding in the sides as you go. Fold the foil in at the ends to keep stuff inside the wrap. Cut in half and eat straight away. If taking to work, leave whole and wrap up like a cracker in baking parchment.

Cucumber, pea & lettuce soup

Prep: 5 mins **Cook:** 15 mins

Serves 4

Ingredients

- 1 tsp rapeseed oil
- small bunch spring onions , roughly chopped
- 1 cucumber , roughly chopped
- 1 large round lettuce , roughly chopped
- 225g frozen peas
- 4 tsp vegetable bouillon
- 4 tbsp bio yogurt (optional)
- 4 slices rye bread

Method

STEP 1

Boil 1.4 litres water in a kettle. Heat the oil in a large non-stick frying pan and cook the spring onions for 5 mins, stirring frequently, or until softened. Add the cucumber, lettuce and peas, then pour in the boiled water. Stir in the bouillon, cover and simmer for 10 mins or until the vegetables are soft but still bright green.

STEP 2

Blitz the mixture with a hand blender until smooth. Serve hot or cold, topped with yogurt (if you like), with rye bread alongside.

Mexican rice & bean salad

Prep: 20 mins **Cook:** 15 mins

Serves 4

Ingredients

- 175g/6oz basmati and wild rice
- 400g can mixed bean salad , drained and rinsed
- bunch spring onions , chopped
- 1 red pepper , deseeded and chopped
- 1 avocado , chopped
- juice 1 lime , plus wedges to serve
- 1 tbsp Cajun spice mix
- small bunch coriander , chopped

Method

STEP 1

Cook the rice following pack instructions. Drain, then cool under cold running water until completely cold. Stir in beans, onions, pepper and avocado.

STEP 2

Mix the lime juice with the Cajun spice mix and some black pepper. Pour over the rice mix, stir in the coriander and serve with extra lime wedges.

Thin-stemmed broccoli with hoisin sauce & fried shallots

Prep: 5 mins **Cook:** 15 mins

Serves 8

Ingredients

- vegetable oil , for shallow frying
- 4 shallots , thinly sliced
- 1 garlic clove , thinly sliced
- 500g thin-stemmed broccoli
- 4 tbsp hoisin sauce

Method

STEP 1

Heat 2.5cm of oil in a small saucepan until a small piece of bread sizzles. Add the shallots and garlic, and fry for about 2 mins or until golden. Drain on kitchen paper and sprinkle with salt.

STEP 2

Bring a large pan of water to the boil. Add the broccoli and blanch for 5-10 mins until just cooked, then drain. Serve immediately on a large platter drizzled with the hoisin sauce and sprinkled with the fried garlic and shallots.

Rich paprika seafood bowl

Prep: 10 mins **Cook:** 20 mins

Serves 4

Ingredients

- 1 tbsp olive oil
- 2 onions , halved and thinly sliced
- 2 celery stalks, finely chopped
- large bunch flat-leaf parsley , leaves and stalks separated
- 2-3 tsp paprika
- 200g roasted red pepper , drained weight, thickly sliced
- 400g can chopped tomato with garlic
- 400g white fish fillet, cut into very large chunks
- few fresh mussels (optional)

Method

STEP 1

Heat the oil in a pan, then add the onions, celery and a little salt. Cover, then gently fry until soft, about 10 mins. Put the parsley stalks, half the leaves, oil and seasoning into a food processor and whizz to a paste. Add this and the paprika to the softened onions, frying for a few mins. Tip in the peppers and tomatoes with a splash of water, then simmer for 10 mins until the sauce has reduced.

STEP 2

Lay the fish and mussels on top of the sauce, put a lid on, then simmer for 5 mins until the fish is just flaking and the mussels have opened – discard any that stay shut. Gently stir the seafood into the sauce, season, then serve in bowls.

One-pan prawn & tomato curry

Prep: 10 mins **Cook:** 20 mins

Serves 4

Ingredients

- 2 tbsp sunflower oil
- 1 large onion , chopped
- large piece ginger , crushed
- 4 garlic cloves , crushed

- ½ red chilli, finely chopped
- 1 tsp golden caster sugar
- 1 tsp black mustard seeds
- 1 tsp ground cumin
- 1 tsp ground coriander
- 1 tsp turmeric
- 1 tbsp garam masala
- 2 tsp malt vinegar
- 400g can chopped tomato
- 400g raw king prawns
- small bunch coriander, chopped
- basmati rice, yogurt, mango chutney and Carrot & cumin salad, to serve

Method

STEP 1

Heat the oil in a deep-sided frying pan and cook the onion for 8-10 mins until it starts to turn golden. Add the ginger, garlic and chilli and cook for 1-2 mins. Stir in the sugar and spices for 1 min, then splash in the vinegar and tomatoes. Season with salt and simmer for 5 mins, stirring, until the sauce thickens.

STEP 2

Stir in the prawns, reduce the heat and cook for 8-10 mins until cooked through – if the sauce gets really thick, add a splash of water. Remove from the heat, stir though most of the coriander. Serve straight from the dish scattered with the remaining coriander and the rice, yogurt, chutney and salad in separate bowls.

Easy Thai beef salad

Prep: 15 mins **Cook:** 5 mins Plus resting

Serves 2

Ingredients

- 300g rump steak, trimmed of fat
- 2 tsp groundnut oil
- juice 1 lime
- 1 red chilli, deseeded and sliced (bird's-eye chillies work well)
- 1 tbsp light brown soft sugar
- 85g bag baby leaf salad
- 140g beansprouts
- 140g red grapes, halved
- steamed rice, to serve (optional)

Method

STEP 1

Rub the steak with 1 tsp oil and season. Fry in a hot pan for 2-2½ mins each side (depending on thickness), for medium rare. Transfer to a plate, cover loosely with foil and rest for 5 mins.

STEP 2

Make the dressing by mixing the lime juice, chilli, sugar and remaining oil in a bowl. Set aside until the sugar dissolves.

STEP 3

Divide the salad leaves, beansprouts and grapes between 2 serving bowls. Thinly slice the steak and add the juices to the dressing. Drizzle this over the salads, toss with the sliced beef and serve immediately with rice, if you like.

Penne with broccoli, lemon & anchovies

Prep: 10 mins **Cook:** 17 mins

Serves 2

Ingredients

- 170g wholemeal penne
- 1 leek, washed and sliced
- 180g broccoli, cut into small florets
- 2 tsp oil from the anchovy can, plus 15g anchovies, chopped
- 1 red pepper, seeded, quartered and sliced
- ½ tsp finely chopped rosemary
- 1 red chilli, seeded and sliced
- 3 garlic cloves, sliced
- ½ lemon, zested and juiced
- 4 tbsp ricotta
- 2 tbsp sunflower seeds

Method

STEP 1

Boil the pasta with the sliced leek for 7 mins, then add the broccoli and boil for 5 mins until everything is just tender.

STEP 2

Meanwhile, heat the oil from the anchovies and fry the red pepper with the rosemary, chilli and garlic in a large non-stick pan for 5 mins until softened.

STEP 3

Drain the pasta, reserving a little water, then tip the pasta and veg into the pan and add the lemon juice and zest, anchovies and ricotta. Toss well over the heat, using the pasta water to moisten. Toss through the sunflower seeds and serve.

Walnut & almond muesli with grated apple

Prep: 10 mins **Cook:** 2 mins

Serves 4

Ingredients

- 85g porridge oats
- 15g flaked almonds
- 15g walnut pieces
- 15g pumpkin seeds
- 1 tsp ground cinnamon
- 80g raisins
- 15g high fibre puffed wheat (we used Good Grain)
- 4 apples , no need to peel, grated
- milk , to serve

Method

STEP 1

Put the porridge oats in a saucepan and heat gently, stirring frequently until they're just starting to toast. Turn off the heat, then add all of the nuts, pumpkin seeds, and cinnamon, then stir everything together well.

STEP 2

Tip into a large bowl, stir to help it cool, then add the raisins and puffed wheat and toss together until well mixed. Tip half into a jar or airtight container and save for another day – it will keep at room temperature. Serve the rest in two bowls, grate over 2 apples and pour over some cold milk (use nut milk if you're vegan) at the table. Save the other apples for the remaining muesli.

Lemony prawn pasta

Prep: 10 mins **Cook:** 15 mins

Serves 4

Ingredients

- 300g short pasta shapes
- 1 head broccoli , cut into small florets
- 200g large cooked prawns , halved
- 3 tbsp crème fraîche or double cream
- juice ½ lemon

Method

STEP 1

Cook the pasta following pack instructions, scooping out a bit of the cooking water as it cooks. Three mins before the pasta is done, add the broccoli to the pan and cook for the 3 mins more. Drain, then tip back into the pan.

STEP 2

Reduce the heat to very low and gently stir through the prawns, crème fraîche, lemon juice and some seasoning. Add a splash of the reserved pasta water if it looks too thick, then serve when everything is really hot.

Minced beef cobbler

Prep: 20 mins **Cook:** 50 mins

Serves 4

Ingredients

- 500g pack extra-lean beef mince
- 1 onion , finely chopped
- 140g baby chestnut mushroom , halved
- 2 tbsp plain flour
- 500ml beef stock
- few shakes Worcestershire sauce
- 140g self-raising flour
- 1 tbsp chopped thyme
- 4 tbsp low-fat natural yogurt
- 140g frozen peas

Method

STEP 1

Heat oven to 180C/160C fan/gas 4. Dry-fry the mince and onion in a large non-stick frying pan over a high heat. Stir frequently to break up the mince, until well browned. Add the mushrooms and plain flour, followed by the stock and Worcestershire sauce. Bring to a simmer, then gently cook for 10 mins.

STEP 2

Meanwhile, to make the cobbles, mix the self-raising flour and thyme together in a bowl. Stir in the yogurt with enough cold water to form a scone-like dough. On a lightly floured surface, roll out to the thickness of about 1.5cm and use a cutter to stamp out 12 x 5cm rounds.

STEP 3

Stir the peas into the mince mixture, then transfer to a baking dish. Randomly place the cobbles on top of the mince, then bake for 20-25 mins, until cobbles are risen and golden brown. This is good served with horseradish sauce.

Tasty cottage pie with parsnip mash

Prep: 1 hr and 15 mins **Cook:** 30 mins

Serves 4

Ingredients

- 250g packet lean minced beef (12% fat)
- 2 onions, chopped
- 4 carrots (about 450g/1lb), peeled and coarsely grated
- 2 tbsp Worcestershire sauce
- 2 tbsp tomato purée
- 2 beef stock, cubes dissolved in 425ml/¾pint boiling water
- 1 tsp cornflour
- 900g potato, peeled and cubed
- 3 parsnips, peeled, cored and chopped
- 2-4 tbsp skimmed milk
- steamed broccoli or Savoy cabbage to serve

Method

STEP 1

Dry fry the mince (without adding any oil) in a non-stick pan until evenly brown and crumbly. Add the onions and carrots and cook over a high heat for 5 minutes, stirring well.

STEP 2

Add the Worcestershire sauce and tomato purée, pour in the stock and bring to the boil, stirring until well mixed. Cover the pan and leave to simmer for 40 minutes, stirring occasionally until the carrots and onions are tender and the stock has reduced. Taste and season. Blend the cornflour with a little water and stir into the mixture, cooking for a minute or until slightly thickened.

STEP 3

Preheat the oven to 200C/Gas 6/ fan oven 180C. While the meat is simmering, cook the potatoes and parsnips in boiling salted water for 15 minutes or until tender. Drain and mash with seasoning and enough milk to make a creamy consistency.

STEP 4

Tip the meat mixture into a 1.4 litre/ 2 1/2 pint ovenproof dish, spoon the mash on top and rough up the surface with a fork. Bake for 30 minutes or until the potato topping is lightly golden. Serve with steamed broccoli or Savoy cabbage.

Turkey & spring onion wraps

Prep: 5 mins No cook

Serves 4

Ingredients

- 2 tbsp reduced-fat mayonnaise
- 2 tbsp pesto
- 4 curly lettuce leaves
- 250g cooked turkey, shredded
- 6 spring onions, shredded
- 12cm chunk cucumber, shredded
- 4 flour tortillas

Method

STEP 1

Mix together the mayonnaise and pesto. Divide the lettuce leaves, turkey, spring onions and cucumber between the tortillas. Drizzle over the pesto dressing, roll up and eat.

Lighter chicken tacos

Prep: 35 mins **Cook:** 25 mins

Serves 4

Ingredients

For the chicken

- 2 tsp rapeseed oil
- 1 tsp ground cumin
- 1 tsp smoked paprika
- 450g skinless chicken breasts, preferably organic

For the salsa

- 4 medium tomatoes, preferably on the vine, halved
- 1 red pepper, quartered
- 1 small red onion, cut into 8 wedges
- ¼ tsp rapeseed oil
- 2 tsp lime juice
- ¼ tsp ground cumin
- good pinch of chilli flakes

For the guacamole

- 2 medium-sized ripe avocados, stoned, peeled and roughly chopped
- 4 tsp lime juice
- 2 spring onions, ends trimmed, finely chopped
- 3 tbsp chopped coriander
- good pinch of chilli flakes

To serve

- 8 corn tacos shells
- 8 tsp 0% Greek yogurt
- 2 Little Gem lettuces, shredded
- chopped coriander
- lime wedges, for squeezing over

Method

STEP 1

Mix the oil with the cumin and paprika on a large plate. Sit the chicken on the plate and rub the spiced oil all over it. Season with pepper and a pinch of salt, then cover and set aside while you prepare the salsa.

STEP 2

Heat the grill to high for 10 mins. Meanwhile, line a large baking tray with foil and lay the tomatoes (cut-side up) on it, along with the pepper and red onion. Brush the oil over the onion, and season the tomatoes and onion with pepper. Grill for 12-15 mins, turning the tomatoes and onion halfway through, until well charred. Remove (leaving the grill on) and set aside to cool – put the pepper in a bowl and cover with cling film so that it's easier to skin later.

STEP 3

For the guacamole, put the avocado in a bowl and briefly mash with a fork, leaving some chunky pieces for texture. Gently mix in the lime juice, spring onions, coriander and chilli flakes. Season with pepper and a pinch of salt.

STEP 4

Re-line the baking tray with foil and lay the chicken on it, plump-side up. Grill for about 10 mins until cooked – there is no need to turn it. Meanwhile, scoop out and discard as much of the seeds and juice from the tomatoes as you can (so the salsa isn't too wet), leaving the pulp and charred skin. When the pepper is cool enough to handle, peel off and discard the skin. Chop the tomatoes and onion, and dice the pepper. Combine in a bowl with the lime juice, cumin, chilli flakes, some pepper and a pinch of salt.

STEP 5

When the chicken is cooked, remove from the grill, cover loosely with foil and set aside for 5 mins.

STEP 6

Heat oven to 180C/160C fan/gas 4. Cut the chicken into chunky slices and spoon over the juices. When ready to serve, lay the taco shells on a baking sheet and warm through for 2-3 mins. Serve the chicken, taco shells, yogurt, lettuce, coriander and lime wedges in separate bowls, so that everyone can build their own tacos.

Chicken & broccoli potato-topped pie

Prep: 35 mins **Cook:** 1 hr and 25 mins

Serves 4

Ingredients

- 750g potatoes, peeled and halved
- 250g broccoli, cut into small florets
- 100ml strong chicken stock
- small bunch tarragon, finely chopped (optional)
- 1-2 tsp Dijon mustard
- 100g frozen peas
- 1 tbsp butter

For the chicken base

- 25g butter
- 25g plain flour
- 250ml milk
- 1 tsp olive oil
- 2-3 (depending on size) skinless chicken thigh fillets, cut into cubes
- 1 skinless chicken breast, cut into cubes
- ⅓ onion, very finely chopped (optional)

Method

STEP 1

For the base, melt the butter in a saucepan, stir in the flour and cook for a few mins, stirring all the time. Now, using a whisk or spatula, carefully stir in the milk, a little at a time, making sure the sauce stays smooth. Bring the mixture to a simmer and cook for a couple of mins until it thickens – it will be very thick. Turn the heat right down and keep cooking for 5 mins, stirring often.

STEP 2

Meanwhile, heat the oil in a non-stick frying pan and fry all of the chicken in batches until it starts to colour lightly at the edges. Scoop out each batch of chicken and put it on a plate. Add the onion to the pan if you are using it, and cook over a low heat until soft. Add the chicken and any juices and the onion to the white sauce, fold it in and cook the mixture for a further 15 mins or until the chicken is cooked through. If you're making the base ahead of time, you can leave it to cool at this stage then freeze in an airtight container for up to a month. (Defrost fully before using in the next step.)

STEP 3

Heat oven to 180C/160C fan/gas 4. Cook the potatoes in boiling water for 10 mins, then drain and cool a little before slicing thickly.

STEP 4

Meanwhile, cook the broccoli until tender, then drain. Heat the chicken base with the stock in a pan until it is just beginning to bubble, then stir in the tarragon (if using) and the mustard. Fold in the broccoli and peas. Tip the chicken mixture into a dish and arrange the potato slices on top, then dot the butter over. Bake for 30-35 mins or until golden.

Chinese chicken noodle soup with peanut sauce

Prep: 15 mins **Cook:** 30 mins

Serves 2

Ingredients

- 1 tbsp sunflower oil
- 4 skinless boneless chicken thighs
- 1 garlic clove, crushed
- 1 thumb-sized piece ginger, grated
- 500ml chicken stock

For the peanut sauce

- 1 tbsp peanut butter
- 1 tsp soy sauce
- 1 tsp honey
- sriracha or other chilli sauce (optional), to serve

- 1 tsp soy sauce
- ½ hispi cabbage, finely sliced
- 150g mushrooms
- 150g straight to wok noodles (we used udon)

Method

STEP 1

Heat the oil in a saucepan over a medium heat, add the chicken and brown a little, so around 2-3 mins, then add the garlic and ginger and stir to coat the chicken. Fry for a further minute, then pour in the chicken stock and soy, bring to the boil, then reduce to a simmer. Cover with a lid and leave to gently bubble for 25-30 mins until the chicken is tender and pulls apart.

STEP 2

Meanwhile, mix the sauce ingredients with a splash of water. When the chicken is ready, lift it out with a slotted spoon and use two forks to shred it on a plate. Add the cabbage, mushrooms and noodles to the pan, turn up the heat, then stir in the chicken, add a dash of sriracha, if using, and ladle into bowls. Top with a drizzle of the peanut sauce and serve.

Crab & lemon spaghetti with peas

Prep: 7 mins **Cook:** 12 mins

Serves 2

Ingredients

- 150g wholemeal spaghetti
- 1 tbsp rapeseed oil
- 2 leeks (220g), cut into lengths then long thin strips
- 1 red chilli , deseeded and finely chopped
- 1 garlic clove , finely grated
- 160g frozen peas
- 1 lemon , zested and 1/2 juiced
- 100g fresh white and brown crabmeat (not dressed)

Method

STEP 1

Cook the spaghetti for 12 mins, or following pack instructions, until al dente. Meanwhile, heat the oil in a large frying pan, add the leeks and chilli and cook for 5 mins. Stir in the garlic, peas, lemon zest and juice, then cook for a few mins.

STEP 2

Drain the pasta, then add to the pan with ¼ mug of pasta water and the crab, then toss everything together until well coated. Spoon into shallow bowls and serve.

Apple pie samosas

Prep: 20 mins **Cook:** 25 mins

Serves 4

Ingredients

- 2 cooking apples , peeled, cored and chopped
- 50g caster sugar
- 1 tsp ground mixed spice
- 50g sultanas
- 4 sheets filo pastry
- 25g low-fat spread (we used Flora Light), melted

Method

STEP 1

Heat oven to 200C/180C fan/gas 6. Place the apples, sugar, mixed spice and sultanas in a saucepan with 2 tbsp water and cook, covered, for 6 mins or until the apples are soft, stirring once or twice. Tip into a shallow dish and spread out to cool slightly.

STEP 2

Cut the sheets of filo in thirds lengthways, then brush lightly with the melted spread. Place a spoonful of the apple filling at the top of each strip, then fold over and over to form triangular parcels. Place on a baking sheet and bake for 15-20 mins until crisp and golden. Serve with low-fat yogurt, if you like.

Banana pancakes

Prep: 5 mins **Cook:** 5 mins

Serves 2 (makes 4)

Ingredients

- 1 large banana
- 2 medium eggs, beaten
- pinch of baking powder (gluten-free if coeliac)
- splash of vanilla extract
- 1 tsp oil
- 25g pecans, roughly chopped
- 125g raspberries

Method

STEP 1

In a bowl, mash 1 large banana with a fork until it resembles a thick purée.

STEP 2

Stir in 2 beaten eggs, a pinch of baking powder (gluten-free if coeliac) and a splash of vanilla extract.

STEP 3

Heat a large non-stick frying pan or pancake pan over a medium heat and brush with ½ tsp oil.

STEP 4

Using half the batter, spoon two pancakes into the pan, cook for 1-2 mins each side, then tip onto a plate. Repeat the process with another ½ tsp oil and the remaining batter.

STEP 5

Top the pancakes with 25g roughly chopped pecans and 125g raspberries.

Green eggs

Prep: 5 mins **Cook:** 15 mins

Serves 2

Ingredients

- 1½ tbsp rapeseed oil, plus a splash extra
- 2 trimmed leeks, sliced
- 2 garlic cloves, sliced
- ½ tsp coriander seeds
- ½ tsp fennel seeds
- pinch of chilli flakes, plus extra to serve
- 200g spinach
- 2 large eggs
- 2 tbsp Greek yogurt
- squeeze of lemon

Method

STEP 1

Heat the oil in a large frying pan. Add the leeks and a pinch of salt, then cook until soft. Add the garlic, coriander, fennel and chilli flakes. Once the seeds begin to crackle, tip in the spinach and turn down the heat. Stir everything together until the spinach has wilted and reduced, then scrape it over to one side of the pan. Pour a little oil into the pan, then crack in the eggs and fry until cooked to your liking.

STEP 2

Stir the yogurt through the spinach mix and season. Pile onto two plates, top with the fried egg, squeeze over a little lemon and season with black pepper and chilli flakes to serve.

Roast pork with couscous & ginger yogurt

Prep: 10 mins **Cook:** 40 mins

Serves 6

Ingredients

- 2 pork fillets , each about 500g/1lb 2oz, trimmed of any fat
- 2 tsp olive oil
- 3 tsp ground cumin
- 1 tsp ground cinnamon
- 4 tsp grated ginger
- 250g couscous
- 100g sultanas
- zest and juice 1 lemon
- small bunch mint , chopped
- 200g fat-free natural yogurt

Method

STEP 1

Heat oven to 190C/170C fan/gas 5. Brown the pork in a non-stick frying pan over a high heat for 4-5 mins, turning twice. Mix the oil, 2 tsp cumin, cinnamon, 2 tsp ginger and some seasoning, then rub all over the pork. Transfer to a roasting tin and roast for 30-35 mins or until the juices run clear when the thickest part is pierced with a skewer.

STEP 2

Mix the couscous with the remaining cumin, the sultanas, lemon zest and juice, then season and pour over 400ml boiling water. Stir well and cover for 5 mins, then stir in the mint.

STEP 3

Stir the remaining ginger and a little seasoning into the yogurt. Thickly slice the pork and serve with the couscous and ginger yogurt.

Lamb & squash biryani with cucumber raita

Prep: 10 mins **Cook:** 25 mins

Serves 4

Ingredients

- 4 lean lamb steaks (about 400g), trimmed of all fat, cut into chunks
- 2 garlic cloves, finely grated
- 8 tsp chopped fresh ginger
- 3 tsp ground coriander
- 4 tsp rapeseed oil
- 4 onions, sliced
- 2 red chillies, deseeded and chopped
- 170g brown basmati rice
- 320g diced butternut squash
- 2 tsp cumin seeds
- 2 tsp vegetable bouillon powder
- 20cm length cucumber, grated
- 100ml bio yogurt
- 4 tbsp chopped mint, plus a few extra leaves
- handful coriander, chopped

Method

STEP 1

Mix the lamb with the garlic, 2 tsp chopped ginger and 1 tsp ground coriander and set aside.

STEP 2

Heat 2 tsp oil in a non-stick pan. Add the onions, the remaining ginger and chilli and stir-fry briefly over a high heat so they start to soften. Add the rice and squash and stir over the heat for a few mins. Tip in all the remaining spices, then stir in 500ml boiling water and the bouillon. Cover the pan and simmer for 20 mins.

STEP 3

Meanwhile, mix the cucumber, yogurt and mint together in a bowl to make a raita. Chill half for later.

STEP 4

About 5 mins before the rice is ready, heat the remaining oil in a non-stick frying pan, add the lamb and stir for a few mins until browned but still nice tender. Toss into the spiced rice with the coriander and serve with the raita and a few mint or coriander leaves on top.

Roasted red pepper & tomato soup with ricotta

Prep: 10 mins **Cook:** 30 mins

Serves 2

Ingredients

- 400g tomatoes , halved
- 1 red onion , quartered
- 2 Romano peppers , roughly chopped
- 2 tbsp good quality olive oil
- 2 garlic cloves , bashed in their skins
- few thyme sprigs
- 1 tbsp red wine vinegar
- 2 tbsp ricotta
- few basil leaves
- 1 tbsp mixed seeds , toasted
- bread , to serve

Method

STEP 1

Heat oven to 200C/180C fan/gas 6. Put the tomatoes, onion and peppers in a roasting tin, toss with the oil and season. Nestle in the garlic and thyme sprigs, then roast for 25-30 mins until all the veg has softened and slightly caramelised. Squeeze the garlic cloves out of their skins into the tin, strip the leaves off the thyme and discard the stalks and garlic skins. Mix the vinegar into the tin then blend everything in a bullet blender or using a stick blender, adding enough water to loosen to your preferred consistency (we used around 150ml).

STEP 2

Reheat the soup if necessary, taste for seasoning, then spoon into two bowls and top each with a spoonful of ricotta, a few basil leaves, the seeds and a drizzle of oil. Serve with bread for dunking.

Creamy yogurt porridge

Prep: 1 min **Cook:** 3 mins

Serves 1

Ingredients

- 3 tbsp (25g) porridge oat
- 150g pot 0% fat probiotic yogurt

Method

STEP 1

Tip 200ml water into a small non-stick pan and stir in porridge oats.

STEP 2

Cook over a low heat until bubbling and thickened. (To make in a microwave, use a deep container to prevent spillage as the mixture will rise up as it cooks, and cook for 3 mins on High.)

STEP 3

Stir in yogurt – or swirl in half and top with the rest. Serve plain or with one of our toppings (see 'goes well with').

Noodles with turkey, green beans & hoisin

Prep: 10 mins **Cook:** 15 mins

Serves 2

Ingredients

- 100g ramen noodles
- 100g green beans , halved
- 3 tbsp hoisin sauce
- juice 1 lime
- 1 tbsp chilli sauce
- 1 tbsp vegetable oil
- 250g turkey mince
- 2 garlic cloves , chopped
- 6 spring onions , sliced diagonally

Method

STEP 1

Boil the noodles following pack instructions, adding the green beans for the final 2 mins. Drain and set aside.

STEP 2

In a small bowl, mix together the hoisin, lime juice and chilli sauce. In a wok or frying pan, heat the oil, then fry the mince until nicely browned. Add the garlic and fry for 1 min more. Stir in the hoisin mixture and cook for a few mins more until sticky. Finally, stir in the noodles, beans and half the spring onions to heat through. Scatter over the remaining spring onions to serve.

Ginger & soy sea bass parcels

Prep: 30 mins **Cook:** 15 mins

Serves 4

Ingredients

- 100ml shaohsing rice wine or dry sherry
- 100ml light soy sauce
- 1 small bunch of spring onions, finely sliced
- 2 garlic cloves, finely chopped
- thumb-sized piece fresh ginger, finely chopped
- 4 sea bass fillets, scaled (about 100g each)
- 3 pak choi, each quartered
- 1 large carrot, shredded into fine strips
- 2 red chillies, 4 spring onions, and thumb-sized piece ginger, cut into fine strips, to serve

Method

STEP 1

In a jug, mix together the wine or sherry with the soy, spring onions, garlic and ginger, then set aside. Lightly score the skin of each sea bass fillet a couple of times.

STEP 2

Lay a square of foil on your work surface with a square of baking parchment the same size on top. Put 3 pak choi quarters just off centre of the paper and top with a quarter of the shredded carrot followed by a sea bass fillet, skin-side up. Spoon over a quarter of the ginger, onion and garlic mixture (don't add the rice wine and soy mixture yet). Fold over the parcel so it becomes a triangle, then, from left to right, begin to seal it by scrunching the edges together. Continue all the way around until there is just a little hole at the end. Pour a quarter of the soy mix through the hole. Scrunch the remaining bit to seal and place on a baking tray. Repeat until all the fish are wrapped, sauced and sealed. Can be prepared a day ahead and chilled.

STEP 3

Heat oven to 200C/180C fan/gas 6 and cook the fish on the tray for 15 mins. Remove from the oven and divide the parcels between four warmed plates. Let your guests open them up themselves so they get a hit of aromatic steam before they tuck in. Pass around some chilli, spring onion and ginger strips to sprinkle over.

Vegetarian bean pot with herby breadcrumbs

Prep: 10 mins **Cook:** 35 mins

Serves 2

Ingredients

- 1 slice crusty bread
- ½ small pack parsley leaves
- ½ lemon , zested
- 2 tbsp olive oil
- pinch chilli flakes (optional)
- 2 leeks , rinsed and chopped into half-moons
- 2 carrots , thinly sliced
- 2 celery sticks , thinly sliced
- 1 fennel bulb , thinly sliced
- 2 large garlic cloves , chopped
- 1 tbsp tomato purée
- few thyme sprigs
- 150ml white wine
- 400g can cannellini beans , drained

Method

STEP 1

Toast the bread, then tear into pieces and put in a food processor with the parsley, lemon zest, ½ tbsp olive oil, a good pinch of salt and pepper and the chilli flakes, if using. Blitz to breadcrumbs. Set aside.

STEP 2

Heat the remaining oil in a pan and add the leeks, carrots, celery and fennel along with a splash of water and a pinch of salt. Cook over a medium heat for 10 mins until soft, then add the garlic and tomato purée. Cook for 1 min more, then add the thyme and white wine. Leave to bubble for a minute, then add the beans. Fill the can halfway with water and pour into the pot.

STEP 3

Bring the cassoulet to the boil, then turn down the heat and leave to simmer for 15 mins before removing the thyme sprigs. Mash half the beans to thicken the stew. Season to taste, then divide between bowls and top with the herby breadcrumbs to serve.

Savoy cabbage with shallots & fennel seeds

Prep: 20 mins **Cook:** 30 mins

Serves 8

Ingredients

- 300g pack small shallots
- 2 tbsp olive oil
- 2 large garlic cloves, sliced
- 1 tsp fennel seeds, lightly crushed
- 1 Savoy cabbage (outer leaves discarded) quartered, cored and shredded
- 150ml hot vegetable stock

Method

STEP 1

Boil the shallots in their skins for 10-15 mins until they are soft but still hold their shape. Leave to cool then slip the skins from the shallots and halve them. Can be prepared a couple of days in advance, then chilled.

STEP 2

Heat the oil in a large non-stick wok, and stir-fry the garlic, fennel seeds and shallots for a couple of mins until the shallots are golden. Remove from the pan.

STEP 3

Add the cabbage to the pan and stir-fry until it starts to wilt a little, then pour in the stock, cover the wok and cook for 3 mins until just tender. Test to see if the cabbage is done to your liking; if not, cook a little longer, then add the shallot mixture, heat through and serve.

Healthy salad Niçoise

Prep: 15 mins **Cook:** 10 mins

Serves 2

Ingredients

- 200g new potato, thickly sliced
- 2 medium eggs
- 100g green bean, trimmed

- 1 romaine lettuce heart, leaves separated and washed
- 8 cherry tomatoes , halved
- 6 anchovies in olive oil, drained well
- 197g can tuna steak in spring water, drained
- 2 tbsp reduced-fat mayonnaise

Method

STEP 1

Bring a large pan of water to the boil. Add the potatoes and the eggs, and cook for 7 mins. Scoop the eggs out of the pan, tip in the green beans and cook for a further 4 mins. Drain the potatoes, beans and eggs in a colander under cold running water until cool. Leave to dry.

STEP 2

Peel the eggs and cut into quarters. Arrange the lettuce leaves in 2 shallow bowls. Scatter over the beans, potatoes, tomatoes and egg quarters. Pat the anchovies with kitchen paper to absorb the excess oil and place on top.

STEP 3

Flake the tuna into chunks and scatter over the salad. Mix the mayonnaise and 1 tbsp cold water in a bowl until smooth. Drizzle over the salad and serve.

Mumbai potato wraps with minted yogurt relish

Prep: 10 mins - 15 mins **Cook:** 35 mins

Serves 4

Ingredients

- 2 tsp sunflower oil
- 1 onion , sliced
- 2 tbsp medium curry powder
- 400g can chopped tomato
- 750g potato , diced
- 2 tbsp spiced mango chutney , plus extra to serve
- 100g low-fat natural yogurt
- 1 tsp mint sauce from a jar
- 8 small plain chapatis
- coriander sprigs, to serve

Method

STEP 1

Heat the sunflower oil in a large saucepan and fry the onion for 6-8 mins until golden and soft. Stir in 1½ tbsp curry powder, cook for 30 secs, then add the tomatoes and seasoning. Simmer, uncovered, for 15 mins.

STEP 2

Meanwhile, add the potatoes and ½ tbsp curry powder to a pan of boiling salted water. Cook for 6-8 mins until just tender. Drain, reserving 100ml of the liquid. Add the drained potatoes and reserved liquid to the tomato sauce along with the mango chutney. Heat through.

STEP 3

Meanwhile, mix together the yogurt and mint sauce, and warm the chapattis following pack instructions.

STEP 4

To serve, spoon some of the potatoes onto a chapatti and top with a few sprigs of coriander. Drizzle with the minted yogurt relish, adding extra mango chutney if you wish, then roll up and eat.

Banana & cinnamon pancakes with blueberry compote

Prep: 10 mins **Cook:** 15 mins

Serves 4

Ingredients

- 65g wholemeal flour
- 1 tsp ground cinnamon , plus extra for sprinkling
- 2 egg , plus 2 egg whites
- 100ml whole milk
- 1 small banana , mashed
- ½ tbsp rapeseed oil
- 320g blueberries
- few mint leaves , to serve

Method

STEP 1

Tip the flour and cinnamon into a bowl, then break in the whole eggs, pour in the milk and whisk together until smooth. Stir in the banana. In a separate bowl, whisk the egg whites until light and fluffy, but not completely stiff, then fold into the pancake mix until evenly incorporated.

STEP 2

Heat a small amount of oil in a large non-stick frying pan, then add a quarter of the pancake mix, swirl to cover the base of the pan and cook until set and golden. Carefully turn the pancake over with a palette knife and cook the other side. Transfer to a plate, then carry on with the rest of the batter until you have four.

STEP 3

To make the compote, tip the berries in a non-stick pan and heat gently until the berries just burst but hold their shape. Serve two warm pancakes with half the berries, then scatter with the mint leaves and sprinkle with a little cinnamon. Chill the remaining pancakes and compote and serve the next day. You can reheat them in the microwave or in a pan.

15-minute chicken pasta

Cook: 15 mins **Serves 4**

Ingredients

- 350g pasta bows (farfalle)
- 300g broccoli , cut into small florets
- 1 tbsp olive oil
- 3 large skinless boneless chicken breasts, cut into bite-sized chunks
- 2 garlic cloves , crushed
- 2 tbsp wholegrain mustard
- juice of 1 large or 2 small oranges
- 25g flaked almond , toasted

Method

STEP 1

Cook the pasta in plenty of boiling salted water according to the packet instructions. Three minutes before the pasta is cooked, throw the broccoli into the pasta water and continue to boil.

STEP 2

While the pasta is cooking, gently heat the oil in a large frying pan or wok. Tip in the chicken and fry, stirring occasionally, until the chicken pieces are cooked and golden, about 8-10 minutes, adding the garlic for the last 2 minutes.

STEP 3

Mix the mustard with the orange juice in a small bowl. Pour the mixture over the chicken, and gently simmer for a minute or two. Drain the pasta and broccoli, reserving 3 tablespoons of the pasta water. Toss the pasta and broccoli with the chicken, stir in the pasta water and the almonds, season well and serve.

Easy turkey paella

Cook: 18 mins - 24 mins **Serves 4**

Ingredients

- 205g jar of paella paste
- 300g paella rice
- 300g pack stir-fry vegetables (without beansprouts)
- 130g pack roast turkey slices

Method

STEP 1

Heat 1 tbsp olive oil in a large sauté pan. Fry the paella paste for 1-2 mins, then tip in the rice and cook for 2 mins more. Add 800ml boiling water, simmer for 12-15 mins or until the liquid has been absorbed, then season to taste.

STEP 2

In another pan, fry the veg in 1 tbsp olive oil on a high heat for 1-2 mins. Add 50ml water, cover and steam for 2-3 mins. Tear the turkey into bite-sized pieces and stir through the rice with the veg.

Teriyaki prawns & broccoli noodles

Prep: 10 mins **Cook:** 10 mins

Serves 2

Ingredients

- 50ml low-sodium soy sauce
- 50ml mirin
- 2 tbsp lemon juice
- 1 ½ tbsp caster sugar
- 200g soba noodle
- 140g thin-stemmed broccoli
- 140g cooked prawn
- 1 small red chilli, thinly sliced

Method

STEP 1

In a small saucepan, heat the soy sauce, mirin, lemon juice and sugar. Simmer for 5 mins until syrupy, then remove from the heat. Bring a large saucepan of salted water to the boil, then cook the noodles and broccoli for about 3 mins, adding the prawns a few secs before draining. Divide the mixture between 2 plates, pour the warm teriyaki sauce over the top, sprinkle with the red chilli and serve.

Spicy mince & lettuce cups

Prep: 10 mins **Cook:** 15 mins Ready in 25 minutes

Serves 4

Ingredients

- 1 tbsp sunflower oil
- large piece fresh root ginger, peeled and grated
- 2 garlic cloves, crushed
- 2 red chillies, deseeded and finely sliced
- 500g minced chicken, turkey or pork
- 85g light brown sugar
- 2 tbsp fish sauce
- juice 1 lime
- 2 lime leaves, finely shredded

To serve

- mix of iceberg lettuce, Little Gem and cos leaves
- large handful mint and coriander leaves, very roughly chopped
- handful toasted peanuts, roughly chopped
- 2 shallots, finely sliced into rings
- 1 lime, cut into wedges

Method

STEP 1

Heat the oil in a large frying pan. Fry the ginger, garlic and chillies for 1 min. Add the mince, then cook on a high heat until golden brown, breaking it up with a wooden spoon as you go. Sprinkle over the brown sugar, fish sauce, lime juice and shredded lime leaves, then cook everything down until sticky.

STEP 2

Tip the mince into a serving bowl, then serve with a bowl of lettuce leaves for wrapping the mince in; the herbs, shallots and peanuts for scattering over; and the lime wedges for squeezing.

Black-eyed bean mole with salsa

Prep: 15 mins **Cook:** 5 mins - 8 mins

Serves 2

Ingredients

For the salsa

- 1 red onion , finely chopped
- 2 large tomatoes , chopped
- 2 tbsp fresh coriander
- ½ lime , zest and juice

For the mole

- 2 tsp rapeseed oil
- 1 red onion , halved and sliced
- 1 garlic clove , finely grated
- 1 tsp ground coriander
- 1 tsp mild chilli powder
- ½ tsp ground cinnamon
- 400g can black-eyed beans in water
- 2 tsp cocoa
- 1 tsp vegetable bouillon
- 1 tbsp tomato purée

Method

STEP 1

Tip all the salsa ingredients into a bowl and stir together.

STEP 2

For the mole, heat the oil in a non-stick pan, add the onion and garlic and fry stirring frequently until softened. Tip in the spices, stir then add the contents of the can of beans with the cocoa, bouillon and tomato purée. Cook, stirring frequently to make quite a thick sauce.

STEP 3

Spoon into shallow bowls, top with the salsa and serve.

Avocado hummus & crudités

Prep: 10 mins No cook

Serves 2

Ingredients

- 1 avocado, peeled and stoned
- 210g chickpeas, drained
- 1 garlic clove, crushed
- pinch chilli flakes, plus extra to serve
- 1 lime, juiced
- handful coriander leaves
- 2 carrots, cut into strips
- 2 mixed peppers, cut into strips
- 160g sugar snap peas

Method

STEP 1

Blitz together the avocado, chickpeas, garlic, chilli flakes and lime juice, and season to taste. Top the hummus with the coriander leaves and a few more chilli flakes, and serve with the carrot, pepper and sugar snap crudités. Make the night before for a great take-to-work lunch.

Breakfast super-shake

Prep: 5 mins no cook

Serves 1

Ingredients

- 100ml full-fat milk
- 2 tbsp natural yogurt
- 1 banana
- 150g frozen fruits of the forest
- 50g blueberries
- 1 tbsp chia seeds
- ½ tsp cinnamon
- 1 tbsp goji berries

- 1 tsp mixed seeds
- 1 tsp honey (ideally Manuka)

Method

STEP 1

Put the ingredients in a blender and blitz until smooth. Pour into a glass and enjoy!

Avocado & strawberry ices

Prep: 5 mins Plus freezing

Serves 4

Ingredients

- 200g ripe strawberries, hulled and chopped
- 1 avocado, stoned, peeled and roughly chopped
- 2 tsp balsamic vinegar
- ½ tsp vanilla extract
- 1-2 tsp maple syrup (optional)

Method

STEP 1

Put the strawberries (save four pieces for the top), avocado, vinegar and vanilla in a bowl and blitz using a hand blender (or in a food processor) until as smooth as you can get it. Have a taste and only add the maple syrup if the strawberries are not sweet enough.

STEP 2

Pour into containers, add a strawberry to each, cover with cling film and freeze. Allow the pots to soften for 5-10 mins before eating.

Salmon pasta salad with lemon & capers

Prep: 10 mins **Cook:** 20 mins

Serves 2

Ingredients

- 85g wholewheat penne
- 1 tbsp rapeseed oil

- 1 large red pepper, roughly chopped
- 2 frozen, skinless wild salmon fillets (about 120g each)
- 1 lemon, zested and juiced
- 2 garlic cloves, finely grated
- 1 shallot, very finely chopped
- 2 tbsp capers
- 6 pitted Kalamata olives, sliced
- 1 tsp extra virgin olive oil
- 2 handfuls rocket

Method

STEP 1

Cook the pasta following pack instructions. Meanwhile, heat the rapeseed oil in a frying pan, add the pepper, cover and leave for about 5 mins until it softens and starts to char a little. Stir, then push the pepper to one side and add the salmon. Cover and fry for 8-10 mins until just cooked.

STEP 2

Meanwhile, mix the lemon zest and juice in a large bowl with the garlic, shallot, capers and olives.

STEP 3

Add the cooked pepper and salmon to the bowl. Drain the pasta and add it too, with black pepper and the olive oil. Toss everything together, flaking the salmon as you do so. If eating now, toss through the rocket; if packing a lunch, leave to cool, then put in a container with the rocket on top and mix through just before eating.

Thai shredded chicken & runner bean salad

Prep: 30 mins **Cook:** 5 mins

Serves 4

Ingredients

- 200g runner beans (or any other green bean), topped and tailed
- 1 red chilli, halved and finely sliced, use a bird's eye chilli for more heat
- 2 shallots, finely sliced
- 1 lemongrass, finely sliced
- 2cm piece ginger, shredded
- 2 cooked, skinless chicken breasts
- small bunch mint leaves
- large bunch Thai basil or coriander
- 1 lime cut in wedges or cheeks, to serve
- steamed jasmine rice, to serve

Coconut dressing

- 100ml coconut cream
- 1 garlic clove, crushed
- 3 tbsp fish sauce
- 1 tsp sugar
- juice 1 lime
- 1 bird's eye chilli, finely diced

Method

STEP 1

Run a potato peeler down either side of the beans to remove any stringy bits. Cut into strips using a bean slicer, or on the diagonal into 2cm pieces. Cook the beans in simmering salted water for 4 mins or until tender but still bright green. Drain and put in a bowl with the chilli, shallots, lemongrass and ginger. Pull the chicken breasts into shreds using your fingers and add to the bowl.

STEP 2

Make the dressing. Mix the coconut with the garlic, fish sauce, sugar, lime and chilli. Tear the mint and Thai basil over the chicken and toss everything together. Pile onto a plate and pour over the dressing. Serve with the lime to squeeze over and jasmine rice.

Squash & chorizo stew

Prep: 10 mins **Cook:** 25 mins

Serves 4

Ingredients

- 140g chorizo, thickly sliced
- 1 onion, chopped
- 680g jar passata
- 1 butternut squash (approx 1kg/2lb 4oz), peeled and cut into 1-2cm chunks
- flat-leaf parsley, chopped

Method

STEP 1

Heat a large pan, add the chorizo, then cook over a high heat for 2 mins until it starts to release its red oil. Lift the chorizo out of the pan, then add the onion and fry for 5 mins until starting to soften.

STEP 2

Tip in the passata, squash and chorizo, bring to the boil, then cover and cook for 15-20 mins until the squash is softened, but not broken up. If you need to, add a little water during cooking. Season to taste, then serve in bowls scattered with parsley.

Miso steak

Prep: 10 mins **Cook:** 10 mins Plus marinating

Serves 2

Ingredients

- 2 tbsp brown miso paste
- 1 tbsp dry sherry or sake
- 1 tbsp caster sugar
- 2 crushed garlic cloves
- 300g/11oz lean steak
- baby spinach, sliced cucumber, celery, radish and toasted sesame seeds, to serve

Method

STEP 1

Tip the miso paste, Sherry or sake, sugar and garlic into a sealable food bag. Season with a generous grinding of black pepper, then squash it all together until completely mixed. Add the steak, gently massage the marinade into the steak until completely coated, then seal the bag. Pop the bag into the fridge and leave for at least 1 hr, but up to 2 days is fine.

STEP 2

To cook, heat a heavy-based frying pan, griddle pan or barbecue until very hot. Wipe the excess marinade off the steak, then sear for 3 mins on each side for medium-rare or a few mins longer if you prefer the meat more cooked. Set aside for 1 min to rest. Carve the beef into thick slices and serve with a crunchy salad made with the spinach, cucumber, celery, radish and sesame seeds.

Beef bulgogi stir-fry

Prep: 10 mins **Cook:** 10 mins

Serves 4

Ingredients

- 4cm/1 ½in piece of ginger
- 4 tbsp soy sauce
- 4 tbsp mirin
- 3 garlic cloves
- 2 tbsp chopped pineapple
- 2 tsp red chilli flakes or Korean chilli powder
- 3 tbsp golden caster sugar
- 3 tsp sesame oil
- 500g sirloin or rump steak , trimmed of fat and sliced
- 1 large onion , cut into half moons
- 1 tbsp toasted sesame seeds
- 200g cooked basmati rice
- chopped spring onions , to serve

Method

STEP 1

Put the ginger, soy, mirin, garlic, pineapple, chilli flakes, sugar and 1 tsp of the sesame oil in a food processor and blend until fine. Pour the marinade into a bowl, add the meat, mix well and leave to sit while you prepare the onion.

STEP 2

Heat the remaining sesame oil in a large wok or frying pan until very hot. Add the onion and stir-fry for a few mins. Add the beef and the marinade, stirring constantly until it's cooked through, about 5 mins. Sprinkle with the sesame seeds and serve with rice and chopped spring onions.

Beetroot & butternut stew

Prep: 20 mins **Cook:** 35 mins

Serves 2

Ingredients

- 250g raw beetroot
- 350g butternut squash , unpeeled
- 1 garlic clove , grated
- 1 small onion , diced
- ¼ tsp cumin seeds
- ½ tsp ground coriander
- 4 cardamom pods , seeds removed and crushed
- 1 tbsp sunflower oil
- ½ tsp cinnamon
- 100g green beans , topped and cut in half

- 50g chard or spinach, stems removed and leaves roughly chopped
- small pack flat-leaf parsley , roughly chopped
- brown rice , to serve (optional)

Method

STEP 1

Peel the beetroot and chop into small pieces. Chop the butternut squash into small pieces. Put them in separate bowls until you need them.

STEP 2

In a large wide-topped saucepan, fry the garlic, onion, cumin seeds, coriander and cardamom pods in the oil for 2 mins on a medium heat. Add 125ml water along with the beetroot and leave for a further 5 mins until the water has simmered away.

STEP 3

Add 250ml water, the butternut squash and cinnamon, and leave to simmer on a medium heat for 10 mins. Add 250ml water and leave to simmer for another 10 mins.

STEP 4

Add 125ml water, the green beans and simmer for another 5 mins until the water has simmered away. Take off the heat and stir in the chard and parsley. Serve by itself or with brown rice for a fuller meal.

Thai cucumber slaw

Prep: 15 mins No cook

Serves 4 - 6

Ingredients

- 2 spring onions , shredded
- zest and juice 1 lime
- 1 ½ tbsp fish sauce
- 2 tsp agave syrup
- 1 cucumber , cut into thin matchsticks
- 1 chinese leaf cabbage , finely sliced
- 1 red chilli , thinly sliced (optional)

Method

STEP 1

Fill a small bowl with cold water and add the spring onions, then set aside – this will make it curl. To make the dressing, combine the lime juice and zest, fish sauce and agave syrup.

STEP 2

Toss together the cucumber, Chinese leaves and dressing, then transfer to a serving dish. Drain the spring onions and pat dry, then scatter over the slaw, and top with the chilli, if you like.

BBQ salad pizza

Prep: 25 mins **Cook:** 20 mins Plus rising time

Serves 2-3

Ingredients

For the pizza dough

- strong white bread flour , plus extra for dusting
- ½ tsp easy or fast-action dried yeast

For the topping

- 3 Little Gem lettuces , cut in half
- 6 spring onions
- 200g Tenderstem broccoli
- oil , for brushing
- 30g walnuts , toasted and roughly chopped

For the dressing

- 75ml buttermilk (if you can't find any, squeeze a little lemon juice into milk and leave for 5 mins to sour)
- 2 tbsp thick Greek yogurt
- 1 tsp Dijon mustard
- ½ garlic clove , crushed
- 1 lemon , zested and juiced

Method

STEP 1

To make the pizza dough, combine the flour, yeast and a big pinch of salt in a large bowl. Pour in 120ml warm water and knead together with well-floured hands to form a smooth dough. Put the dough back in its bowl, cover with a tea towel and leave somewhere warm to double in size. Can be made the night before and kept chilled overnight.

STEP 2

For the buttermilk dressing, whisk together all the ingredients, adding lemon juice and some seasoning to taste. The dressing can be made the day before.

STEP 3

Get your barbecue searingly hot. Brush the broccoli, spring onions and the cut side of the lettuce with a little oil, then put all the vegetables on the barbecue and cook until charred – broccoli will take the longest, between 8-10 mins. Have a plate ready so you can remove them when they're cooked.

STEP 4

On a lightly floured surface, roll the pizza dough into a circle, about 30cm in diameter. Flour a large piece of foil, put the dough on top and carefully place on the barbecue. Put the lid on the barbecue and cook the dough, with the lid on throughout, for 6-8 mins, flipping halfway, or until cooked through – it may take slightly longer if your barbecue has lost some heat. Pile the charred veg on top of the dough, drizzle over some of the dressing (leaving some to dip the crusts), then scatter over the toasted walnuts and lemon zest to serve.

Courgetti bolognese

Prep: 15 mins **Cook:** 1 hr

Serves 4

Ingredients

- 2 tbsp olive oil
- 500g turkey mince (thigh or breast)
- 1 large onion , finely chopped
- 1 garlic clove , crushed
- 2 large carrots , peeled and diced
- 150g pack button mushrooms , roughly chopped
- 1 tbsp tomato purée
- 2 x 400g cans chopped tomatoes
- 2 chicken stock cubes
- 1 tbsp soy sauce
- 4 large courgettes
- grated pecorino or parmesan , to serve
- handful basil leaves

Method

STEP 1

Heat 1 tbsp of the olive oil in a large saucepan and add the turkey mince. Fry until browned, then scoop into a bowl and set aside.

STEP 2

Add the onion to the pan and cook on a low heat for 8-10 mins until tender. Then add the garlic, stirring for 1 min or so, followed by the carrot and the mushrooms, stirring for about 3 mins, until softened. Tip the turkey mince back into the pan, add the tomato purée, give everything a quick stir and tip in the chopped tomatoes. Fill 1 can with water and pour into the pan. Crumble over the chicken stock cubes and bring to the boil. Once boiling, lower the heat and simmer for about 1 hr, until the sauce has thickened and the veg is tender.

STEP 3

When the bolognese is nearly ready, stir through the soy sauce and some seasoning. Spiralize your courgettes on the large noodle attachment. Heat a large frying pan with the remaining 1 tbsp olive oil and add your courgetti. Cook until slightly softened, for 2-3 mins. Season with salt and serve topped with the turkey bolognese, grated pecorino and basil leaves.

Lighter aubergine Parmigiana

Prep: 35 mins **Cook:** 55 mins

Serves 4

Ingredients

- 2 tbsp rapeseed oil , plus 1 tsp
- 2 tbsp lemon juice
- 3 aubergines (750g/1lb 10oz total weight), stalk ends trimmed, cut into 1cm/1/2in lengthways slices
- 1 small onion , chopped
- 3 garlic cloves , finely chopped
- 400g can plum tomatoes
- 225g can plum tomatoes
- 1 tbsp tomato purée
- 2 tbsp chopped fresh oregano
- 100g ricotta
- 50g mozzarella , torn into small pieces
- handful basil leaves , roughly torn
- 2 medium tomatoes , sliced
- 25g vegetarian-style parmesan , grated

Method

STEP 1

Heat oven to 200C/180C fan/gas 6. Measure the 2 tbsp of oil into a small bowl. Brush just a little of it onto 2 large, non- stick baking sheets (if you only have 1 tray, bake the aubergines in batches). Mix the lemon juice into the measured oil. Lay the aubergine slices snugly in a single layer on the baking sheets, brush the tops with half the oil and lemon, season with pepper and bake for 20 mins. Turn the slices over, give the remaining oil and lemon mixture a good stir as it will have separated, and brush it over again. Season with pepper and bake for 10-15 mins more or until softened.

STEP 2

Meanwhile, heat the remaining 1 tsp oil in a medium saucepan. Add the onion and garlic and fry for 3-4 mins, stirring often, until the onion is softened and starting to brown. Tip in the cans of tomatoes, stir to break them up, then mix in the purée, pepper and a pinch of salt. Simmer uncovered for about 10-12 mins until thickened and saucy, then stir in the oregano.

STEP 3

Spread a little of the tomato sauce in the bottom of a shallow ovenproof dish (about 25 x 20 x 5cm). Start by laying a third of the aubergine slices widthways across the dish, spread over a third of the remaining sauce and put half the ricotta on top in small spoonfuls, then half the mozzarella. Scatter over half the torn basil and season well with pepper. Repeat the layering of aubergine slices, tomato sauce, ricotta, mozzarella and basil, and finish with the final aubergine slices, the sliced tomatoes and the last of the sauce. Season with pepper and scatter over the Parmesan. Bake for about 20 mins, or until the cheese is golden and the juices are bubbling.

Yogurt parfaits with crushed strawberries & amaretti

Prep: 10 mins **Serves 6**

Ingredients

- 400g punnet strawberries , chopped
- 4 tbsp caster sugar
- 500g pot low-fat Greek yogurt
- 12 small amaretti biscuits , crushed

Method

STEP 1

In a small bowl, mix the strawberries with half the sugar, then roughly mash them with a fork so they are juicy. Mix the remaining sugar into the yogurt, then layer up 6 glasses with amaretti biscuits, yogurt and strawberries.

Slow-cooker ham with sticky ginger glaze

Prep: 20 mins **Cook:** 7 hrs and 20 mins

Serves 6 - 8

Ingredients

- 1 onion, thickly sliced
- 10 cloves, plus extra for studding
- 1 medium gammon joint, approx 1.3kg
- 1.5 litre bottle ginger beer
- 1 tbsp English mustard
- 3 tbsp ginger preserve

Method

STEP 1

Put the onion and 10 cloves in the base of the slow cooker then nestle in the gammon joint. Pour over the ginger beer then cover and cook on LOW for 7 hours until the gammon is tender, but still holding its shape. You can cool then chill the gammon at this stage if you prefer.

STEP 2

Heat the oven to 200C/180C fan/ gas 6. Carefully remove the skin from the gammon leaving a layer of fat behind. Score the fat in a diamond pattern with a sharp knife, making sure you don't cut into the meat, then stud the centre of each diamond with cloves.

STEP 3

Mix the mustard and ginger preserve in a bowl, spoon or brush over the gammon then bake for 20 mins until golden and sticky. If roasting from cold you will need to add another 20 mins to the cooking time.

Wild salmon with coconut chutney & green pilau

Prep: 15 mins **Cook:** 35 mins

Serves 2

Ingredients

- 1 tsp rapeseed oil
- 1 onion, sliced
- 25g ginger, cut into thin matchsticks
- 2 garlic cloves, chopped
- 1 green chilli, deseeded and sliced
- ⅔ small pack coriander
- handful mint leaves
- 20g creamed coconut
- 1 lime, zested and 1/2 juiced
- 50g brown basmati rice
- 2 x 100g skinless wild salmon fillets, thawed if frozen
- head of spring greens (about 175g), stalks trimmed, finely shredded (remove outer leaves if tough)
- 125g frozen peas
- 1 tbsp ground coriander

Method

STEP 1

Heat oven to 200C/180C fan/ gas 6. Heat the oil in a large non-stick wok and add the onion, ginger, garlic and chilli. Cook briefly over a high heat to mix everything, then cover and leave to cook gently for about 10 mins until the onions are soft. Scoop two spoonfuls of the mixture into a bowl, add the coriander, mint, coconut, lime zest and juice with 1 tbsp water and blitz to a purée with a stick bender.

STEP 2

Meanwhile, boil the rice for 20 mins, then drain.

STEP 3

Spread half the coconut mixture over the fish and wrap up in a parcel of foil. Bake for 10 mins.

STEP 4

Carry on cooking the onions, uncovered this time, until they start to brown. Add the spring greens and stir-fry for a few mins until softened. Add the rice and peas with the ground coriander and cook until the veg is tender. If the mixture starts to stick, add 1 tbsp water. Stir through the remaining coconut mixture, then serve with the fish.

Bean, ham & egg salad

Prep: 15 mins **Cook:** 15 mins

Serves 4

Ingredients

- 2 eggs, hard-boiled
- 500g baby potato
- 200g green bean
- 200g frozen peas, defrosted
- 175g lean ham, shredded

For the dressing

- juice ½ lemon
- 1tbsp wholegrain mustard
- 1tbsp honey
- crusty bread, to serve (optional)

Method

STEP 1

Peel and quarter the eggs. Cook the potatoes in a large pan of boiling water for 8-10 mins or until tender. Tip in the beans for the final 3 mins, then add the peas for the final min. Drain all the veg, cool under cold running water, then drain really well.

STEP 2

For the dressing, mix the juice, mustard and honey together. Season, then pour over the veg. Fold through the ham and top with the eggs. Serve with bread, if you like.

Lemony mushroom pilaf

Prep: 10 mins **Cook:** 30 mins

Serves 4

Ingredients

- 500ml vegetable stock
- 1 onion, sliced
- 300g mixed mushrooms, sliced
- 2 garlic cloves, crushed
- 200g mixed basmati rice and wild rice
- zest and juice 1 lemon
- small bunch snipped chives
- 6 tbsp light soft cheese with garlic and herbs

Method

STEP 1

Put 2 tbsp of the stock in a non-stick pan, then cook the onion for 5 mins until softened – add a splash more stock if it starts to dry out. Add mushrooms and garlic and cook for 2 mins more. Add the rice and lemon zest and juice, mixing well. Pour in remaining stock and seasoning and bring to the boil. Turn down, cover and simmer for 25-30 mins until rice is tender. Stir through half each of the chives and soft cheese, then serve topped with the remaining chives and soft cheese.

Ultimate toad-in-the-hole with caramelised onion gravy

Prep: 20 mins **Cook:** 40 mins plus 2 hrs resting

Serves 4 - 6

Ingredients

- 140g plain flour
- 4 large eggs
- 300ml semi-skimmed milk
- 1 tbsp wholegrain mustard
- handful of woody herbs, leaves picked and chopped (we used 6 sage leaves, 4 rosemary sprigs and 4 thyme sprigs), plus a handful, fried until crispy, to serve (optional)
- 2 tbsp sunflower oil
- 8 rashers smoked streaky bacon
- 8 fat sausages (we used Cumberland but use your favourite variety)
- 2 red onions, cut into wedges
- cooked green vegetables (optional), to serve
- mash (optional), to serve

For the gravy

- drizzle of sunflower oil
- 2 red onions, halved and thinly sliced
- 1 tbsp golden caster sugar
- 2 tbsp balsamic vinegar

- 2 tbsp plain flour
- 250ml red wine
- 500ml chicken or beef stock

Method

STEP 1

Tip the flour into a large jug or bowl. Crack in the eggs, one at a time, whisking as you do. Pour in the milk and continue whisking until you have a smooth, lump-free batter. Add the mustard, herbs and some seasoning, then cover and set aside for 2 hrs, or chill overnight.

STEP 2

Heat oven to 220C/200C fan/gas 7. Heat the oil in a large metal roasting tin or enamel baking dish, roughly 30 x 22cm, with high-ish sides. Wrap a rasher of bacon around each sausage and pop them in the dish with the onion wedges. Place on the middle shelf of the oven (make sure the top shelf is removed to allow space for the batter to rise later). Cook for 15-20 mins until the sausages and bacon are browning and sizzling.

STEP 3

Meanwhile, make the gravy. Drizzle a little oil into a saucepan. Add the sliced onions and cook slowly for 15 mins. Stir every now and then until they are soft and caramelised. Add the sugar and balsamic vinegar, and cook for 5 mins more until sticky.

STEP 4

The batter should be the consistency of double cream - if it has become a little thick, add a splash of cold water. Take the batter to the oven, open the door, carefully pull out the shelf and quickly pour the batter around the sausages. Close the oven and do not open it again for at least 25 mins.

STEP 5

To finish the gravy, stir the flour into the onions to make a paste, cooking for 1-2 mins. Continue stirring while you splash in the wine, a little at a time, until you have a smooth, thick sauce. Increase the heat and bubble for a few mins until reduced by about half. Add the stock and some seasoning, and continue bubbling for 10 mins while the toad cooks.

STEP 6

By now the toad should be puffed up and deep golden brown. If not, continue cooking - but don't open the oven as it will sink. Serve scattered with the crisp herbs (if using), with the gravy, green veg, and mash, if you like.

Turkey burgers with beetroot relish

Prep: 15 mins **Cook:** 10 mins

Serves 4

Ingredients

- 500g pack turkey mince
- ½ tsp dried thyme or 2 tsp fresh
- 1 lemon

For the relish

- 250g cooked peeled beetroot (not in vinegar), finely diced
- 1 small red onion, finely chopped
- 2 tbsp chopped parsley
- 2 tsp olive oil
- 2 tsp wholegrain mustard
- Little Gem lettuce, to serve
- wholemeal pitta bread, to serve

Method

STEP 1

Tip turkey into a bowl with the thyme. Finely grate in the zest from the lemon and add a little seasoning. Use your hands to mix the ingredients well, then shape into 4 patties. Chill until ready to cook. Can be frozen for up to 1 month.

STEP 2

Mix the beetroot with the juice from ½ the lemon, onion, parsley, oil and mustard. Grill, griddle or barbecue the burgers for about 6 mins each side and serve with the beetroot relish, lettuce and pitta breads.

Berry bake with passion fruit drizzle

Prep: 15 mins **Cook:** 30 mins

Serves 6

Ingredients

- 100g/4oz low-fat spread
- 85g caster sugar
- grated zest and juice 1 lemon
- 1 egg
- 140g self-raising flour
- 1 tsp baking powder
- 4 tbsp low-fat natural yogurt, plus extra to serve (optional)
- 200g apple sauce
- 140g raspberries, blueberries or blackberries (or a mixture)
- 50g demerara sugar
- 2 passion fruits, halved and pulp scooped out

Method

STEP 1

Heat the oven to 180C/160C fan/gas 4. Lightly grease a medium baking dish with 1 tsp of the spread. Put the remaining spread, caster sugar, lemon zest, egg, flour, baking powder and yogurt in a mixing bowl. Whisk together for 2 mins until pale and fluffy. Stir in the apple sauce – this might make the mixture look curdled, but don't worry. Gently fold in the berries, then pour the batter into the prepared dish and level the surface. Bake for 25-30 mins until the sponge is golden brown and firm in the centre.

STEP 2

Meanwhile, mix lemon juice, demerara sugar and passion fruit pulp together. Remove pudding from the oven, lightly prick the surface with a fork and drizzle over passion fruit mixture. Serve warm with low-fat vanilla ice cream or the yogurt.

Prawn & pak choi stir-fry

Prep: 5 mins **Cook:** 6 mins

Serves 2

Ingredients

- 2 tbsp sesame oil
- 100g mangetout
- 1 carrot, finely sliced
- 200g pak choi, washed and sliced
- 2 spring onions, sliced on the diagonal
- 300g straight-to-wok egg noodles
- 150g cooked king prawns
- 2 tbsp soy sauce, plus extra to serve, (optional)
- 1 tbsp sesame seeds, toasted
- 1 red chilli, sliced, to serve (optional)

Method

STEP 1

Heat 1 tbsp sesame oil in a large wok or frying pan over a medium-high heat and toss in the mangetout and carrot. Cook for a few mins until starting to soften and brown, then add the pak choi and spring onions. Add the noodles and prawns, use tongs to combine, and warm through.

STEP 2

Pour in the soy sauce and remaining sesame oil, and toss to coat. Just before serving, scatter over the sesame seeds and chilli. Serve with extra soy sauce, if you like.

Mushroom & chickpea burgers

Prep: 10 mins **Cook:** 20 mins

Serves 4

Ingredients

- 1 tbsp olive oil
- 250g chestnut mushroom, finely chopped
- 2 garlic cloves, crushed
- 1 bunch spring onions, sliced
- 1 tbsp medium curry powder
- zest and juice ½ lemon
- 400g can chickpea, rinsed and drained
- 85g fresh wholemeal breadcrumb
- 6 tbsp 0% Greek yogurt
- pinch ground cumin
- 2 mixed-grain muffins or rolls, toasted and halved
- 2 plum tomatoes, sliced
- handful rocket leaves

Method

STEP 1

Heat 1 tsp oil in a non-stick frying pan and cook the mushroom, garlic and spring onion for 5 mins. Mix in the curry powder, lemon zest and juice and cook for 2 mins or until mixture looks quite dry. Tip out onto a plate to cool slightly.

STEP 2

Use a potato masher or fork to mash the chickpeas in a bowl, leaving a few chunky pieces. Add the mushroom mix and the crumbs, then shape into 4 patties. Fry in the remaining oil for 3-4 mins on each side until crisp and browned.

STEP 3

Mix the yogurt with the cumin. Place half a muffin on each plate, then spread with the yogurt. Top with the burgers, a few slices of tomato and a little rocket.

Asian pulled chicken salad

Prep: 20 mins No cook

Serves 5

Ingredients

- 1 small roasted chicken, about 1kg
- ½ red cabbage, cored and finely sliced
- 3 carrots, coarsley grated or finely shredded
- 5 spring onions, finely sliced on the diagonal

- 2 red chillies, halved and thinly sliced
- small bunch coriander, roughly chopped, including stalks
- 2 heaped tbsp roasted salted peanuts, roughly crushed

For the dressing

- 3 ½ tbsp hoisin sauce
- 1 ½ tbsp toasted sesame oil

Method

STEP 1

Combine the dressing ingredients in a small bowl and set aside.

STEP 2

Remove all the meat from the chicken, shred into large chunks and pop in a large bowl. Add the cabbage, carrots, spring onions, chillies and half the coriander. Toss together with the dressing and pile onto a serving plate, then scatter over the remaining coriander and peanuts.

Curtido

Prep: 15 mins **Cook:** 5 mins plus chilling

Serves 4

Ingredients

- 1 small white cabbage (around 680g), finely shredded
- 1 red onion , finely sliced
- 2 carrots , thinly sliced lengthways
- 50ml apple cider vinegar
- 2 tsp golden caster sugar
- ½ small pack coriander , leaves only, roughly chopped

Method

STEP 1

Mix the cabbage with the onion and carrots in a heatproof bowl. Heat the vinegar, sugar and 1 tsp salt in a pan over a low heat until dissolved, then pour over the vegetables and mix well.

STEP 2

Put the slaw in the fridge for at least 30 mins or until ready to serve. Just before serving, stir through the coriander leaves and season well, to taste.

Goat's cheese, tomato & olive triangles

Prep: 5 mins No cook

Serves 2

Ingredients

- 3 triangular bread thins
- 50g soft goat's cheese
- 2 x 5cm lengths of cucumber , thinly sliced lengthways
- 3 tomatoes , sliced

- 4 Kalamata olives, finely chopped
- 2 small handfuls rocket leaves

Method

STEP 1

Follow our triangular bread-thins recipe to make your own.

STEP 2

Cut the bread thins in half, put cut-side up and spread with the goat's cheese. Top with the cucumber and tomato, then scatter over the olives and top with the rocket. Eat straight away or pack into lunchboxes for later.

Pork & rosemary lasagne

Prep: 40 mins **Cook:** 35 mins

Serves 4

Ingredients

- 1 tsp olive oil, plus extra for greasing
- 400g lean minced pork (less than 5% fat)
- 1 onion, finely chopped
- 2 sticks celery, finely chopped
- 1 tsp dried rosemary
- 150ml white wine
- 425ml chicken stock
- 2 tbsp tomato purée
- 400g can chopped tomato
- 1 tsp cornflour
- 2 x 250g tubs quark
- 250ml skimmed milk
- freshly grated nutmeg
- 10 dried lasagne sheets, about 175g/6oz in total
- 15g/½oz freshly grated parmesan (about 5 tbsp)

Method

STEP 1

Preheat the oven to 190C/Gas 5/fan oven 170C. Heat the oil in a non-stick pan, add the pork and quickly fry until starting to become brown and crumbly. Add the onion, celery, rosemary and wine and bring to the boil. Cover and gently cook for 10 minutes, until softened.

STEP 2

Add the stock, tomato purée, canned tomatoes, and season. Stir well, then bring to the boil, cover and simmer for 30 minutes by which time it will be nicely pulpy. Blend the cornflour to a paste with a few drops of water, then add to the pan and cook briefly until slightly thickened. Remove from the heat.

STEP 3

Tip the Quark into a bowl. Give it a stir, then stir in the milk, nutmeg, seasoning.

STEP 4

Brush a 1.4 litre/2½ pint oblong dish with a little oil. Spoon a third of the meat over the base, then cover with 2 sheets of lasagne, breaking them to fit, if necessary. Try to avoid overlapping. Spread with a third of the sauce, a little parmesan, then 2 more sheets of lasagne. Repeat layers twice more, omitting the last layer of lasagne and finishing with the sauce.

STEP 5

Sprinkle with remaining parmesan and bake for 30-35 minutes, until golden and tender.

Turkey & coriander burgers with guacamole

Prep: 15 mins **Cook:** 15 mins

Serves 4

Ingredients

- 400g turkey mince
- 1 tsp Worcestershire sauce
- 85g fresh breadcrumb
- 1 tbsp chopped coriander
- 1 red onion , finely chopped
- 1 large ripe avocado , or 2 small
- 1 chilli , deseeded and finely chopped
- juice 1 lime
- 4 ciabatta rolls, cut in half
- 1 tsp sunflower oil
- 8 hot peppadew peppers, roughly chopped

Method

STEP 1

Mix the mince, Worcestershire sauce, breadcrumbs, half each of the coriander and onion, and some seasoning until combined. Form into 4 burgers, then chill until ready to cook.

STEP 2

To make the guacamole, mash the avocado with the remaining coriander and onion, the chilli and lime juice, and season.

STEP 3

Heat a griddle pan or barbecue until hot. Griddle the rolls, cut-side down, for 1 min, then keep warm. Brush the burgers with the oil to keep them from sticking. Cook for 7-8 mins on each side until charred and cooked through. Fill the rolls with the burgers, guacamole and peppadews.

Curried spinach, eggs & chickpeas

Prep: 15 mins **Cook:** 35 mins

Serves 2

Ingredients

- 1 tbsp rapeseed oil
- 1 onion, thinly sliced
- 1 garlic clove, crushed
- 3cm piece ginger, peeled and grated
- 1 tsp ground turmeric
- 1 tsp ground coriander
- 1 tsp garam masala
- 1 tbsp ground cumin
- 450g tomatoes, chopped
- 400g can chickpeas, drained
- 1 tsp sugar
- 200g spinach
- 2 large eggs
- 3 tbsp natural yogurt
- 1 red chilli, finely sliced
- ½ small bunch of coriander, torn

Method

STEP 1

Heat the oil in a large frying pan or flameproof casserole pot over a medium heat, and fry the onion for 10 mins until golden and sticky. Add the garlic, ginger, turmeric, ground coriander, garam masala, cumin and tomatoes, and fry for 2 mins more. Add the chickpeas, 100ml water and the sugar and bring to a simmer. Stir in the spinach, then cover and cook for 20-25 mins. Season to taste.

STEP 2

Cook the eggs in a pan of boiling water for 7 mins, then rinse under cold running water to cool. Drain, peel and halve. Swirl the yogurt into the curry, then top with the eggs, chilli and coriander. Season.

Spicy chickpeas

Prep: 5 mins **Cook:** 25 mins

Serves 4

Ingredients

- 400g can chickpea , drained and dried
- 1 tsp vegetable oil
- 1 tbsp chilli powder

Method

STEP 1

Tip the chickpeas into a bowl with the vegetable oil and chilli powder and mix until the chickpeas are coated with chilli. Transfer to a baking sheet, spread out the chickpeas, then cook for 25 mins. Remove from the oven and allow to cool. Sprinkle with sea salt before serving.

Sweet potato falafels with coleslaw

Prep: 20 mins **Cook:** 50 mins

Serves 4

Ingredients

For the falafels

- 1 large or 2 small sweet potatoes , about 700g/1lb 9oz in total
- 1 tsp ground cumin
- 2 garlic cloves , chopped
- 2 tsp ground coriander
- handful coriander leaves , chopped
- juice ½ lemon
- 100g plain or gram flour
- 1 tbsp olive oil
- 4 wholemeal pitta breads
- 4 tbsp reduced-fat hummus

For the coleslaw

- 2 tbsp red wine vinegar
- 1 tbsp golden caster sugar
- 1 small onion, finely sliced
- 1 medium carrot, grated
- ¼ each white and red cabbage, shredded

Method

STEP 1

Heat oven to 200C/180C fan/gas 6. Microwave sweet potato whole for 8-10 mins until tender. Leave to cool a little, then peel. Put the potato, cumin, garlic, ground and fresh coriander, lemon juice and flour into a large bowl. Season, then mash until smooth. Using a tablespoon, shape mix and into 20 balls. Put on an oiled baking sheet, bake for around 15 mins until the bases are golden brown, then flip over and bake for 15 mins more until brown all over.

STEP 2

Meanwhile, stir the vinegar and sugar together in a large bowl until the sugar has dissolved, toss through the onion, carrot and cabbage, then leave to marinate for 15 mins. To serve, toast the pittas, then split. Fill with salad, a dollop of hummus and the falafels.

Zesty haddock with crushed potatoes & peas

Prep: 15 mins **Cook:** 20 mins

Serves 4

Ingredients

- 600g floury potato, unpeeled, cut into chunks
- 140g frozen peas
- 2 ½ tbsp extra-virgin olive oil
- juice and zest ½ lemon
- 1 tbsp capers, roughly chopped
- 2 tbsp snipped chives
- 4 haddock or other chunky white fish fillets, about 120g each (or use 2 small per person)
- 2 tbsp plain flour
- broccoli, to serve

Method

STEP 1

Cover the potatoes in cold water, bring to the boil, then turn to a simmer. Cook for 10 mins until tender, adding peas for the final min of cooking. Drain and roughly crush together, adding plenty of seasoning and 1 tbsp oil. Keep warm.

STEP 2

Meanwhile, for the dressing, mix 1 tbsp oil, the lemon juice and zest, capers and chives with some seasoning.

STEP 3

Dust the fish in the flour, tapping off any excess and season. Heat remaining oil in a non-stick frying pan. Fry the fish for 2-3 mins on each side until cooked, then add the dressing and warm through. Serve with the crush and broccoli.

Wild salmon veggie bowl

Prep: 10 mins no cook

Serves 2

Ingredients

- 2 carrots
- 1 large courgette
- 2 cooked beetroot , diced
- 2 tbsp balsamic vinegar
- ⅓ small pack dill , chopped, plus some extra fronts (optional)
- 1 small red onion , finely chopped
- 280g poached or canned wild salmon
- 2 tbsp capers in vinegar, rinsed

Method

STEP 1

Shred the carrots and courgette into long spaghetti strips with a julienne peeler or spiralizer, and pile onto two plates.

STEP 2

Stir the beetroot, balsamic vinegar, chopped dill and red onion together in a small bowl, then spoon on top of the veg. Flake over chunks of the salmon and scatter with the capers and extra dill, if you like.

Linguine with avocado, tomato & lime

Prep: 20 mins **Cook:** 10 mins

Serves 2

Ingredients

- 115g wholemeal linguine
- 1 lime, zested and juiced
- 1 avocado, stoned, peeled, and chopped
- 2 large ripe tomatoes, chopped
- ½ pack fresh coriander, chopped
- 1 red onion, finely chopped
- 1 red chilli, deseeded and finely chopped (optional)

Method

STEP 1

Cook the pasta according to pack instructions – about 10 mins. Meanwhile, put the lime juice and zest in a medium bowl with the avocado, tomatoes, coriander, onion and chilli, if using, and mix well.

STEP 2

Drain the pasta, toss into the bowl and mix well. Serve straight away while still warm, or cold.

Stuffed cherry peppers

Prep: 10 mins No cook

Makes 20

Ingredients

- 3 grilled artichokes, from a jar
- handful of rocket
- 2 tbsp crumbled feta
- 20 drained pickled cherry peppers

Method

STEP 1

Finely chop the artichokes and a handful of rocket. Mix together with the crumbled
Spoon the mixture into the pickled cherry peppers and serve.

Garden veg pasta ✓

Prep: 10 mins **Cook:** 15 mins

Serves 4

Ingredients

- 350g penne
- 140g broccoli , cut into small florets
- 100g sugar snap pea , halved
- 2 courgettes , diced
- 1 tbsp olive oil
- 100g light cream cheese
- 50g grated parmesan (or vegetarian alternative), plus extra to serve
- zest and juice 1 lemon
- large handful basil

Method

STEP 1

Cook the penne according to pack instructions, adding the broccoli florets and sugar snap peas to the pan for the final 3 mins.

STEP 2

Meanwhile, gently fry the courgettes in oil for 7-8 mins until soft and tinged pale gold. When the penne and vegetables are almost ready, remove a ladleful of cooking water from the pan. Add 6 tbsp of this to the pan of courgettes, along with the cream cheese, Parmesan, lemon zest, half the lemon juice and seasoning. Stir to make a smooth, creamy sauce.

STEP 3

Drain the penne and vegetables, then mix with the creamy sauce, adding the basil, extra lemon juice and seasoning to taste. Serve in warmed bowls.

White fish with spicy beans and chorizo

Prep: 5 mins **Cook:** 15 mins

Serves 4

Ingredients

- 1 tbsp olive oil
- 1 onion , chopped
- small rosemary sprig, leaves finely chopped
- 25g chorizo or other spicy sausage, chopped
- 2 fat garlic cloves , crushed
- 700g/1lb 9oz bottle passata
- 410g can cannellini bean in water, drained
- 200g/7oz shredded green cabbage
- pinch sugar
- 4 skinless chunky fillets haddock or cod

Method

STEP 1

Heat the oil in a large frying pan, then soften the onion for 5 mins. Add the rosemary, chorizo and garlic, then fry for 2 mins more until the chorizo is starting to crisp. Tip in the passata, beans, cabbage and sugar, season, then simmer for 5 mins.

STEP 2

Add the fish to the pan, leaving the tops of the fillets peeking out of the sauce, then cover with a lid and leave to cook for 3-5 mins or until the flesh flakes easily. Delicious served with crusty bread.

Salmon noodle soup

Prep: 15 mins **Cook:** 20 mins

Serves 4

Ingredients

- 1l low-salt chicken stock
- 2 tsp Thai red curry paste
- 100g flat rice noodle
- 150g pack shiitake mushroom , sliced
- 125g pack baby corn , sliced
- 2 skinless salmon fillets , sliced
- juice 2 limes
- 1 tbsp reduced-salt soy sauce
- pinch brown sugar
- small bunch coriander , chopped

Method

STEP 1

Pour the stock into a large pan, bring to the boil, then stir in the curry paste. Add the noodles and cook for 8 mins. Tip in the mushrooms and corn and cook for 2 mins more.

STEP 2

Add the salmon to the pan and cook for 3 mins or until cooked through. Remove from the heat and stir in the lime juice, soy sauce and a pinch of sugar. Ladle into 4 bowls and sprinkle over the coriander just before you serve.

Swedish meatballs

Prep: 10 mins **Cook:** 25 mins plus cooling and chilling

Serves 4

Ingredients

- 2 tbsp rapeseed oil
- 1 onion, finely chopped
- 1 small garlic clove, finely grated
- 375g lean pork mince
- 1 medium egg yolk
- grating of nutmeg
- 50g fine fresh breadcrumbs
- 300ml hot low-salt beef stock
- ½ tbsp Dijon mustard
- 2 tbsp fat-free natural yogurt
- 400g spring greens, shredded
- lingonberry or cranberry sauce, to serve

Method

STEP 1

Put 1 tbsp rapeseed oil in a frying pan over a medium heat. Add the onion and fry for 10 mins or until soft and translucent. Add the garlic and cook for 1 min. Leave to cool.

STEP 2

Mix the cooled onions, pork mince, egg yolk, a good grating of nutmeg and the breadcrumbs in a bowl with your hands until well combined. Form into 12 balls and chill for 15 mins.

STEP 3

Heat the remaining oil in a frying pan and fry the meatballs for 5 mins over a medium heat, turning often until golden. Pour over the stock and bubble for 8-10 mins or until it has reduced a little. Stir through the mustard and yogurt.

STEP 4

Steam the greens for 5 mins or until tender. Serve the meatballs with the greens and a dollop of the sauce.

Speedy red pepper chana masala

Prep: 5 mins **Cook:** 15 mins

Serves 4

Ingredients

- 1 tbsp rapeseed oil
- 3 garlic cloves , thinly sliced
- 3 tbsp tikka masala curry paste
- 2 tsp nigella seeds
- 400g can chopped tomatoes
- 400g can chickpeas
- 460g jar roasted red peppers , drained and chopped

Method

STEP 1

Heat the rapeseed oil in a large pan. Add the garlic, fry for 30 secs, then add the tikka masala curry paste and nigella seeds.

STEP 2

Stir for another 30 secs, then add the chopped tomatoes, chickpeas and roasted red peppers. Simmer for 10 mins, adding a splash of water if it looks too thick.

Individual summer puddings

Prep: 25 mins **Cook:** 8 mins plus 4 hrs chilling

Serves 2

Ingredients

- 350g mixed berry , fresh or frozen (we used raspberries, blackberries, redcurrants, blueberries and strawberries)
- 2 tbsp golden caster sugar

To serve

- 2 tbsp extra-thick double cream
- 2 tsp icing sugar , sifted

- zest 1 lemon
- sunflower oil , for greasing
- 3-4 slices slightly stale white bread , crusts removed

Method

STEP 1

Tip all the berries, apart from the strawberries, into a saucepan. Sprinkle over the sugar and stir. Set over a low heat and cook until the sugar has dissolved and the fruit has started to release its juices. Increase the heat, bring the mixture to the boil, then simmer for 2 mins until the fruit is soft and you have lots of deep red juices. Quarter the strawberries and stir into the berries, along with the lemon zest. Remove the pan from the heat and strain the fruit through a sieve, reserving the juices. Meanwhile, lightly oil 2 x 175ml dariole moulds (or 2 large teacups) and line with cling film. Using a pastry cutter, stamp out 2 small circles of bread to fit in the base of each mould. Dip one side into the reserved juices while still hot, and place, juice-side down, into the bottom of the lined mould. Cut another 2 larger circles from the bread, and slice the remainder into 2.5cm-wide strips that are the same height as the mould. Dip the strips into the juices and use to line the sides of the moulds in the same way, pressing each piece in place and overlapping slightly.

STEP 2

Pack the strained fruit into the bread-lined moulds, reserving some fruit and juices for serving. Fold over any strips of bread that protrude from the mould, then dip the final 2 circles of bread in the juices and top the puddings to seal. Cover with cling film and push down firmly with the palm of your hand. Pop in the fridge to chill for at least 4 hrs, preferably overnight.

STEP 3

When ready to serve, whip together the cream and icing sugar. Turn the puddings out onto plates, top with the reserved fruit and juices, and serve with the sugared cream.

Creamy seafood stew

Prep: 5 mins **Cook:** 25 mins

Serves 4

Ingredients

- 1 tbsp olive oil
- 1 onion , chopped
- 2 celery sticks, chopped
- 1 garlic clove , crushed
- 175ml white wine
- 300ml chicken stock
- 1 tbsp cornflour , mixed to a paste with 1 tbsp cold water
- 400g bag frozen seafood mix , defrosted
- small bunch dill , chopped
- 5 tbsp half-fat crème fraîche
- garlic bread, to serve

Method

STEP 1

Heat the oil in a large frying pan and cook the onion and celery until soft but not coloured, about 10 mins. Throw in the garlic and cook for 1 min more. Pour in the wine and simmer on a high heat until most has disappeared.

STEP 2

Pour in the stock and cornflour mix and simmer for 5-10 mins, stirring often until thickened. Season, then add the seafood and most of the dill. Simmer for a few mins until piping hot, then stir in the crème fraîche.

STEP 3

Meanwhile, cook the garlic bread following pack instructions. Divide the stew into warm bowls and scatter with the remaining dill. Serve with garlic bread for dipping into the stew.

Steamed trout with mint & dill dressing

Prep: 10 mins **Cook:** 25 mins

Serves 2

Ingredients

- 120g new potatoes , halved
- 170g pack asparagus spears , woody ends trimmed
- 1 ½ tsp vegetable bouillon powder made up to 225ml with water

For the dressing

- 4 tbsp bio yogurt
- 1 tsp cider vinegar
- ¼ tsp English mustard powder

- 80g fine green beans , trimmed
- 80g frozen peas
- 2 skinless trout fillets
- 2 slices lemon

- 1 tsp finely chopped mint
- 2 tsp chopped dill

Method

STEP 1

Put the new potatoes on to simmer in a pan of boiling water until tender. Cut the asparagus in half to shorten the spears and slice the ends without the tips. Tip the bouillon into a wide non-stick pan. Add the asparagus and beans, then cover and cook for 5 mins.

STEP 2

Add the peas to the pan, then top with the trout and lemon slices. Cover again and cook for 5 mins more until the fish flakes really easily, but is still juicy.

STEP 3

Meanwhile, mix the yogurt with the vinegar, mustard powder, mint and dill. Stir in 2-3 tbsp of the fish cooking juices. Put the veg and any remaining pan juices in bowls, top with the fish and herb dressing, then serve with the potatoes.

Poached beef & noodles (Gyudon)

Prep: 15 mins **Cook:** 20 mins

Serves 4

Ingredients

- 100ml Japanese or other soy sauce
- 100ml mirin
- 100ml saké
- 200ml vegetable or dashi stock
- 2 tbsp caster sugar

- 2 medium onions, cut into half moons
- 400g beef rump steak, fat removed, thinly sliced
- 100g glass vermicelli noodles

To serve

- steamed Japanese rice
- pickled ginger
- 3 spring onions, chopped
- shichimi togarashi chilli powder (optional, available from Asian supermarkets or online)

Method

STEP 1

In a saucepan, bring the soy, mirin, sake, vegetable stock and sugar to the boil. Let simmer for a few mins, then add the onions. Cook for 10 mins until brown. Add the steak and simmer for 5 mins on a medium heat.

STEP 2

Rinse the noodles and drain. Add to the meat and broth, and cook for 5 mins. Serve with rice, pickled ginger, spring onions and a little chili powder, if you like.

Rice noodle & turkey salad with lime-chilli dressing

Prep: 20 mins **Cook:** 10 mins

Serves 4

Ingredients

- 100g dried thin rice noodle
- 1 red chilli , seeds removed, thinly sliced
- 2 carrots , shredded
- 1 small red onion , thinly sliced into half moons

For the lime-chilli dressing

- 2 tbsp fish sauce
- 2 tbsp light brown sugar
- juice 4 limes
- 1 garlic clove , crushed

- handful coriander leaves, roughly chopped
- handful mint leaves, roughly chopped
- cooking oil spray
- 500g turkey mince

Method

STEP 1

Pour boiling water over the noodles and allow to sit for 5 mins. Drain, rinse under cold water and put in a large bowl, along with the chilli, carrots, onion and herbs.

STEP 2

To make the lime-chilli dressing, mix all the ingredients together in a small bowl or a screw-top jar.

STEP 3

Heat a non-stick frying pan or wok over a high heat until extremely hot. Lightly coat with oil and fry the turkey until nicely browned, breaking into chunks as you go. Add the noodle mixture, pour the dressing over the salad and mix well.

Egg & soldiers

Prep: 2 mins **Cook:** 5 mins

Serves 1

Ingredients

- 1 soft-boiled egg
- 7 spears of steamed asparagus

Method

STEP 1

Cut the soft-boiled egg in half and serve with the steamed asparagus for dipping.

Hearty lamb & barley soup

Prep: 10 mins **Cook:** 25 mins

Serves 4

Ingredients

- 1 tsp olive oil
- 200g lamb neck fillet, trimmed of fat and cut into small pieces
- ½ large onion, finely chopped
- 50g pearl barley
- 600g mixed root vegetable (we used potato, parsnip and swede, cubed)
- 2 tsp Worcestershire sauce
- 1 ¾ 1 litre lamb or beef stock
- 1 thyme sprig
- 100g green bean (frozen are fine), finely chopped

Method

STEP 1

Heat the oil in a large saucepan. Season the lamb, then fry for a few mins until browned. Add the onion and barley, then gently fry for 1 min. Add the veg, cook for 2 more mins, then add the Worcestershire sauce, stock and thyme. Cover, then simmer for 20 mins.

STEP 2

When everything is cooked, spoon about a quarter of the soup into a separate pan. Purée with a stick blender (or put into a normal blender and whizz), then stir it back into the rest of the soup. Add the green beans, simmer for 3 mins, then ladle the soup into bowls and serve with granary bread.

Haddock & leek au gratin with sweetcorn mash

Prep: 10 mins **Cook:** 50 mins

Serves 2

Ingredients

- 350g potatoes, quartered
- 195g can sweetcorn in water
- 240g bag ready-washed spinach
- 2 leeks, thickly sliced
- 300ml skimmed milk, plus 3 tbsp
- 15g unsalted butter
- 15g plain flour
- ½ tsp English mustard
- 75g mature reduced-fat cheese, grated
- 2 x 125g fillets of skinless haddock

Method

STEP 1

Heat oven to 200C/180 fan/gas 6. Boil the potatoes for 15-20 mins until tender, then drain. Reserve 3 tbsp corn and blitz the rest (with its juice) using a hand blender or a food processor until completely smooth, then mash into the potatoes. Cook the spinach following pack instructions – if you have a microwave, choose this method.

STEP 2

Put the leeks in a pan with the 300ml milk and the butter. Cook gently, part-covered, for 8 mins until the leeks are tender. (Keep an eye on things as milk can easily boil over.) Mix the 3 tbsp milk with the flour and mustard, then stir into the leek mixture – keep stirring until thickened. Take off the heat and stir in three-quarters of the cheese.

STEP 3

Squeeze as much liquid as you can from the spinach, then arrange on the base of 2 gratin dishes. Place a fish fillet on top of each, then spoon over the leek & cheese sauce. Top with the sweetcorn mash. Mix the remaining corn and cheese, and scatter on top. Place the dishes on a baking tray and cook for 25 mins until the fish flakes when tested and the top is golden.

Lemon chicken with fruity olive couscous

Prep: 20 mins **Cook:** 8 mins

Serves 4

Ingredients

- 4 skinless chicken breasts
- juice 2 lemons
- 2 tbsp olive oil

For the couscous

- 200g couscous
- 85g sultana
- 250ml hot chicken stock
- 1 tsp dried chilli flakes
- 3 garlic cloves, crushed
- 85g pitted green olive
- 400g can chickpeas, drained
- 2 tbsp chopped flat-leaf parsley

Method

STEP 1

Butterfly the chicken breasts by cutting through the thickest part of the breast, stopping 1cm before the edge, then opening out like a book. Whisk together the lemon juice, olive oil, chilli flakes and garlic. Pour half over the chicken and marinate for 15 mins.

STEP 2

Meanwhile, put the couscous and sultanas in a bowl, then pour over the stock. Cover the bowl with cling film and leave for 5 mins.

STEP 3

Heat a griddle or non-stick frying pan, remove the chicken from the marinade and cook for 4 mins on each side until golden and cooked through.

STEP 4

Fluff up the couscous with a fork and stir in the olives, chickpeas, parsley and the other half of the marinade. Season and serve with the chicken.

Moroccan pomegranate & roast veg salad

Prep: 10 mins **Cook:** 40 mins

Serves 2

Ingredients

- 2 small sweet potatoes, cut into chunks

- 2 red onions, roots kept intact, cut into wedges
- 1 large parsnip, peeled and chopped into chunks
- 2 large carrots, peeled and chopped into chunks
- 1 tbsp ras-el-hanout
- 1 tbsp olive oil
- 100g bag baby spinach
- 110g pack pomegranate seeds
- 50g light feta cheese, crumbled
- 4 tbsp balsamic vinegar

Method

STEP 1

Heat oven to 200C/180C fan/gas 6, line a large baking tray with baking parchment. In a large bowl, toss together all the veg with the ras el hanout, olive oil, salt and pepper. Arrange in a single layer on the baking tray. roast, turning once, for 40 mins until tender and starting to char.

STEP 2

Once cooked, allow to cool for 10 mins then toss with the spinach leaves, pomegranate seeds, feta and vinegar.

Steamed fish with ginger & spring onion

Prep: 10 mins **Cook:** 20 mins

Serves 4

Ingredients

- 100g pak choi
- 4 x 150g fillets firm white fish
- 5cm piece ginger, finely shredded
- 2 garlic cloves, finely sliced
- 2 tbsp low-salt soy sauce
- 1 tsp mirin rice wine
- 1 bunch spring onions, finely shredded
- handful coriander, chopped
- brown rice, to serve
- 1 lime, cut into wedges, to serve

Method

STEP 1

Heat oven to 200C/180C fan/gas 6. Cut a large rectangle of foil, big enough to make a large envelope. Place the pak choi on the foil, followed by the fish, then the ginger and garlic. Pour over the soy sauce and rice wine, then season.

STEP 2

Fold over foil and seal the 3 edges, then put on a baking sheet. Cook for 20 mins, open the parcel and scatter over the spring onions and coriander. Serve with brown rice and squeezed lime juice.

Italian borlotti bean, pumpkin & farro soup

Prep: 15 mins **Cook:** 35 mins

Serves 6

Ingredients

- 4 tbsp extra virgin olive oil , plus extra to serve
- 1 onion , finely chopped
- 1 celery stick , cut into chunks
- 750g pumpkin or squash, peeled, deseeded and cut into small chunks
- 1 carrot , peeled and cut into chunks
- 3 garlic cloves , chopped
- 3 tbsp tomato purée
- 1.2l chicken stock or vegetable stock
- 75g farro or mixed grains (such as barley or spelt)
- 50-80g parmesan rinds or vegetarian alternative (optional), plus a few shavings to serve
- 400g can borlotti beans , drained
- 2 handfuls baby spinach
- 2 tbsp chopped parsley or 8 whole sage leaves

Method

STEP 1

Heat the oil in a heavy-bottomed saucepan. Add the onion, celery, pumpkin or squash and carrot and cook until the vegetables have some colour. Add a splash of water and some seasoning, then cover the pan and let the vegetables cook over a very low heat for 5 mins.

STEP 2

Add the garlic and cook for another couple of mins, then add the tomato purée, stock, mixed grains, parmesan rinds, if using, and some seasoning. Simmer for about 15 mins (or until the grains are cooked), adding the beans for the final 5 mins. In the last few mins, add the spinach, then taste for seasoning.

STEP 3

If you want to use sage, fry the leaves in a little olive oil before adding to the s
you prefer to use parsley, you can ju   t directly to the soup. Serve with shaving
parmesan and a drizzle of extra virgin olive oil on top of each bowlful. Remove the
parmesan rinds and serve.

Strawberry cheesecakes

Prep: 10 mins **Serves 4**

Ingredients

- 85g low-fat biscuit (we used WeightWatchers ginger biscuits)
- 200g tub extra-light soft cheese
- 200g tub 0% fat Greek yogurt
- 4 tbsp caster sugar
- few drops vanilla extract
- 2 tbsp good-quality strawberry jam
- 100g strawberry , hulled and sliced

Method

STEP 1

Put the biscuits in a plastic bag and bash with a rolling pin until you have chunky crumbs. Divide between 4 glasses or small bowls.

STEP 2

Beat the soft cheese, yogurt, sugar and vanilla together until smooth, then spoon over the crumbs and chill until you are ready to serve.

STEP 3

Stir the jam in a bowl until loose, then gently stir in the strawberries. Divide the strawberries between the cheesecakes and serve.

Spiced chickpea soup

Prep: 10 mins **Cook:** 25 mins

Serves 4

Ingredients

- 1 tbsp olive oil
- 1 onion , chopped

- 2 garlic cloves, crushed
- 1 red chilli, deseeded and roughly chopped
- 1 tbsp grated fresh ginger
- 1 tsp cumin
- 1 tsp ras-el-hanout
- ¼ tsp cinnamon
- 200g roasted red pepper, from a jar
- 2 x 400g cans chopped tomato
- 400ml vegetable stock
- 400g can chickpea, drained and rinsed
- 2 preserved lemons, rind chopped (discard the pulp and seeds)
- 1 tbsp clear honey
- 50g wholewheat couscous

Method

STEP 1

Heat the oil in a large lidded pan. Add the onion and garlic, put on the lid and cook for 5 mins, stirring halfway through. Stir the chilli, ginger, cumin, ras el hanout and cinnamon into the pan and cook for 1 min. Add the peppers, tomatoes and stock. Bring to the boil, turn down to a simmer, put on the lid and cook for 10 mins.

STEP 2

Blitz the soup with a stick blender, or in a food processor until smooth. Return to the pan and add more liquid to thin the soup, if you like. Stir in the chickpeas, preserved lemons, honey and some seasoning. If eating straight away, add the couscous and heat through for 5 mins. (If taking to work, add the couscous just before reheating).

Moroccan roast lamb with roasted roots & coriander

Prep: 15 mins **Cook:** 55 mins

Serves 4

Ingredients

- ½ leg of lamb, around 800g
- 2 red onions, cut into wedges
- 1 butternut squash, skin left on, cut into wedges
- 1 celeriac, peeled and cut into wedges
- 2½ tbsp cold pressed rapeseed oil
- 2 tbsp ras el hanout
- 8 garlic cloves, skin on

- 1 small bunch coriander
- ½ tsp cumin seeds
- 1 lemon, zested and juiced
- 1/2 green chilli, deseeded

Method

STEP 1

Take the lamb out of the fridge while you chop the onions, squash and celeriac. Heat oven to 200C/180C fan/gas 6. Trim any excess fat off the leg of lamb, then cut a few slashes into the meat. Rub ½ tbsp oil and 1 tbsp ras el hanout over the lamb and season with salt and pepper. Put the onion, celeriac, butternut squash into a large roasting tin with the garlic. Toss with the remaining ras el hanout, remaining oil and some salt and pepper. Nestle the lamb into the tin and put in the oven to roast for 40 mins.

STEP 2

Take the lamb out of the oven and leave to rest. Put the veg back in the oven for 20 mins. Meanwhile, blitz the coriander, cumin seeds, lemon zest, lemon juice and green chilli together in a mini food processor until finely chopped and vivid green.

STEP 3

Carve the lamb, put on a platter, then pile on the veg. Sprinkle over some of the coriander mixture before taking the platter to the table for everyone to help themselves.

Asparagus & new potato frittata

Prep: 10 mins **Cook:** 12 mins

Serves 3

Ingredients

- 200g new potatoes, quartered
- 100g asparagus tips
- 1 tbsp olive oil
- 1 onion, finely chopped
- 6 eggs, beaten
- 40g cheddar, grated
- rocket or mixed leaves, to serve

Method

STEP 1

Heat the grill to high. Put the potatoes in a pan of cold salted water and bring to the boil. Once boiling, cook for 4-5 mins until nearly tender, then add the asparagus for a final 1 min. Drain.

STEP 2

Meanwhile, heat the oil in an ovenproof frying pan and add the onion. Cook for about 8 mins until softened.

STEP 3

Mix the eggs with half the cheese in a jug and season well. Pour over the onion in the pan, then scatter over the asparagus and potatoes. Top with the remaining cheese and put under the grill for 5 mins or until golden and cooked through. Cut into wedges and serve from the pan with salad.

Cashew curry

Prep: 20 mins **Cook:** 1 hr

Serves 3

Ingredients

- 1 small onion , chopped
- 3-4 garlic cloves
- thumb-sized piece ginger , peeled and roughly chopped
- 3 green chillies , deseeded
- small pack coriander , leaves picked and stalk roughly chopped
- 100g unsalted cashews
- 2 tbsp coconut oil
- 1 ½ tbsp garam masala
- 400g can chopped tomatoes
- 450ml chicken stock
- 3 large chicken breasts (about 475g), any visible fat removed, chopped into chunks
- 155g fat-free Greek yogurt
- 10ml single cream (optional)

To serve

- 165g boiled or steamed greens (choose from spinach, kale, runner beans, asparagus or broccoli)

Method

STEP 1

Put the onion, garlic, ginger, chillies and coriander stalks in a small food processor and blitz to a paste.

STEP 2

Heat a large, non-stick frying pan over a medium heat. Add the cashews and toast for 1-2 mins until light golden. Set aside and return the pan to the heat. Add the oil and stir-fry the paste for 5 mins to soften. Add the garam masala and cook for a further 2 mins.

STEP 3

Add the tomatoes and stock to the pan. Mix well, then tip into a blender with the cashews and blitz until smooth. Return to the pan, season and bring to the boil, then lower to a simmer.

STEP 4

Cook for 30 mins until the sauce has thickened then add the chicken, cover with a lid and simmer for another 15 mins, until the chicken is cooked through. Add the yogurt and cream (if using), and stir well to make a creamy sauce.

STEP 5

Scatter with the coriander leaves and serve with the greens.

Veggie kofta pittas with pick & mix sides

Prep: 20 mins **Cook:** 30 mins

Serves 6

Ingredients

- 2 onions, chopped
- 2 garlic cloves, crushed
- 1 Cal cooking spray, for frying
- 2 x 400g cans chickpeas, drained
- 100g fresh brown breadcrumbs
- 1 large egg
- 2 tsp ground cumin
- 2 tsp ground coriander

- zest 1 lemon , 1 tbsp juice, plus extra wedges to serve
- 85g baby spinach
- toasted pitta breads , to serve

For the carrot & tomato salad

- 200g carrots , coarsely grated
- 200g tomatoes , diced
- ½ red onion , finely chopped

- 175g fat-free natural or Greek yogurt , to serve
- pickled chillies or jalapeños (optional), to serve

- 2 tbsp red wine vinegar
- 1 tsp sugar

Method

STEP 1

Soften the onions and garlic with a few sprays of 1 Cal cooking spray and a splash of water in a non-stick pan. Once really soft, tip into a food processor with the chickpeas, breadcrumbs, egg, spices, lemon zest and juice, and plenty of seasoning. Pulse until fairly smooth, then add 30g of the spinach and pulse until finely chopped. Shape the mixture into 12 sausage-shaped koftas and put on a baking-parchment-lined baking tray. Chill while you heat oven to 200C/180C fan/gas 6.

STEP 2

Spray the koftas a few times more with cooking spray, then bake for 20-25 mins until crisp and golden.

STEP 3

Meanwhile, mix together all the carrot salad ingredients with some seasoning. Put the remaining spinach in a bowl and warm the pittas following pack instructions.

STEP 4

Serve the koftas with warm pittas, extra spinach, carrot salad, fat-free yogurt and pickled chillies, if you like.

Little spicy veggie pies

Prep: 10 mins **Cook:** 55 mins

Serves 4

Ingredients

- 2 tbsp rapeseed oil
- 2 tbsp finely chopped ginger
- 3 tbsp Korma curry powder
- 3 large garlic cloves, grated
- 2 x 400g cans chickpeas, undrained
- 320g carrots, coarsely grated
- 160g frozen sweetcorn
- 1 tbsp vegetable bouillon powder
- 4 tbsp tomato purée
- 250g bag spinach, cooked

For the topping

- 750g potatoes, peeled and cut into 3cm chunks
- 1 tsp ground coriander
- 10g fresh coriander, chopped
- 150g coconut yogurt

Method

STEP 1

To make the topping, boil the potatoes for 15-20 mins until tender then drain, reserving the water, and mash with the ground and fresh coriander and yogurt until creamy.

STEP 2

While the potatoes are boiling, heat the oil in a large pan, add the ginger and fry briefly, tip in the curry powder and garlic, stirring quickly as you don't want it to burn, then tip in a can of chickpeas with the water from the can. Stir well, then mash in the pan to smash them up a bit, then tip in the second can of chickpeas, again with the water from the can, along with the carrots, corn, bouillon and tomato purée. Simmer for 5-10 mins, adding some of the potato water, if needed, to loosen.

STEP 3

Heat the oven to 200C/180C fan/gas 6. Spoon the filling into four individual pie dishes (each about 10cm wide, 8cm deep) and top with the mash, smoothing it to seal round the edges of the dishes. If you're following our Healthy Diet Plan, bake two for 25 mins until golden, and cook half the spinach, saving the rest of the bag for another day. Cover and chill the remaining two pies to eat another day. Will keep in the fridge for four days. If freezing, to reheat, bake from frozen for 40-45 mins until golden and piping hot.

Best Yorkshire puddings

Prep: 5 mins **Cook:** 20 mins

Makes 8 large puds or 24 small

Ingredients

- 140g plain flour (this is about 200ml/7fl oz)
- 4 eggs (200ml/7fl oz)
- 200ml milk
- sunflower oil , for cooking

Method

STEP 1

Heat oven to 230C/fan 210C/gas 8.

STEP 2

Drizzle a little sunflower oil evenly into two 4-hole Yorkshire pudding tins or two 12-hole non-stick muffin tins and place in the oven to heat through.

STEP 3

To make the batter, tip 140g plain flour into a bowl and beat in 4 eggs until smooth.

STEP 4

Gradually add 200ml milk and carry on beating until the mix is completely lump-free. Season with salt and pepper.

STEP 5

Pour the batter into a jug, then remove the hot tins from the oven. Carefully and evenly pour the batter into the holes.

STEP 6

Place the tins back in the oven and leave undisturbed for 20-25 mins until the puddings have puffed up and browned.

STEP 7

Serve immediately. You can now cool them and freeze for up to 1 month.

Coleslaw with tahini yogurt dressing

Prep: 15 mins No cook

Serves 6

Ingredients

- 1 ½ tbsp tahini paste
- 5 tbsp Greek-style natural yogurt
- ½ garlic clove, crushed
- 1 small red cabbage, quartered and finely sliced
- 3 small carrots, cut into fine matchsticks
- 1 small onion, halved and finely sliced

Method

STEP 1

Put the tahini, yogurt, garlic, and some seasoning in a large bowl and mix until smooth. The dressing will thicken so add 2-3 tbsps cold water to loosen it. Add the vegetables to the dressing, and toss together until everything is well coated.

Harissa-crumbed fish with lentils & peppers

Prep: 15 mins **Cook:** 15 mins

Serves 4

Ingredients

- 2 x 200g pouches cooked puy lentils
- 200g jar roasted red peppers, drained and torn into chunks

- 50g black olives , from a jar, roughly chopped
- 1 lemon , zested and cut into wedges
- 3 tbsp olive or rapeseed oil
- 4 x 140g cod fillets (or another white fish)
- 100g fresh breadcrumbs
- 1 tbsp harissa
- ½ small pack flat-leaf parsley , chopped

Method

STEP 1

Heat oven to 200C/180C fan/gas 6. Mix the lentils, peppers, olives, lemon zest, 2 tbsp oil and some seasoning in a roasting tin. Top with the fish fillets. Mix the breadcrumbs, harissa and the remaining oil and put a few spoonfuls on top of each piece of fish. Bake for 12-15 mins until the fish is cooked, the topping is crispy and the lentils are hot. Scatter with the parsley and squeeze over the lemon wedges.

Turkey minestrone

Prep: 15 mins **Cook:** 40 mins

Serves 6

Ingredients

- 2 tsp olive oil
- 100g smoked bacon lardons
- 1 red onion , finely chopped
- 1 carrot , finely chopped
- 1 celery stick , finely chopped
- 2 garlic cloves , finely chopped
- 2 bay leaves
- 2 thyme sprigs
- 300g celeriac (or any other root veg), cut into cubes
- 200g potato , cut into cubes
- 400g can borlotti beans , drained and rinsed
- 1 ½l chicken stock or turkey stock, (fresh is best)
- 350g cooked turkey
- 100g orzo
- 75g curly kale , shredded

Method

STEP 1

Heat 1 tsp of oil in a large saucepan. Add the bacon and fry over a medium-to-high heat for 4-5 mins or until golden, then set aside.

STEP 2

Put the remaining oil, the onion, carrot, celery and a pinch of salt in the pan. Cook gently over a low heat for 8-10 mins, stirring occasionally, until the veg is soft but not coloured. Add the garlic and herbs, and cook for 2 mins more

STEP 3

Tip in the celeriac, potato, borlotti beans and chicken stock. Bring to the boil, then simmer, uncovered, for 10-15 mins. Add the cooked turkey, orzo and the bacon, and cook for 10 mins.

STEP 4

Just before serving, tip in the kale, give everything a good stir and return to the heat for about 2 mins or until the kale has wilted.

Hake & seafood cataplana

Prep: 15 mins **Cook:** 35 mins

Serves 2

Ingredients

- 2 tbsp cold-pressed rapeseed oil
- 1 onion, halved and thinly sliced
- 250g salad potatoes, cut into chunks
- 1 large red pepper, deseeded and chopped
- 1 courgette (200g), thickly sliced
- 2 tomatoes, chopped (150g)
- 2 large garlic cloves, finely grated
- 1 tbsp cider vinegar (optional)
- 2 tsp vegetable bouillon powder
- 2 skinless hake fillets (pack size 240g)
- 150g pack ready-cooked mussels (not in shells)
- 60g peeled prawns
- large handful of parsley, chopped

Method

STEP 1

Heat the oil in a wide non-stick pan with a tight-fitting lid. Fry the onions and potatoes for about 5 mins, or until starting to soften. Add the peppers, courgettes, tomatoes and garlic, then stir in the vinegar, if using, the bouillon and 200ml water. Bring to a simmer, cover and cook for 25 mins, or until the peppers and courgettes are very tender (if your pan doesn't have a tight-fitting lid, wet a sheet of baking parchment and place over the stew before covering – this helps keep in the juices).

STEP 2

Add the hake fillets, mussels and prawns, then cover and cook for 5 mins more, or until the fish flakes easily when tested with a fork. Scatter over the parsley and serve.

Lamb with buckwheat noodles & tomato dressing

Prep: 15 mins **Cook:** 25 mins

Serves 2

Ingredients

- 12 cherry tomatoes , quartered
- 1 tsp fish sauce
- juice and zest 1 lime
- 1 tbsp sweet chilli sauce
- 100g buckwheat noodle
- 2 tsp rapeseed oil
- 1 red onion , halved and sliced
- 1 carrot , cut into matchsticks
- 1 red pepper , deseeded and sliced
- 100g shredded white cabbage
- 200g lean lamb loin fillet or steaks, diced
- 4 tbsp chopped fresh mint

Method

STEP 1

Lightly squash the tomatoes with the fish sauce, lime juice and zest, and the chilli sauce. Cook the noodles following pack instructions.

STEP 2

Meanwhile, heat the oil in a wok and stir-fry the onion, carrot and pepper for 5 mins or until softening. Add the cabbage and cook for a few mins more. Remove the vegetables from the pan, add the lamb and cook for 5-8 mins so that it is still tender and juicy. Take the pan off the heat, toss in the noodles, vegetables, tomato dressing and mint, and serve.

Paneer jalfrezi with cumin rice

Prep: 20 mins **Cook:** 30 mins

Serves 4

Ingredients

- 2 tsp cold-pressed rapeseed oil
- 1 large and 1 medium onion , large one finely chopped and medium one cut into wedges
- 2 large garlic cloves , chopped
- 50g ginger , peeled and shredded
- 2 tsp ground coriander
- 2 tsp cumin seeds
- 400g can chopped tomatoes
- 1 tbsp vegetable bouillon powder
- 135g paneer , chopped
- 2 large peppers , seeded and chopped
- 1 red or green chilli , deseeded and sliced
- 25g coriander , chopped

For the rice

- 260g brown basmati rice
- 1 tsp cumin seeds

Method

STEP 1

Heat 1 tsp oil a large non-stick frying pan and fry the chopped onions, garlic and half the ginger for 5 mins until softened. Add the ground coriander and cumin seeds and cook for 1 min more, then tip in the tomatoes, half a can of water and the bouillon. Blitz everything together with a stick blender until very smooth, then bring to a simmer. Cover and cook for 15 mins.

STEP 2

Meanwhile, cook the rice and cumin seeds in a pan of boiling water for 25 mins, or until tender.

STEP 3

Heat the remaining oil in a non-stick wok and fry the paneer until lightly coloured. Remove from the pan and set aside. Add the peppers, onion wedges and chilli to the pan and stir-fry until the veg is tender, but still retains some bite. Mix the stir-fried veg and paneer into the sauce with the chopped coriander, then serve with the rice. If you're following our Healthy Diet Plan, eat two portions of the curry and rice, then chill the rest for another day. Will keep for up to three days, covered, in the fridge. To serve on the second night, reheat the leftover portions in the microwave until piping hot.

Spicy tuna & cottage cheese jacket

Prep: 10 mins **Cook:** 1 hr

Serves 1

Ingredients

- 225g can tuna, drained
- ½ red chilli, chopped
- 1 spring onion, sliced
- handful halved cherry tomatoes
- ½ small bunch coriander, chopped
- 1 medium-sized jacket potato
- 150g low-fat cottage cheese

Method

STEP 1

Preheat the oven to 180C/Gas 4/fan oven 160C. Prick the potato several times with a fork and put it straight onto a shelf in the hottest part of the oven. Bake for approximately 1 hour, or until it is soft inside.

STEP 2

Mix tuna with chilli, spring onion, cherry tomatoes and coriander. Split jacket potato and fill with the tuna mix and cottage cheese.

Tomato, onion & cucumber raita

Prep: 10 mins **Cook:** 5 mins

Serves 8

Ingredients

- 1 ripe tomato, chopped into 1cm dice
- ¼ red onion, finely chopped
- 85g cucumber, finely chopped
- a large handful chopped coriander
- 1 tsp cumin seeds, toasted and coarsely ground

- 450g plain yogurt, whisked until smooth
- sugar, to taste

Method

STEP 1

Stir together the tomato, red onion, cucumber, coriander, cumin seeds, plain yogurt, and a large pinch of sugar. Season to taste, adding more sugar if it is particularly sour.

Low 'n' slow rib steak with Cuban mojo salsa

Prep: 20 mins **Cook:** 3 hrs and 20 mins

Serves 2

Ingredients

- 1 rib steak on the bone or côte du boeuf (about 800g)
- 1 tbsp rapeseed oil
- 1 garlic clove
- 2 thyme sprigs
- 25g butter, chopped into small pieces
- sweet potato fries
- a dressed salad, to serve

For the mojo salsa

- 2 limes
- 1 small orange
- ½ small bunch mint, finely chopped
- small bunch coriander, finely chopped
- 4 spring onions, finely chopped
- 1 small garlic clove, crushed
- 1 fat green chilli, finely chopped
- 4 tbsp extra virgin rapeseed oil or olive oil

Method

STEP 1

Leave the beef at room temperature for about 1 hr before you cook it. Heat oven to 60C/40C fan/gas 1/4 if you like your beef medium rare, or 65C/45C fan/gas 1/4 for medium. (Cooking at these low temperatures will be more accurate in an electric oven than in a gas one. If using gas, put the oven on the lowest setting you have, and be aware that the cooking time may be shorter.)

STEP 2

Put the unseasoned beef in a heavy-based ovenproof frying pan. Cook in the middle of the oven for 3 hrs undisturbed.

STEP 3

Meanwhile, make the salsa. Zest the limes and orange into a bowl. Cut each in half and place, cut-side down, in a hot pan. Cook for a few mins until the fruits are charred, then squeeze the juice into the bowl. Add the other ingredients and season well.

STEP 4

When the beef is cooked, it should look dry on the surface, and dark pink in colour. If you have a meat thermometer, test the internal temperature – it should be 58-60C. Remove the pan from the oven and set over a high heat on the hob. Add the oil and sear the meat on both sides for a few mins until caramelised. Sear the fat for a few mins too. Smash the garlic clove with the heel of your hand and add this to the pan with the thyme and butter. When the butter is foaming, spoon it over the beef and cook for another 1-2 mins. Transfer the beef to a warm plate, cover with foil, and leave to rest for 5-10 mins. Carve away from the bone and into slices before serving with the salsa, fries and salad.

Herbed pork fillet with roast vegetables

Total time 1 hr and 45 mins Takes around 1½ - 1¾ hours

Serves 4

Ingredients

- 4 medium parsnips, peeled and quartered lengthways
- 1 butternut squash (about 650g/1lb 7oz), peeled, seeded and cut into chunks
- 2 red onions, each cut into 8 wedges
- 1 tbsp olive oil
- grated zest of 1 lemon
- 2 tsp pork seasoning or dried mixed Italian herbs
- 500g lean pork tenderloin, in one or two pieces
- 1 medium Bramley apple
- 400ml hot chicken stock

Method

STEP 1

Preheat the oven to 200C/ gas 6/fan 180C. Put all the vegetables into a roasting tin. Drizzle with the olive oil, season with salt and pepper, then toss everything together.

STEP 2

On a plate, mix together the lemon zest and pork seasoning or herbs. Roll the pork tenderloin in the mixture, then put it on top of the vegetables. Roast for 40 minutes.

STEP 3

Peel and core the apple and cut it into chunks. Scatter the pieces into the roasting tin, then pour in the hot stock and cook for a further 15-20 minutes. Slice the pork, arrange on a platter with the veg, then spoon the pan juices on top.

Charred broccoli, lemon & walnut pasta

Prep: 5 mins **Cook:** 15 mins

Serves 2

Ingredients

- 1 head broccoli , cut into small florets and stalk cut into small pieces
- 3 tsp olive oil
- 150g penne or fusilli
- 2 garlic cloves , crushed
- 1 tbsp roughly chopped walnuts
- pinch of chilli flakes
- ½ lemon , zested and juiced

Method

STEP 1

Heat the grill to high. Put the broccoli on a baking tray and drizzle over 1 tsp of the oil. Season, and toss together. Grill for 8-10 mins, tossing around halfway through, until crispy and charred.

STEP 2

Cook the pasta in salted water following pack instructions. Drain, reserving a cup of the cooking water.

STEP 3

In a frying pan, heat the remaining 2 tsp oil over a medium heat, and fry the garlic, walnuts and chilli for 3-4 mins until golden.

STEP 4

Tip in the pasta, broccoli, lemon zest and juice, reserving a little of the zest. Add a splash of the reserved cooking water and toss everything together to coat the pasta. Serve in warmed bowls with the remaining lemon zest scattered over.

Chicken, chickpea & lemon casserole

Total time 40 mins Ready in 35-40 minutes

Serves 2

Ingredients

- 175g new potato , halved (Charlotte would work well)
- 1 medium onion , thinly sliced
- 2 slices lemon , chopped
- 2 garlic cloves , roughly chopped
- 1 tsp ground cumin
- 1 tsp ground cinnamon
- 450ml chicken stock
- large skinless, boneless chicken thighs , trimmed of all fat and cut into cubes
- ½ x can chickpea
- handful fresh coriander , chopped

Method

STEP 1

Put the potatoes, onion, lemon and garlic into a casserole or heavy saucepan. Sprinkle over the ground spices and season lightly. Toss together then pour over the stock. Bring to the boil and simmer for 12 mins or until potatoes are tender.

STEP 2

Add the chicken and chickpeas, cover the saucepan and simmer gently for a further 10-12 mins or until the chicken is cooked through. Check the seasoning and stir in the coriander. Serve with steamed green beans or broccoli.

Chicken gumbo

Prep: 25 mins **Cook:** 35 mins

Serves 4

Ingredients

- 1 tbsp olive oil
- 500g skinless, boneless chicken thigh , cut into chunks
- 1 onion , chopped
- 1 green pepper , deseeded and chopped
- 3 celery sticks, finely chopped
- 1 garlic clove , finely chopped
- ¼ tsp cayenne pepper
- 1 tsp smoked paprika
- 1 tsp ground cumin
- 1 tsp dried thyme
- 1 bay leaf
- 1 heaped tbsp plain flour
- 400g can chopped tomato
- 400ml chicken stock
- 100g okra , cut into 2cm rounds
- small handful sage , leaves chopped
- crusty bread or microwave rice, to serve

Method

STEP 1

Heat the oil in a large pan over a medium high heat. Add the chicken and cook in batches for about 5 mins to brown all over. Remove the chicken with a slotted spoon and set aside.

STEP 2

Add the onion, green pepper and celery to the pan, put on the lid and cook for 5 mins, stirring occasionally until softened a little. Stir in the garlic, spices, thyme and bay leaf and cook for 1 min until fragrant. Return the chicken and any juices to the pan with the flour, stirring to coat everything. Pour in the tomatoes and stock, and bring to the boil, cook for 5 mins, then add the okra and half the sage. Turn down to a simmer, put on the lid and cook for 10 mins. Then season and serve, scattering the rest of the sage over.

Smoky chickpeas on toast

Prep: 2 mins **Cook:** 10 mins

Serves 2

Ingredients

- 1 tsp olive oil or vegetable oil, plus a drizzle
- 1 small onion or banana shallot, chopped
- 2 tsp chipotle paste
- 250ml passata
- 400g can chickpeas, drained
- 2 tsp honey
- 2 tsp red wine vinegar
- 2-4 slices good crusty bread
- 2 eggs

Method

STEP 1

Heat ½ tsp of the oil in a pan. Tip in the onion and cook until soft, about 5-8 mins, then add the chipotle paste, passata, chickpeas, honey and vinegar. Season and bubble for 5 mins.

STEP 2

Toast the bread. Heat the remaining oil in a frying pan and fry the eggs. Drizzle the toast with a little oil, then top with the chickpeas and fried eggs.

Frazzled chorizo & rocket linguine

Prep: 5 mins **Cook:** 15 mins

Serves 2

Ingredients

- 140g linguine
- 4 small cooking chorizo, cut into small chunks
- 2 tbsp capers, drained
- juice 1 lemon
- 50g bag rocket

Method

STEP 1

Cook the linguine following pack instructions. Meanwhile, put the chorizo in a cold frying pan over a low heat, then gradually increase it. Enough oil will be released by the chorizo to brown it without adding extra.

STEP 2

Stir and fry the chorizo until it is completely frazzled, then lift it out onto a plate.

STEP 3

Add the capers to the frying pan and cook for 1 min. Scoop them out and discard any excess oil.

STEP 4

Drain the pasta and add the chorizo and capers along with the lemon juice and rocket. Season and toss everything together.

Pasta with chilli tomatoes & spinach

Prep: 10 mins **Cook:** 20 mins

Serves 2

Ingredients

- 2 tsp olive oil
- 1 onion , finely chopped
- 2 garlic cloves , crushed
- ½ tsp dried chilli flakes
- 200g wholemeal penne pasta
- 400g can chopped tomato
- 100ml red wine
- ½ tsp dried oregano
- 125g bag young spinach leaves
- 25g parmesan or vegetarian alternative, grated

Method

STEP 1

Heat the oil in a non-stick frying pan and gently fry the onion, garlic and chilli flakes, stirring regularly, for 5 mins (add a little water if they begin to stick).

STEP 2

Cook pasta following pack instructions. Add the tomatoes, wine and oregano to the frying pan and stir to combine. Bring to a gentle simmer and cook, stirring occasionally, for 10 mins.

STEP 3

Shake the spinach into the pan and cook for 1-2 mins until wilted. Drain the pasta and tip into the pan with the sauce. Toss to combine, sprinkle with cheese and serve.

Prawn sweet chilli noodle salad

Prep: 10 mins **Cook:** 5 mins

Serves 4 - 6

Ingredients

- 3 nests medium egg noodles
- ½ large cucumber
- bunch spring onions , finely sliced
- 100g cherry tomato , halved
- 1 green chilli , deseeded, finely chopped
- 200g cooked king prawns , defrosted if frozen
- zest and juice 2 limes
- 4 tbsp sweet chilli sauce
- 100g baby spinach leaves
- 25g roasted cashew

Method

STEP 1

Boil the noodles for 4 mins, then drain. Cool under running water, then drain again. Put into a large bowl, then using scissors, cut into shorter lengths.

STEP 2

Halve cucumber lengthways, then scoop out the seeds. Slice into halfmoons and add to the noodles with the onions, tomatoes, chilli and prawns.

STEP 3

Mix the lime zest, juice and chilli sauce to make a dressing and fold through noodles. Put a handful of spinach onto each serving plate, top with the noodles and cashews.

Pickled red onion & radish

Prep: 10 mins **Cook:** 2 mins plus resting

Serves 6

Ingredients

- 1 large red onion
- 12 small radishes
- 1 tbsp golden caster sugar
- 100ml cider vinegar

Method

STEP 1

Slice 1 large red onion into thin rings and 12 small radishes into thin slices. Stir in 1 tbsp salt and 1 tbsp golden caster sugar and leave for 20 mins. Warm 100ml cider vinegar and 50ml water in a small saucepan, then pour over the vegetables. Stir to dissolve the sugar and salt, then leave to cool.

Baked asparagus risotto

Prep: 10 mins **Cook:** 45 mins

Serves 4

Ingredients

- 2 tsp olive oil
- 1 small onion, chopped
- 300g risotto rice
- 400ml can asparagus soup
- 850ml vegetable stock
- small bunch parsley, chopped
- 300g asparagus, ends trimmed
- 10 cherry tomatoes, halved
- 25g parmesan (or vegetarian alternative), grated

Method

STEP 1

Heat oven to 200C/180C fan/gas 6. Heat the oil in an ovenproof casserole dish, add the onion and cook for 5 mins until softened. Add the rice and cook for 1 min more, stirring to coat in the oil. Tip in the soup and stock, season and stir well to combine, then bring to the boil. Cover and place in the oven.

STEP 2

Bake for 15 mins, then remove the dish from the oven, give the rice a good mix, stirring in the parsley. Place the asparagus and tomatoes on top of the rice. Return to the oven, uncovered, for a further 15 mins. Scatter with the cheese to serve.

Creamy chicken & asparagus braise

Prep: 10 mins **Cook:** 20 mins - 25 mins

Serves 2

Ingredients

- 1 tbsp rapeseed oil
- 2 skinless chicken breasts (about 150g each)
- 10 medium asparagus spears , each cut into 3
- 1 large or 2 small leeks , well washed and thickly sliced
- 3 celery sticks , sliced
- 200ml reduced-salt vegetable bouillon
- 140g frozen peas
- 1 egg yolk
- 4 tbsp natural bio yogurt
- 1 garlic clove , finely grated
- ⅓ small pack fresh tarragon , chopped
- new potatoes , to serve (optional)

Method

STEP 1

Heat the oil in a large non-stick frying pan and fry the chicken for 5 mins, turning to brown both sides.

STEP 2

Add the asparagus (reserve the tips), leeks and celery, pour in the bouillon and simmer for 10 mins. Add the asparagus tips and peas, and cook for 5 mins more.

STEP 3

Meanwhile, stir the egg yolk with the yogurt and garlic. Stir the yogurt mixture into the vegetables and add the tarragon. Divide between two warm plates, then place the chicken on top of the vegetables. Serve with new potatoes, if you like.

Prawn jambalaya

Prep: 10 mins **Cook:** 35 mins

Serves 2

Ingredients

- 1 tbsp rapeseed oil
- 1 onion , chopped
- 3 celery sticks , sliced
- 100g wholegrain basmati rice
- 1 tsp mild chilli powder
- 1 tbsp ground coriander
- ½ tsp fennel seeds
- 400g can chopped tomatoes
- 1 tsp vegetable bouillon powder
- 1 yellow pepper , roughly chopped
- 2 garlic cloves , chopped
- 1 tbsp fresh thyme leaves
- 150g pack small prawns , thawed if frozen
- 3 tbsp chopped parsley

Method

STEP 1

Heat the oil in a large, deep frying pan. Add the onion and celery, and fry for 5 mins to soften. Add the rice and spices, and pour in the tomatoes with just under 1 can of water. Stir in the bouillon powder, pepper, garlic and thyme.

STEP 2

Cover the pan with a lid and simmer for 30 mins until the rice is tender and almost all the liquid has been absorbed. Stir in the prawns and parsley, cook briefly to heat through, then serve.

Asparagus & broad bean lasagne

Prep: 35 mins **Cook:** 1 hr and 10 mins

Serves 4

Ingredients

- 225ml whole milk
- 320g frozen baby broad beans
- 3 garlic cloves , chopped
- 30g pack fresh basil , roughly chopped
- ½ lemon , zested
- 4 spring onions , chopped
- 1 tsp vegetable bouillon powder
- 6 wholemeal lasagne sheets
- 320g frozen peas
- 2 x 300g tubs low-fat cottage cheese
- 1 egg
- whole nutmeg , for grating
- 250g asparagus , woody ends trimmed
- 25g parmesan or vegetarian alternative, finely grated

Method

STEP 1

Heat oven to 180C/160C fan/gas 4. Heat the milk in a pan until just boiling, then tip in the beans (add a splash of water to cover if you need to). Cook for 3 mins to defrost, then add the garlic, basil, lemon zest, spring onions and bouillon, then blitz for a few mins with a hand blender until smooth.

STEP 2

Spoon half the purée into a 20 x 26cm ovenproof dish. Top with 3 lasagne sheets, the remaining purée, and the peas, then the remaining lasagne sheets.

STEP 3

Whisk the cottage cheese with the egg and a good grating of nutmeg. Pour over the lasagne, then press in the asparagus and scatter over the parmesan. Bake for 1 hr until golden and a knife easily slides through. Can be kept chilled for two days.

Mediterranean turkey-stuffed peppers

Prep: 20 mins **Cook:** 30 mins

Serves 2

Ingredients

- 2 red peppers (about 220g)
- 1 ½ tbsp olive oil, plus an extra drizzle
- 240g lean turkey breast mince (under 8% fat)
- ½ small onion, chopped
- 1 garlic clove, grated
- 1 tsp ground cumin
- 3-4 mushrooms, sliced
- 400g can chopped tomatoes
- 1 tbsp tomato purée
- 1 chicken stock cube
- handful fresh oregano leaves
- 60g mozzarella, grated
- 150g green vegetables (spinach, kale, broccoli, mangetout or green beans), to serve

Method

STEP 1

Heat oven to 190C/170C fan/gas 5. Halve the peppers lengthways, then remove the seeds and core but keep the stalks on. Rub the peppers with a drizzle of olive oil and season well. Put on a baking tray and roast for 15 mins.

STEP 2

Meanwhile, heat 1 tbsp olive oil in a large pan over a medium heat. Fry the mince for 2-3 mins, stirring to break up the chunks, then tip onto a plate.

STEP 3

Wipe out your pan, then heat the rest of the oil over a medium-high heat. Add the onion and garlic, stir-fry for 2-3 mins, then add the cumin and mushrooms and cook for 2-3 mins more.

STEP 4

Tip the mince back into the pan and add the chopped tomatoes and tomato purée. Crumble in the stock cube and cook for 3-4 mins, then add the oregano and season. Remove the peppers from the oven and fill them with as much of the mince as you can. (Don't worry if some spills out it – it will go satisfyingly crisp in the oven.) Top with the cheese and return to the oven for 10-15 mins until the cheese starts to turn golden.

STEP 5

Carefully slide the peppers onto a plate and serve alongside a pile of your favourite greens blanched, boiled or steamed.

Super-quick sesame ramen

Prep: 5 mins **Cook:** 10 mins

Serves 1

Ingredients

- 80g pack instant noodles (look for an Asian brand with a flavour like sesame)
- 2 spring onions , finely chopped
- ½ head pak choi
- 1 egg
- 1 tsp sesame seeds
- chilli sauce , to serve

Method

STEP 1

Cook the noodles with the sachet of flavouring provided (or use stock instead of the sachet, if you have it). Add the spring onions and pak choi for the final min.

STEP 2

Meanwhile, simmer the egg for 6 mins from boiling, run it under cold water to stop it cooking, then peel it. Toast the sesame seeds in a frying pan.

STEP 3

Tip the noodles and greens into a deep bowl, halve the boiled egg and place on top. Sprinkle with sesame seeds, then drizzle with the sauce or sesame oil provided with the noodles, and chilli sauce, if using.

Ginger, sesame and chilli prawn & broccoli stir-fry

Prep: 5 mins **Cook:** 10 mins

Serves 2

Ingredients

- 250g broccoli , thin-stemmed if you like, cut into even-sized florets
- 2 balls stem ginger , finely chopped, plus 2 tbsp syrup from the jar
- 3 tbsp low-salt soy sauce
- 1 garlic clove , crushed
- 1 red chilli , a little thinly sliced, the rest deseeded and finely chopped
- 2 tsp sesame seeds
- ½ tbsp sesame oil
- 200g raw king prawns
- 100g beansprouts
- cooked rice or noodles, to serve

Method

STEP 1

Heat a pan of water until boiling. Tip in the broccoli and cook for just 1 min – it should still have a good crunch. Meanwhile, mix the stem ginger and syrup, soy sauce, garlic and finely chopped chilli.

STEP 2

Toast the sesame seeds in a dry wok or large frying pan. When they're nicely browned, turn up the heat and add the oil, prawns and cooked broccoli. Stir-fry for a few mins until the prawns turn pink. Pour over the ginger sauce, then tip in the beansprouts. Cook for 30 seconds, or until the beansprouts are heated thoroughly, adding a splash more soy or ginger syrup, if you like. Scatter with the sliced chilli and serve over rice or noodles.

Slow cooker shepherd's pie

Prep: 1 hr **Cook:** 5 hrs

Serves 4

Ingredients

- 1 tbsp olive oil
- 1 onion, finely chopped
- 3-4 thyme sprigs
- 2 carrots, finely diced
- 250g lean (10%) mince lamb or beef
- 1 tbsp plain flour
- 1 tbsp tomato purée
- 400g can lentils, or white beans
- 1 tsp Worcestershire sauce

For the topping

- 650g potatoes, peeled and cut into chunks
- 250g sweet potatoes, peeled and cut into chunks
- 2 tbsp half-fat crème fraîche

Method

STEP 1

Heat the slow cooker if necessary. Heat the oil in a large frying pan. Tip the onions and thyme sprigs and fry for 2-3 mins. Then add the carrots and fry together, stirring occasionally until the vegetables start to brown. Stir in the mince and fry for 1-2 mins until no longer pink. Stir in the flour then cook for another 1-2 mins. Stir in the tomato purée and lentils and season with pepper and the Worcestershire sauce, adding a splash of water if you think the mixture is too dry. Scrape everything into the slow cooker.

STEP 2

Meanwhile cook both lots of potatoes in simmering water for 12-13 minutes or until they are cooked through. Drain well and then mash with the crème fraîche. Spoon this on top of the mince mixture and cook on Low for 5 hours - the mixture should be bubbling at the sides when it is ready. Crisp up the potato topping under the grill if you like.

Vietnamese chicken noodle soup

Prep: 20 mins **Cook:** 25 mins

Serves 6

Ingredients

- 1 tbsp vegetable oil
- 3 shallots, sliced
- 3 garlic cloves, sliced
- 1 lemongrass stalk, chopped
- 2.5cm piece ginger, sliced
- 3 star anise
- 1 cinnamon stick
- 1 tsp coriander seeds
- ¼ tsp Chinese five spice
- ¼ tsp black peppercorns
- 1 tsp caster sugar
- 1 tbsp fish sauce
- 1.25 - 1.5 litres good quality fresh chicken stock
- 3 large chicken breasts (about 500g)

To serve

- 450g rice noodles
- 4 spring onions, finely sliced on an angle
- 1 carrot, shredded or peeled into ribbon with a vegetable peeler
- 2 large handfuls (150g) mung bean sprouts
- large bunch coriander, chopped
- small bunch mint, leaves chopped
- 1 red chilli, thinly sliced (optional)
- 2 tbsp crispy fried shallots (optional)
- 1 kaffir lime leaf, tough central stalk removed, very finely sliced, (optional)
- 1 lime, cut into wedges

Method

STEP 1

Heat the oil in a small frying pan on medium heat and gently cook the shallots and garlic until caramelised and golden brown (about 4-5 mins).

STEP 2

In a large saucepan, add the caramelised shallots and garlic, lemongrass, ginger, star anise, cinnamon stick, coriander seeds, Chinese five-spice, peppercorns, sugar, fish sauce, chicken stock and chicken breasts. Cover with a lid and bring to a very gentle simmer for about 15 mins.

STEP 3

Meanwhile, cook the noodles, following pack instructions, until just cooked through (do not over-cook). Rinse under cold water to prevent them sticking together. Drain and divide between serving bowls.

STEP 4

Strain the soup through a sieve. Discard the spices. Shred the chicken and keep to one side. Return soup to the pot and bring to a boil. Season to taste with more fish sauce if needed.

STEP 5

To serve, ladle piping hot soup into bowls of noodles and chicken, and top with spring onion, carrot, bean sprouts, and herbs, plus the chilli, crispy shallots and kaffir lime leaf if using. Serve with a lime wedge to squeeze over, and more fish sauce and chilli to taste.

Cod with cucumber, avocado & mango salsa salad

Prep: 5 mins **Cook:** 8 mins

Serves 2

Ingredients

- 2 x skinless cod fillets
- 1 lime, zested and juiced
- 1 small mango, peeled, stoned and chopped (or 2 peaches, stoned and chopped)
- 1 small avocado, stoned, peeled and sliced
- ¼ cucumber, chopped
- 160g cherry tomatoes, quartered
- 1 red chilli, deseeded and chopped
- 2 spring onions, sliced
- handful chopped coriander

Method

STEP 1

Heat oven to 200C/180C fan/gas 6. Put the fish in a shallow ovenproof dish and pour over half the lime juice, with a little of the zest, then grind over some black pepper. Bake for 8 mins or until the fish flakes easily but is still moist.

STEP 2

Meanwhile, put the rest of the ingredients, plus the remaining lime juice and zest, in a bowl and combine well. Spoon onto plates and top with the cod, spooning over any juices in the dish.

Easy soup maker lentil soup

Prep: 5 mins **Cook:** 30 mins

Serves 4

Ingredients

- 750ml vegetable or ham stock
- 75g red lentils
- 3 carrots, finely chopped
- 1 medium leek, sliced (150g)
- small handful chopped parsley, to serve

Method

STEP 1

Put the stock, lentils, carrots and leek into a soup maker, and press the 'chunky soup' function. Make sure you don't fill it above the max fill line. The soup will look a little foamy to start, but don't worry – it will disappear once cooked.

STEP 2

Once the cycle is complete, check the lentils are tender, and season well. Scatter over the parsley to serve.

Singapore noodles with prawns

Prep: 10 mins **Cook:** 10 mins

Serves 2

Ingredients

- 2 nests thin vermicelli rice noodles
- 1 tbsp light soy sauce
- 1 tbsp oyster sauce
- 2 tsp mild curry powder
- 1 tbsp sesame oil
- 1 garlic clove, chopped
- 1 red chilli, thinly sliced (deseeded if you don't like it too hot)
- thumb-sized piece ginger, grated
- 1 medium onion, sliced
- 1 red pepper or yellow pepper, cut into thin batons
- 4 spring onions, cut in half lengthways then into batons
- 8 raw king prawns
- 1 large egg, beaten
- coriander leaves, to serve

Method

STEP 1

Soak the rice noodles in warm water for 5 mins until softened but still al dente. Drain and set aside.

STEP 2

In a small bowl, mix together the soy, oyster sauce and curry powder.

STEP 3

In a large wok, add half the oil and fry the garlic, chilli and ginger until golden, about 2 mins. Add the remaining oil, onion, pepper, spring onions, prawns and noodles and stir-fry for a few mins. Push everything to one side, add the egg and scramble. Add the soy sauce mixture, toss again for a few more mins, then remove from the heat. Sprinkle over the coriander leaves before serving.

Ginger chicken & green bean noodles

Prep: 10 mins **Cook:** 15 mins

Serves 2

Ingredients

- ½ tbsp vegetable oil
- 2 skinless chicken breasts, sliced
- 200g green beans, trimmed and halved crosswise
- thumb-sized piece of ginger, peeled and cut into matchsticks
- 2 garlic cloves, sliced

- 1 ball stem ginger, finely sliced, plus 1 tsp syrup from the jar
- 1 tsp cornflour, mixed with 1 tbsp water
- 1 tsp dark soy sauce, plus extra to serve (optional)
- 2 tsp rice vinegar
- 200g cooked egg noodles

Method

STEP 1

Heat the oil in a wok over a high heat and stir-fry the chicken for 5 mins. Add the green beans and stir-fry for 4-5 mins more until the green beans are just tender, and the chicken is just cooked through.

STEP 2

Stir in the fresh ginger and garlic, and stir-fry for 2 mins, then add the stem ginger and syrup, the cornflour mix, soy sauce and vinegar. Stir-fry for 1 min, then toss in the noodles. Cook until everything is hot and the sauce coats the noodles. Drizzle with more soy, if you like, and serve.

Spicy meatballs with chilli black beans

Prep: 20 mins **Cook:** 25 mins

Serves 4

Ingredients

- 1 red onion, halved and sliced
- 2 garlic cloves, sliced
- 1 large yellow pepper, quartered, deseeded and diced
- 1 tsp ground cumin
- 2-3 tsp chipotle chilli paste
- 300ml reduced-salt chicken stock
- 400g can cherry tomatoes
- 400g can black beans or red kidney beans, drained
- 1 avocado, stoned, peeled and chopped
- juice ½ lime

For the meatballs

- 500g pack turkey breast mince
- 50g porridge oats
- 2 spring onions, finely chopped
- 1 tsp ground cumin
- 1 tsp coriander
- small bunch coriander, chopped, stalks and leaves kept separate
- 1 tsp rapeseed oil

Method

STEP 1

First make the meatballs. Tip the mince into a bowl, add the oats, spring onions, spices and the coriander stalks, then lightly knead the ingredients together until well mixed. Shape into 12 ping-pong- sized balls. Heat the oil in a non-stick frying pan, add the meatballs and cook, turning them frequently, until golden. Remove from the pan.

STEP 2

Tip the onion and garlic into the pan with the pepper and stir-fry until softened. Stir in the cumin and chilli paste, then pour in the stock. Return the meatballs to the pan and cook, covered, over a low heat for 10 mins. Stir in the tomatoes and beans, and cook, uncovered, for a few mins more. Toss the avocado chunks in the lime juice and serve the meatballs topped with the avocado and coriander leaves.

Golden goose fat potatoes & parsnips

Prep: 15 mins **Cook:** 2 hrs and 10 mins

Serves 6

Ingredients

- 1 ½kg Maris Piper potatoes, cut into large chunks
- 600g parsnips, peeled and cut into large chunks
- 100g goose fat
- handful rosemary sprigs (optional)

Method

STEP 1

Tip the potatoes into a large pan of cold salted water and bring to the boil. Turn the heat down slightly and keep the water bubbling gently for 3 mins, then add the parsnips and continue to simmer for 3 mins more. Drain everything and leave until cool enough to handle, then separate the parsnips and the potatoes.

STEP 2

Heat oven to 200C/180C fan/gas 6 with a large roasting tin containing the goose fat inside. When the goose fat is hot, remove the tin from the oven. Carefully tip in the potatoes and turn them so they're completely coated in fat. Place the tin back in the oven and leave undisturbed for 1 hr. Remove the tin from the oven, add the parsnips and gently turn everything together.

STEP 3

Increase oven temperature to 220C/200C fan/gas 8. Roast everything for 20 mins, then turn the parsnips and potatoes again with the rosemary, if using, and roast for about another 15 mins until everything is golden and crisp. Sprinkle with sea salt and scoop into a warm serving dish.

Soup maker tomato soup

Prep: 5 mins **Cook:** 30 mins

Serves 2

Ingredients

- 500g ripe tomatoes , off the vine and quartered or halved
- 1 small onion , chopped
- ½ small carrot , chopped
- ½ celery stick, chopped
- 1 tsp tomato purée
- pinch of sugar
- 450ml vegetable stock

Method

STEP 1

Put all the ingredients into the soup maker and press the 'smooth soup' function. Make sure you don't fill the soup maker above the max fill line.

STEP 2

Once the cycle is complete, season well, and check the soup for sweetness. Add a little more sugar, salt or tomato puree for depth of colour, if you like.

Slow cooker lasagne

Prep: 1 hr and 15 mins **Cook:** 3 hrs

Serves 4

Ingredients

- 2 tsp rapeseed oil
- 2 onions, finely chopped
- 4 celery sticks (about 175g), finely diced
- 4 carrots (320g), finely diced
- 2 garlic cloves, chopped
- 400g lean (5% fat) mince beef
- 400g can chopped tomatoes
- 2 tbsp tomato purée
- 2 tsp vegetable bouillon
- 1 tbsp balsamic vinegar
- 1 tbsp fresh thyme leaves
- 6 wholewheat lasagne sheets (105g)

For the sauce

- 400ml whole milk
- 50g wholemeal flour
- 1 bay leaf
- generous grating of nutmeg
- 15g finely grated parmesan

Method

STEP 1

Heat the slow cooker if necessary. Heat the oil in a large non-stick pan and fry the onions, celery, carrots and garlic for 5-10 mins, stirring frequently until softened and starting to colour. Tip in the meat and break it down with a wooden spoon, stirring until it browns. Pour in the tomatoes with a quarter of a can of water, the tomato purée, bouillon, balsamic vinegar, thyme and plenty of black pepper, return to the boil and cook for 5 mins more.

STEP 2

Spoon half the mince in the slow cooker and top with half the lasagne, breaking it where necessary so it covers as much of the meat layer as possible. Top with the rest of the meat, and then another layer of the lasagne. Cover and cook on Low while you make the sauce.

STEP 3

Tip the milk and flour into a pan with the bay leaf and nutmeg and cook on the hob, whisking continuously until thickened. Carry on cooking for a few mins to cook the flour. Remove the bay leaf and stir in the cheese. Pour onto the pasta and spread out with a spatula, then cover and cook for 3 hours until the meat is cooked and the pasta is tender. Allow to settle for 10 mins before serving with salad.

Turkey meatloaf

Prep: 15 mins **Cook:** 55 mins

Serves 4

Ingredients

- 1 tbsp olive oil
- 1 large onion , finely chopped
- 1 garlic clove , crushed
- 2 tbsp Worcestershire sauce
- 2 tsp tomato purée , plus 1 tbsp for the beans
- 500g turkey mince (thigh is best)
- 1 large egg , beaten
- 85g fresh white breadcrumbs
- 2 tbsp barbecue sauce , plus 4 tbsp for the beans
- 2 x 400g cans cannellini beans
- 1-2 tbsp roughly chopped parsley

Method

STEP 1

Heat oven to 180C/160C fan/gas 4. Heat the oil in a large frying pan and cook the onion for 8-10 mins until softened. Add the garlic, Worcestershire sauce and 2 tsp tomato purée, and stir until combined. Set aside to cool.

STEP 2

Put the turkey mince, egg, breadcrumbs and cooled onion mix in a large bowl and season well. Mix everything to combine, then shape into a rectangular loaf and place in a large roasting tin. Spread 2 tbsp barbecue sauce over the meatloaf and bake for 30 mins.

STEP 3

Meanwhile, drain 1 can of beans only, then pour both cans into a large bowl. Add the remaining barbecue sauce and tomato purée. Season and set aside.

STEP 4

When the meatloaf has had its initial cooking time, scatter the beans around the outside and bake for 15 mins more until the meatloaf is cooked through and the beans are piping hot. Scatter over the parsley and serve the meatloaf in slices.

All-in-one chicken with wilted spinach

Prep: 20 mins **Cook:** 1 hr

Serves 2

Ingredients

- 2 beetroot, peeled and cut into small chunks
- 300g celeriac, cut into small chunks
- 2 red onions, quartered
- 8 garlic cloves, 4 crushed, the rest left whole, but peeled
- 1 tbsp rapeseed oil
- 1½ tbsp fresh thyme leaves, plus extra to serve
- 1 lemon, zested and juiced
- 1 tsp fennel seeds
- 1 tsp English mustard powder
- 1 tsp smoked paprika
- 4 tbsp bio yogurt
- 4 bone-in chicken thighs, skin removed
- 260g bag spinach

Method

STEP 1

Heat oven to 200C/180C fan/gas 6. Tip the beetroot, celeriac, onions and whole garlic cloves into a shallow roasting tin. Add the oil, 1 tbsp thyme, half the lemon zest, fennel seeds and a squeeze of lemon juice, then toss together. Roast for 20 mins while you prepare the chicken.

STEP 2

Stir the mustard powder and paprika into 2 tbsp yogurt in a bowl. Add half the crushed garlic, the remaining lemon zest and thyme, and juice from half the lemon. Add the chicken and toss well until it's coated all over. Put the chicken in the tin with the veg and roast for 40 mins until the chicken is cooked through and the vegetables are tender.

STEP 3

About 5 mins before the chicken is ready, wash and drain the spinach and put it in a pan with the remaining crushed garlic. Cook until wilted, then turn off the heat and stir in the remaining yogurt. Scatter some extra thyme over the chicken and vegetables, then serve.

Green chowder with prawns

Prep: 10 mins **Cook:** 20 mins - 30 mins

Serves 4

Ingredients

- 1 tbsp olive oil
- 1 onion , finely chopped
- 1 celery stick , finely chopped
- 1 garlic clove
- 300g petit pois
- 200g pack sliced kale
- 2 potatoes , finely chopped
- 1 low-salt chicken stock cube (we used Kallo)
- 100g cooked North Atlantic prawns

Method

STEP 1

Heat the oil in a saucepan over a medium heat. Add the onion and celery and cook for 5-6 mins until softened but not coloured. Add the garlic and cook for a further min. Stir in the petit pois, kale and potatoes, then add the stock cube and 750ml water. Bring to the boil and simmer for 10-12 mins until the potatoes are soft.

STEP 2

Tip ¾ of the mixture into a food processor and whizz until smooth. Add a little more water or stock if it's too thick. Pour the mixture back into the pan and add half the prawns.

STEP 3

Divide between four bowls and spoon the remaining prawns on top. Can be frozen for up to a month. Add the prawns once defrosted.

Easy chicken stew

Prep: 10 mins **Cook:** 50 mins

Serves 4

Ingredients

- 1 tbsp olive oil

- 1 bunch spring onions, sliced, white and green parts separated
- 1 small swede (350g), peeled and chopped into small pieces
- 400g potatoes, peeled and chopped into small pieces
- 8 skinless boneless chicken thighs
- 1 tbsp Dijon mustard
- 500ml chicken stock
- 200g Savoy cabbage or spring cabbage, sliced
- 2 tsp cornflour (optional)
- crusty bread or cheese scones, to serve (optional)

Method

STEP 1

Heat the oil in a large saucepan. Add the white spring onion slices and fry for 1 min to soften. Tip in the swede and potatoes and cook for 2-3 mins more, then add the chicken, mustard and stock. Cover and cook for 35 mins, or until the vegetables are tender and the chicken cooked through.

STEP 2

Add the cabbage and simmer for another 5 mins. If the stew looks too thin, mix the cornflour with 1 tbsp cold water and pour a couple of teaspoonfuls into the pan; let the stew bubble and thicken, then check again. If it's still too thin, add a little more of the cornflour mix and let the stew bubble and thicken some more.

STEP 3

Season to taste, then spoon the stew into deep bowls. Scatter over the green spring onion slices and serve with crusty bread or warm cheese scones, if you like.

Healthy bolognese

Prep: 5 mins **Cook:** 20 mins

2 generously, 4 as a snack

Ingredients

- 100g wholewheat linguine
- 2 tsp rapeseed oil
- 1 fennel bulb, finely chopped
- 2 garlic cloves, sliced
- 200g pork mince with less than 5% fat
- 200g whole cherry tomatoes
- 1 tbsp balsamic vinegar
- 1 tsp vegetable bouillon powder

- generous handful chopped basil

Method

STEP 1

Bring a large pan of water to the boil, then cook the linguine following pack instructions, about 10 mins.

STEP 2

Meanwhile, heat the oil in a non-stick wok or wide pan. Add the fennel and garlic and cook, stirring every now and then, until tender, about 10 mins.

STEP 3

Tip in the pork and stir-fry until it changes colour, breaking it up as you go so there are no large clumps. Add the tomatoes, vinegar and bouillon, then cover the pan and cook for 10 mins over a low heat until the tomatoes burst and the pork is cooked and tender. Add the linguine and basil and plenty of pepper, and toss well before serving.

Fennel spaghetti

Prep: 15 mins **Cook:** 30 mins

Serves 2

Ingredients

- 1 tbsp olive oil , plus extra for serving
- 1 tsp fennel seeds
- 2 small garlic cloves , 1 crushed, 1 thinly sliced
- 1 lemon , zested and juiced
- 1 fennel bulb , finely sliced, fronds reserved
- 150g spaghetti
- ½ pack flat-leaf parsley , chopped
- shaved parmesan (or vegetarian alternative), to serve (optional)

Method

STEP 1

Heat the oil in a frying pan over a medium heat and cook the fennel seeds until they pop. Sizzle the garlic for 1 min, then add the lemon zest and half the fennel slices. Cook for 10-12 mins or until the fennel has softened.

STEP 2

Meanwhile, bring a pan of salted water to the boil and cook the pasta for 1 min less than pack instructions. Use tongs to transfer the pasta to the frying pan along with a good splash of pasta water. Increase the heat to high and toss well. Stir through the remaining fennel slices, the parsley and lemon juice, season generously, then tip straight into two bowls to serve. Top with the fennel fronds, extra olive oil and parmesan shavings, if you like.

Carrot & ginger soup

Prep: 15 mins **Cook:** 25 mins - 30 mins

Serves 4

Ingredients

- 1 tbsp rapeseed oil
- 1 large onion, chopped
- 2 tbsp coarsely grated ginger
- 2 garlic cloves, sliced
- ½ tsp ground nutmeg
- 850ml vegetable stock
- 500g carrot (preferably organic), sliced
- 400g can cannellini beans (no need to drain)

Supercharged topping

- 4 tbsp almonds in their skins, cut into slivers
- sprinkle of nutmeg

Method

STEP 1

Heat the oil in a large pan, add the onion, ginger and garlic, and fry for 5 mins until starting to soften. Stir in the nutmeg and cook for 1 min more.

STEP 2

Pour in the stock, add the carrots, beans and their liquid, then cover and simmer for 20-25 mins until the carrots are tender.

STEP 3

Scoop a third of the mixture into a bowl and blitz the remainder with a hand blender or in a food processor until smooth. Return everything to the pan and heat until bubbling. Serve topped with the almonds and nutmeg.

Thai prawn & ginger noodles

Prep: 15 mins **Cook:** 15 mins plus soaking

Serves 2

Ingredients

- 100g folded rice noodles (sen lek)
- zest and juice 1 small orange
- 1½-2 tbsp red curry paste
- 1-2 tsp fish sauce
- 2 tsp light brown soft sugar
- 1 tbsp sunflower oil
- 25g ginger, scraped and shredded
- 2 large garlic cloves, sliced
- 1 red pepper, deseeded and sliced
- 85g sugar snap peas, halved lengthways
- 140g beansprouts
- 175g pack raw king prawns
- handful chopped basil
- handful chopped coriander

Method

STEP 1

Put the noodles in a bowl and pour over boiling water to cover them. Set aside to soak for 10 mins. Stir together the orange juice and zest, curry paste, fish sauce, sugar and 3 tbsp water to make a sauce.

STEP 2

Heat the oil in a large wok and add half the ginger and the garlic. Cook, stirring, for 1 min. Add the pepper and stir-fry for 3 mins more. Toss in the sugar snaps, cook briefly, then pour in the curry sauce. Add the beansprouts and prawns, and continue cooking until the prawns just turn pink. Drain the noodles, then toss these into the pan with the herbs and remaining ginger. Mix until the noodles are well coated in the sauce, then serve.

Squash & spinach fusilli with pecans

Prep: 10 mins **Cook:** 40 mins

Serves 2

Ingredients

- 160g butternut squash, diced
- 3 garlic cloves, sliced
- 1 tbsp chopped sage leaves
- 2 tsp rapeseed oil
- 1 large courgette, halved and sliced
- 6 pecan halves
- 115g wholemeal fusilli
- 125g bag baby spinach

Method

STEP 1

Heat oven to 200C/180C fan/gas 6. Toss the butternut squash, garlic and sage in the oil, then spread out in a roasting tin and cook in the oven for 20 mins, add the courgettes and cook for a further 15 mins. Give everything a stir, then add the pecans and cook for 5 mins more until the nuts are toasted and the vegetables are tender and starting to caramelise.

STEP 2

Meanwhile, boil the pasta according to pack instructions – about 12 mins. Drain, then tip into a serving bowl and toss with the spinach so that it wilts in the heat from the pasta. Add the roasted veg and pecans, breaking up the nuts a little, and toss again really well before serving.

Lighter chicken cacciatore

Prep: 15 mins **Cook:** 50 mins

Serves 4

Ingredients

- 1 tbsp olive oil
- 3 slices prosciutto, fat removed, chopped
- 1 medium onion, chopped
- 2 garlic cloves, finely chopped
- 2 sage sprigs
- 2 rosemary sprigs

- 4 skinless chicken breasts (550g total weight), preferably organic
- 150ml dry white wine
- 400g can plum tomatoes in natural juice
- 1 tbsp tomato purée
- 225g chestnut mushrooms, quartered or halved if large
- small handful chopped flat-leaf parsley, to serve

Method

STEP 1

Heat the oil in a large non-stick frying pan. Tip in the prosciutto and fry for about 2 mins until crisp. Remove with a slotted spoon, letting any fat drain back into the pan, and set aside. Put the onion, garlic and herbs in the pan and fry for 3-4 mins.

STEP 2

Spread the onion out in the pan, then lay the chicken breasts on top. Season with pepper and fry for 5 mins over a medium heat, turning the chicken once, until starting to brown on both sides and the onion is caramelising on the bottom of the pan. Remove the chicken and set aside on a plate. Raise the heat, give it a quick stir and, when sizzling, pour in the wine and let it bubble for 2 mins to reduce slightly.

STEP 3

Lower the heat to medium, return the prosciutto to the pan, then stir in the tomatoes (breaking them up with your spoon), tomato purée and mushrooms. Spoon 4 tbsp of water into the empty tomato can, swirl it around, then pour it into the pan. Cover and simmer for 15-20 mins or until the sauce has thickened and reduced slightly, then return the chicken to the pan and cook, uncovered, for about 15 mins or until the chicken is cooked through. Season and scatter over the parsley to serve.

Cod puttanesca with spinach & spaghetti

Prep: 10 mins **Cook:** 17 mins

Serves 2

Ingredients

- 100g wholemeal spaghetti
- 1 large onion , sliced
- 1 tbsp rapeseed oil
- 1 red chilli , deseeded and sliced

- 2 garlic cloves, chopped
- 200g cherry tomatoes, halved
- 1 tsp cider vinegar
- 2 tsp capers
- 5 Kalamata olives, halved
- ½ tsp smoked paprika
- 2 skinless cod fillet or loins
- 160g spinach leaves
- small handful chopped parsley, to serve

Method

STEP 1

Boil the spaghetti for 10 mins until al dente, adding the spinach for the last 2 mins. Meanwhile, fry the onion in the oil in a large non-stick frying pan with a lid until tender and turning golden. Stir in the chilli and garlic, then add the tomatoes.

STEP 2

Add the vinegar, capers, olives and paprika with a ladleful of the pasta water. Put the cod fillets on top, then cover the pan and cook for 5-7 mins until the fish just flakes. Drain the pasta and wilted spinach and pile on to plates, then top with the fish and sauce. Sprinkle over some parsley to serve.

Sesame chicken & prawn skewers

Prep: 15 mins **Cook:** 5 mins Plus marinating

Makes 20

Ingredients

- thumb-sized piece ginger, grated
- 1 large garlic clove, grated
- 1 tsp honey
- 1½ tsp soy sauce
- 1 tsp sesame oil
- ½ lime, juiced
- 1 tbsp sesame seeds
- 1 skinless chicken breast, cut into 10 pieces
- 10 raw king prawns
- 1 broccoli head, cut into 20 florets
- 20 cocktail skewers

Method

STEP 1

Combine the ginger, garlic, honey, soy sauce, sesame oil, lime juice and sesame seeds. Divide between two bowls, then add the chicken pieces to one and the prawns to the other. Toss both mixtures well, then leave to marinate in the fridge for 15 mins.

STEP 2

Cook the chicken in a frying pan over a medium-high heat for 3 mins, then push to one side and add the prawns to the other side of the pan. Cook for 2 mins until the prawns are pink and the chicken is cooked through (use two separate pans if anyone you're cooking for has an allergy or is a pescatarian). Put the broccoli in a microwaveable bowl with a splash of water, then cover and cook on high for 5 mins.

STEP 3

Thread half of the skewers with chicken and broccoli and the other half with prawns and broccoli.

Charred spring onions & teriyaki tofu

Prep: 5 mins **Cook:** 25 mins

Serves 2

Ingredients

- 150g wholegrain rice
- 50ml soy sauce
- 2 tbsp mirin
- ½ tsp grated ginger
- 1 tsp honey
- 350g firm tofu (we used Cauldron)
- 1 bunch spring onions , ends trimmed
- 2 tsp sunflower oil
- ½ tsp sesame seeds
- 1 red chilli , sliced (optional)

Method

STEP 1

Cook the rice according to pack instructions. Pour the soy sauce, mirin, ginger and honey into a small saucepan and add 50ml water. Bring to a simmer and cook for around 5 mins or until slightly thickened. Remove from the heat and set aside until needed.

STEP 2

If your tofu doesn't feel very firm, you'll need to press it. To do this, wrap the block of in a few layers of kitchen paper, then weigh it down with a heavy pan or tray for 10-15 – the longer you press it, the firmer it will be. Cut the tofu into thick slices.

STEP 3

Heat a griddle pan over high heat and lightly brush the tofu and spring onions with the oil. Griddle the tofu and spring onion until deep char lines appear on both sides (around 4 mins each side) – you may have to do this in batches depending on the size of your griddle pan.

STEP 4

Divide the cooked rice between two plates, top with the tofu and spring onion, then drizzle with the teriyaki sauce. Garnish with the sesame seeds and sliced red chilli, if using.

Hearty pasta soup

Prep: 5 mins **Cook:** 25 mins

Serves 4

Ingredients

- 1 tbsp olive oil
- 2 carrots, chopped
- 1 large onion, finely chopped
- 1l vegetable stock
- 400g can chopped tomato
- 200g frozen mixed peas and beans
- 250g pack fresh filled tortellini (we used spinach and ricotta)
- handful of basil leaves (optional)
- grated parmesan (or vegetarian alternative), to serve

Method

STEP 1

Heat oil in a pan. Fry the carrots and onion for 5 mins until starting to soften. Add the stock and tomatoes, then simmer for 10 mins. Add the peas and beans with 5 mins to go.

STEP 2

Once veg is tender, stir in the pasta. Return to the boil and simmer for 2 mins until the pasta is just cooked. Stir in the basil, if using. Season, then serve in bowls topped with a sprinkling of Parmesan and slices of garlic bread.

Slow cooker mushroom risotto

Prep: 30 mins **Cook:** 1 hr

Serves 4

Ingredients

- 1 onion, finely chopped
- 1 tsp olive oil
- 250g chestnut mushrooms, sliced
- 1l vegetable stock
- 50g porcini
- 300g wholegrain rice
- small bunch parsley, finely chopped
- grated vegetarian parmesan-style cheese to serve

Method

STEP 1

Heat the slow cooker if necessary. Fry the onion in the oil in a frying pan with a splash of water for 10 minutes or until it is soft but not coloured. Add the mushroom slices and stir them around until they start to soften and release their juices.

STEP 2

Meanwhile pour the stock into a saucepan and add the porcini, bring to a simmer and then leave to soak. Tip the onions and mushrooms into the slow cooker and add the rice, stir it in well. Pour over the stock and porcini leaving any bits of sediment in the saucepan (or pour the mixture through a fine sieve).

STEP 3

Cook on High for 3 hours, stirring halfway. and then check the consistency – the rice should be cooked. If it needs a little more liquid stir in a splash of stock. Stir in the parsley and season. Serve with the parmesan.

Spicy meatball tagine with bulgur & chickpeas

Prep: 10 mins **Cook:** 45 mins plus chilling

Serves 4

Ingredients

- 2 onions, 1 quartered, 1 halved and sliced
- 2 tbsp tomato purée
- 2 garlic cloves
- 1 egg
- 1 tbsp chilli powder
- 500g pack extra-lean beef mince
- 2 tsp rapeseed oil
- 4 large carrots, cut into batons
- 1 tsp ground cumin
- 2 tsp ground coriander
- 400g can chopped tomatoes
- 1 lemon, zest removed with a potato peeler, then chopped
- 12 Kalamata olives, chopped
- 1 tbsp vegetable bouillon powder
- ⅓ pack fresh coriander, chopped

For the bulgur

- 200g bulgur wheat
- 400g can chickpeas
- 2 tsp vegetable bouillon powder
- 2 tsp ground coriander

Method

STEP 1

Put the quartered onion in the food processor and process to finely chop it. Add the minced beef, 1 tbsp tomato purée, the garlic, egg and chilli powder and blitz to make a smoothish paste. Divide the mixture into 26 even-sized pieces and roll into balls.

STEP 2

Heat the oil in a large frying pan and cook the meatballs for about 5-10 mins to lightly brown them. Tip from the pan onto a plate.

STEP 3

Now add the sliced onion and carrots to the pan and stir fry briefly in the pan juices to soften them a little. Add the spices and pour in the tomatoes with 1 ½ cans of water then stir in the chopped lemon zest, remaining tomato purée, olives and bouillon powder. Return the meatballs to the pan then cover and cook for 15 mins until the carrots are just tender. Stir in the coriander.

STEP 4

While the tagine is cooking, tip the bulgur into a pan with the chickpeas and water from the can. Add 2 cans of water, the bouillon and coriander. Cover and cook for 10 mins until the bulgur is tender and the liquid had been absorbed. If you're doing the Healthy Diet

Plan (serving two people), serve half with half of the tagine and chill the remainder for another night if you like.

Herb & garlic pork with summer ratatouille

Prep: 15 mins **Cook:** 25 mins

4 (or 2 with leftovers for other meals)

Ingredients

- 2 tsp rapeseed oil
- 2 red onions, halved and sliced
- 2 peppers (any colour), diced
- 1 large aubergine, diced
- 2 large courgettes, halved and sliced
- 2 garlic cloves, chopped

- 400g can chopped tomatoes
- 2 tsp vegetable bouillon
- 1 thyme spig
- handful basil, stalks chopped, leaves torn and kept separate

For the pork

- 475g pork tenderloin, fat trimmed off, cut into 2 equal pieces
- 2 garlic cloves, crushed

- 1 tbsp thyme leaves, plus a few sprigs to decorate
- 1 tsp rapeseed oil
- brown rice or new potatoes, to serve

Method

STEP 1

Heat the oil in a large non-stick pan and fry the onions for 5 mins or until softened. Stir in the peppers, aubergine, courgettes and garlic, and cook, stirring, for a few mins. Tip in the tomatoes and 1 can of water, then stir in the bouillon, thyme and basil stalks. Cover and simmer for 20 mins or until tender. Stir through the basil leaves.

STEP 2

Meanwhile, rub the pork with the garlic, then scatter with the thyme and some black pepper, patting it so it sticks all over. Heat the oil in a non-stick frying pan and cook the pork for about 12 mins, turning frequently so it browns on all sides, until tender but still moist. Cover and rest for 5 mins.

STEP 3

If you're making this as part of the Healthy Diet Plan, set aside half of the pork to use in the curried pork bulghar salad later in the week and store in the fridge once cooled. Chill the half of the ratatouille and use it to make the ratatouille pasta salad with rocket for another day. If you are serving four you can skip this step.

STEP 4

To serve, slice the pork and serve with the ratatouille, some brown rice or new potatoes and some extra thyme.

Peri-peri chicken pilaf

Prep: 20 mins **Cook:** 40 mins

Serves 4

Ingredients

- 1 tbsp olive oil
- pack of 6 skinless boneless chicken thighs , cut into large chunks
- 2 tbsp peri-peri seasoning
- 1 onion , finely chopped
- 2 garlic cloves , crushed
- 350g basmati rice
- 500ml hot chicken stock
- 3 peppers (any colour you like), sliced into strips
- 3 large tomatoes , deseeded and roughly chopped
- small pack parsley , roughly chopped
- 2 red chillies , sliced (optional)
- ½ lemon , cut into wedges, to serve

Method

STEP 1

Heat the oil in a large pan over a medium heat. Rub the chicken with 1 tbsp of the peri-peri and brown in the pan for 1 min each side until golden. Transfer to a plate and set aside.

STEP 2

Add the onion to the pan and cook on a gentle heat for 8-10 mins until soft. Add the garlic and remaining peri-peri, and give everything a stir. Tip in the rice and stir to coat.

STEP 3

Add the stock and return the chicken to the pan. Add the peppers and cover with a lid, then simmer gently for 25 mins until cooked. About 5 mins before the end of cooking, add the tomatoes.

STEP 4

Stir through the parsley, scatter over the chillies (if you like it spicy) and serve with lemon wedges.

Chicken & sweetcorn soup

Prep: 10 mins **Cook:** 2 hrs and 15 mins

Serves 2

Ingredients

- 1 chicken carcass
- 4 thin slices fresh ginger, plus 1 tbsp finely grated
- 2 onions, quartered
- 3 garlic cloves, finely grated
- 2 tsp apple cider vinegar
- 325g can sweetcorn
- 3 spring onions, whites thinly sliced, greens sliced at an angle
- 100g cooked chicken, shredded
- 2 tsp tamari
- 2 eggs, beaten
- few drops sesame oil, to serve (optional)

Method

STEP 1

Boil a large kettle of water. Break the carcass into a big non-stick pan and add the ginger slices, onion and two-thirds of the garlic. Cook, stirring, for about 2 mins – the meat will stick to the base of the pan, but this will add to the flavour. Pour in 1.5 litres of boiling water, stir in the vinegar, then cover and simmer for 2 hrs.

STEP 2

Put a large sieve over a bowl and pour through the contents of the pan. Measure the liquid in the bowl – you want around 450ml. If you have too much, return to the pan and boil with the lid off to reduce it. Transfer the onion from the sieve to a bowl with three-quarters of the sweetcorn. Blitz until smooth with a hand blender.

STEP 3

Return the broth to the pan, and tip in the puréed corn, remaining sweetcorn and garlic, the grated ginger, the whites of the spring onions and the chicken. Simmer for 5 mins, then stir in the tamari. Turn off the heat, and quickly drizzle in the egg, stirring a little to create egg threads. Season with pepper, then ladle into the bowls. Top with the spring onion greens and a few drops of sesame oil, if using.

Yaki udon

Prep: 10 mins **Cook:** 5 mins

Serves 2

Ingredients

- 250g dried udon noodles (400g frozen or fresh)
- 2 tbsp sesame oil
- 1 onion, thickly sliced
- ¼ head white cabbage, roughly sliced
- 10 shiitake mushrooms
- 4 spring onions, finely sliced

- For the sauce
- 4 tbsp mirin
- 2 tbsp soy sauce
- 1 tbsp caster sugar
- 1 tbsp Worcestershire sauce (or vegetarian alternative)

Method

STEP 1

Boil some water in a large saucepan. Add 250ml cold water and the udon noodles. (As they are so thick, adding cold water helps them to cook a little bit slower so the middle cooks through). If using frozen or fresh noodles, cook for 2 mins or until al dente; dried will take longer, about 5-6 mins. Drain and leave in the colander.

STEP 2

Heat 1 tbsp of the oil, add the onion and cabbage and sauté for 5 mins until softened. Add the mushrooms and some spring onions, and sauté for 1 more min. Pour in the remaining sesame oil and the noodles. If using cold noodles, let them heat through before adding the ingredients for the sauce – otherwise tip in straight away and keep stir-frying until sticky and piping hot. Sprinkle with the remaining spring onions.

Basic lentils

Prep: 10 mins **Cook:** 45 mins

Makes 6 portions

Ingredients

- 2 tbsp coconut oil
- 2 onions , chopped
- 4 garlic cloves , chopped
- large piece of ginger , chopped
- 300g red split lentils
- 1 tsp turmeric
- 2 tomatoes , roughly chopped
- 1 tsp coriander seeds
- 1 tsp cumin seeds
- 1 tsp black mustard seeds
- 1 lemon , juiced

Method

STEP 1

Melt 1 tbsp coconut oil in a large saucepan. Add the onion and a pinch of salt, and cook for 8 mins. Stir in the garlic and ginger and cook for a few mins more. Add the lentils, turmeric and tomatoes, stir to combine, then pour in 1 litre of water. Bring to the boil, then turn down and simmer for 25-30 mins, stirring occasionally, until the lentils are tender.

STEP 2

Heat the rest of the oil in a frying pan. When it's very hot, add the spices and fry for a min or so until fragrant, then stir them through. Add the lemon juice and season to taste. Will keep for four days in the fridge, or freeze it in batches and use to make our lentil kedgeree, lentil fritters, or spinach dhal with harissa yogurt.

Baked piri-piri tilapia with crushed potatoes

Prep: 10 mins **Cook:** 25 mins

Serves 4

Ingredients

- 600g small new potatoes
- 2 red peppers, cut into chunky pieces
- 1 tbsp red wine vinegar
- drizzle of extra virgin olive oil

- 4 large pieces tilapia or cod

For the piri-piri sauce

- 6 hot pickled peppers (I used Peppadew)
- 1 tsp chilli flakes
- 2 garlic cloves
- green salad, to serve
- juice and zest 1 lemon
- 1 tbsp red wine vinegar
- 2 tbsp extra virgin olive oil
- 1 tbsp smoked paprika

Method

STEP 1

Heat oven to 220C/200C fan/gas 7. Boil the potatoes until knife-tender, then drain. Spread out on a large baking tray and gently crush with the back of a spatula. Add the peppers, drizzle with the vinegar and oil, season well and roast for 25 mins.

STEP 2

Put the piri-piri ingredients in a food processor with some salt. Purée until fine, then pour into a bowl. Put the fish on a baking tray and spoon over some of the piri-piri sauce. Season and bake for the final 10 mins of the potatoes' cooking time. Serve everything with the extra sauce and a green salad on the side.

Parma pork with potato salad

Prep: 15 mins **Cook:** 15 mins

Serves 2

Ingredients

- 175g new potatoes (we used Jersey Royals), scrubbed and thickly sliced
- 3 celery sticks, thickly sliced
- 3 tbsp bio yogurt
- 2 gherkins (about 85g each), sliced
- ¼ tsp caraway seeds
- ½ tsp Dijon mustard
- 2 x 100g pieces lean pork tenderloin
- 2 tsp chopped sage
- 2 slices Parma ham
- 1 tsp rapeseed oil
- 2 tsp balsamic vinegar
- 2 handfuls salad leaves

Method

STEP 1

Bring a pan of water to the boil, add the potatoes and celery and cook for 8 mins. Meanwhile, mix the yogurt, guerkins, caraway and mustard in a bowl. When the potatoes and celery are cooked, drain and set aside for a few mins to cool a little.

STEP 2

Bash the pork pieces with a rolling pin to flatten them. Sprinkle over the sage and some pepper, then top each with a slice of Parma ham. Heat the oil in a non-stick pan, add the pork and cook for a couple of mins each side, turning carefully. Add the balsamic vinegar and let it sizzle in the pan.

STEP 3

Stir the potatoes and celery into the dressing and serve with the pork, with some salad leaves on the side.

Red lentil, chickpea & chilli soup

Prep: 10 mins **Cook:** 25 mins

Serves 4

Ingredients

- 2 tsp cumin seeds
- large pinch chilli flakes
- 1 tbsp olive oil
- 1 red onion, chopped
- 140g red split lentils
- 850ml vegetable stock or water
- 400g can tomatoes, whole or chopped
- 200g can chickpeas or ½ a can, drained and rinsed (freeze leftovers)
- small bunch coriander, roughly chopped (save a few leaves, to serve)
- 4 tbsp 0% Greek yogurt, to serve

Method

STEP 1

Heat a large saucepan and dry-fry 2 tsp cumin seeds and a large pinch of chilli flakes for 1 min, or until they start to jump around the pan and release their aromas.

STEP 2

Add 1 tbsp olive oil and 1 chopped red onion, and cook for 5 mins.

STEP 3

Stir in 140g red split lentils, 850ml vegetable stock or water and a 400g can tomatoes, then bring to the boil. Simmer for 15 mins until the lentils have softened.

STEP 4

Whizz the soup with a stick blender or in a food processor until it is a rough purée, pour back into the pan and add a 200g can drained and rinsed chickpeas.

STEP 5

Heat gently, season well and stir in a small bunch of chopped coriander, reserving a few leaves to serve. Finish with 4 tbsp 0% Greek yogurt and extra coriander leaves.

Low-sugar lime & basil green juice

Prep: 5 mins no cook

Serves 1

Ingredients

- 70ml chilled apple and elderflower juice
- 50g baby spinach
- 20g basil leaves
- 6cm piece of cucumber (about 100g), chopped
- 1 lime, zested and juiced

Method

STEP 1

Pour the apple juice into a large jug then add the spinach, basil, cucumber, lime and 100ml chilled water.

STEP 2

Blitz really well with a hand blender until very smooth. Pour into a glass and drink straightaway.

Rustic vegetable soup

Prep: 15 mins **Cook:** 30 mins

Serves 4

Ingredients

- 1 tbsp rapeseed oil
- 1 large onion, chopped
- 2 carrots, chopped
- 2 celery sticks, chopped
- 50g dried red lentils
- 1½ l boiling vegetable bouillon (we used Marigold)
- 2 tbsp tomato purée
- 1 tbsp chopped fresh thyme
- 1 leek, finely sliced
- 175g bite-sized cauliflower florets
- 1 courgette, chopped
- 3 garlic cloves, finely chopped
- ½ large Savoy cabbage, stalks removed and leaves chopped
- 1 tbsp basil, chopped

Method

STEP 1

Heat the oil in a large pan with a lid. Add the onion, carrots and celery and fry for 10 mins, stirring from time to time until they are starting to colour a little around the edges. Stir in the lentils and cook for 1 min more.

STEP 2

Pour in the hot bouillon, add the tomato purée and thyme and stir well. Add the leek, cauliflower, courgette, and garlic, bring to the boil, then cover and leave to simmer for 15 mins.

STEP 3

Add the cabbage and basil and cook for 5 mins more until the veg is just tender. Season with pepper, ladle into bowls and serve. Will keep in the fridge for a couple of days. Freezes well. Thaw, then reheat in a pan until piping hot.

Garlicky mushroom penne

Prep: 20 mins **Cook:** 15 mins

Serves 2

Ingredients

- 210g can chickpeas , no need to drain
- 1 tbsp lemon juice
- 1 large garlic clove
- 1 tsp vegetable bouillon
- 2 tsp tahini
- ¼ tsp ground coriander
- 115g wholemeal penne
- 2 tsp rapeseed oil
- 2 red onions , halved and sliced
- 200g closed cup mushrooms , roughly chopped
- ½ lemon , juiced
- generous handful chopped parsley

Method

STEP 1

To make the hummus, tip a 210g can chickpeas with the liquid into a bowl and add 1 tbsp lemon juice, 1 large garlic clove, 1 tsp vegetable bouillon, 2 tsp tahini and ¼ tsp ground coriander.

STEP 2

Blitz to a wet paste with a hand blender, still retaining some texture from the chickpeas.

STEP 3

Cook 115g wholemeal penne pasta according to the pack instructions.

STEP 4

Meanwhile, heat 2 tsp rapeseed oil in a non-stick wok or large frying pan and add 2 halved and sliced red onions and 200g roughly chopped closed cup mushrooms, stirring frequently until softened and starting to caramelise.

STEP 5

Toss together lightly, squeeze over the juice of ½ a lemon and serve, adding a dash of water to loosen the mixture a little if needed. Scatter with a generous handful of chopped parsley.

Miso aubergines

Prep: 5 mins **Cook:** 50 mins

Serves 2

Ingredients

- 2 small aubergines, halved
- vegetable oil, for roasting and frying
- 50g brown miso
- 100g giant couscous
- 1 red chilli, thinly sliced
- ½ small pack coriander, leaves chopped

Method

STEP 1

Heat oven to 180C/160C fan/ gas 4. With a sharp knife, criss-cross the flesh of the aubergines in a diagonal pattern, then place on a baking tray. Brush the flesh with 1 tbsp vegetable oil.

STEP 2

Mix the miso with 25ml water to make a thick paste. Spread the paste over the aubergines, then cover the tray with foil and roast in the centre of the oven for 30 mins.

STEP 3

Remove the foil and roast the aubergines for a further 15-20 mins, depending on their size, until tender.

STEP 4

Meanwhile, bring a saucepan of salted water to the boil and heat 1/2 tbsp vegetable oil over a medium-high heat in a frying pan. Add the couscous to the frying pan, toast for 2 mins until golden brown, then tip into the pan of boiling water and cook for 8-10 mins until tender (or following pack instructions). Drain well. Serve the aubergines with the couscous, topped with the chilli and a scattering of coriander leaves.

Balsamic beef with beetroot & rocket

Prep: 15 mins **Cook:** 25 mins

Serves 2

Ingredients

- 240g beef sirloin, fat trimmed
- 1 tbsp balsamic vinegar
- 2 tsp thyme leaves
- 2 garlic cloves, 1 finely grated, 1 sliced
- 2 tsp rapeseed oil
- 2 red onions, halved and sliced
- 175g fine beans, trimmed
- 2 cooked beetroot, halved and cut into wedges
- 6 pitted Kalamata olives, quartered
- 2 handfuls rocket

Method

STEP 1

Beat the steak with a rolling pin until it is about the thickness of two £1 coins, then cut into two equal pieces. In a bowl, mix the balsamic, thyme, grated garlic, half the oil and a grinding of black pepper. Place the steaks in the marinade and set aside.

STEP 2

Heat the remaining 1 tsp oil in a large non-stick frying pan, and fry the onions and garlic for 8-10 mins, stirring frequently, until soft and starting to brown. Meanwhile, steam the beans for 4-6 mins or until just tender.

STEP 3

Push the onion mixture to one side in the pan. Lift the steaks from the bowl, shake off any excess marinade, and sear in the pan for 2½-3 mins, turning once, until cooked but still a little pink inside. Pile the beans onto plates and place the steaks on top. Add the beetroot wedges, olives and remaining marinade to the pan and cook briefly to heat through, then spoon on top and around the steaks. Add the rocket and serve.

Chicken & pearl barley risotto

Prep: 5 mins **Cook:** 40 mins

Serves 2

Ingredients

- 1 tsp sunflower oil
- 2 chicken thighs , skinless, bone in
- 2 carrots , chopped
- 2 celery sticks , chopped
- 1 onion , chopped
- 1 garlic clove , crushed
- 140g pearl barley

For the green dressing

- ½ x 60g bag fresh rocket leaves
- small handful mint , leaves only
- small handful flat-leaf parsley
- juice 1 lemon
- 1 tsp capers

Method

STEP 1

Heat a large saucepan over a medium-high heat and add the oil. Add the chicken and fry for 5 mins or until well-browned on all sides. Tip in the vegetables and cook for a further 5 mins until starting to soften. Add the garlic and pearl barley, then pour over 500ml water. Cover and leave to simmer for 25-30 mins, stirring occasionally.

STEP 2

Meanwhile, put all the dressing ingredients in the small bowl of a food processor and blitz until very finely chopped. Transfer to a bowl and set aside until serving.

STEP 3

When the pearl barley is soft, but still with a little bite, and most of the liquid has been absorbed, it's ready to serve. Season to taste and divide the risotto between two plates, adding spoonfuls of the dressing, to serve.

Low-sugar granola

Prep: 10 mins **Cook:** 30 mins - 35 mins

Makes 500g

Ingredients

- 200g rolled oats
- 150g bag mixed nuts
- 150g mixed seeds
- 1 orange, zested
- 2 tsp mixed spice
- 2 tsp cinnamon
- 2 tbsp cold pressed rapeseed oil
- 1½ tbsp maple syrup

Method

STEP 1

Heat oven to 160C/140C fan/gas 4. Mix all the ingredients in a bowl with a pinch of salt, then spread out on a baking tray.

STEP 2

Roast for 30-35 mins until golden, pulling the tray out of the oven twice while cooking to give everything a good stir – this will help the granola toast evenly. Leave to cool. Will keep in an airtight container for one month.

Chunky butternut mulligatawny

Prep: 25 mins **Cook:** 40 mins

Serves 6

Ingredients

- 2 tbsp olive or rapeseed oil
- 2 onions, finely chopped
- 2 dessert apples, peeled and finely chopped
- 3 celery sticks, finely chopped
- ½ small butternut squash, peeled, seeds removed, chopped into small pieces
- 2-3 heaped tbsp gluten-free curry powder (depending on how spicy you like it)
- 1 tbsp ground cinnamon

- 1 tbsp nigella seeds (also called black onion or kalonji seeds)
- 2 x 400g cans chopped tomatoes
- 1 ½l gluten-free chicken or vegetable stock
- 140g basmati rice
- small pack parsley , chopped
- 3 tbsp mango chutney , plus a little to serve, if you like (optional)
- natural yogurt , to serve

Method

STEP 1

Heat the oil in your largest saucepan. Add the onions, apples and celery with a pinch of salt. Cook for 10 mins, stirring now and then, until softened. Add the butternut squash, curry powder, cinnamon, nigella seeds and a grind of black pepper. Cook for 2 mins more, then stir in the tomatoes and stock. Cover with a lid and simmer for 15 mins.

STEP 2

By now the vegetables should be tender but not mushy. Stir in the rice, pop the lid back on and simmer for another 12 mins until the rice is cooked through. Taste and add more seasoning if needed. Stir through the parsley and mango chutney, then serve in bowls with yogurt and extra mango chutney on top, if you like.

Creamy leek & bean soup

Prep:10 mins **Cook:**20 mins

Serves 4

Ingredients

- 1 tbsp rapeseed oil
- 600g leeks , well washed and thinly sliced
- 1l hot vegetable bouillon
- 2 x 400g cans cannellini beans , drained
- 2 large garlic cloves , finely grated
- 100g baby spinach
- 150ml full-fat milk

Method

STEP 1

Heat the oil in a large pan, add the leeks and cook on a low-medium heat for 5 mins. Pour in the bouillon, tip in the beans, cover and simmer for 10 mins.

STEP 2

Stir in the garlic and spinach, cover the pan and cook for 5 mins more until the spinach has wilted but still retains its fresh green colour.

STEP 3

Add the milk and plenty of pepper, and blitz with a stick blender until smooth. Ladle into bowls and chill the remainder.

Healthy stuffing balls

Prep: 20 mins **Cook:** 45 mins

Serves 8, makes about 12

Ingredients

- 1 tbsp olive oil
- 1 large onion , finely chopped
- 2 sticks celery , stringed and finely chopped
- 2 garlic cloves , finely chopped
- 15g dried apricots , roughly chopped
- 75g peeled chestnuts
- 75g almonds
- 100g wholemeal bread , crusts removed and roughly torn (about 6 slices)
- large bunch parsley , chopped
- large pinch dried sage
- 1 egg

Method

STEP 1

Heat oven to 200C/180C fan/gas 6. Gently heat the oil in a shallow saucepan then add the onion, celery and garlic. Keep everything sizzling on a medium heat for 15 mins until soft. Tip into a food processor with the rest of the ingredients, except the egg, plus a small pinch of salt, if you like. Pulse until everything is chopped, then add the egg and pulse until combined. Use wet hands to roll the mixture into walnut-sized balls, then place on a baking sheet lined with baking parchment.

STEP 2

Bake in the oven for 25-30 mins until golden and hot through. Will freeze for up to three months; defrost fully before reheating.

Raspberry tea ice lollies

Prep: 10 mins plus 4 hrs freezing

Serves 6

Ingredients

- 100g raspberries
- 3 raspberry teabag
- 1 tbsp maple syrup
- juice of 1 lime

Method

STEP 1

Put the raspberries, raspberry tea bags and maple syrup in a bowl, then pour over 350ml boiling water. Leave to infuse for 10 mins, then remove the tea bags, stir in the lime juice and leave to cool. Pour into six ice lolly moulds and freeze for at least 4 hrs, or overnight.

Moroccan harira

Prep: 15 mins **Cook:** 40 mins

Serves 4

Ingredients

- 1-2 tbsp rapeseed oil
- 2 large onions , finely chopped
- 4 garlic cloves , chopped
- 2 tsp turmeric
- 2 tsp cumin
- ½ tsp cinnamon
- 2 red chillies , deseeded and sliced
- 500g carton passata
- 1.7l reduced-salt vegetable bouillon
- 175dried green lentils
- 2 carrots , chopped into small pieces
- 1 sweet potato , peeled and diced
- 5 celery sticks , chopped into small pieces
- ⅔ small pack coriander , few sprigs reserved, the rest chopped
- 1 lemon , cut into 4 wedges, to serve

Method

STEP 1

Heat the oil in a large non-stick sauté pan over a medium heat and fry the onions and garlic until starting to soften. Tip in the spices and chilli, stir briefly, then pour in the passata and stock. Add the lentils, carrots, sweet potato and celery, and bring to the boil.

STEP 2

Cover the pan and leave to simmer for 30 mins, then cook uncovered for a further 5-10 mins until the vegetables and lentils are tender. Stir in the chopped coriander and serve in bowls with lemon wedges for squeezing over, and the reserved coriander sprinkled over.

Healthy gravy

Prep: 5 mins **Cook:** 25 mins

Serves 8

Ingredients

- 1 tsp sunflower oil
- 1 large onion, chopped
- 3 large carrots, chopped
- 1 tbsp ketchup
- handful dried porcini mushrooms
- 3 tbsp balsamic vinegar
- 1l low-salt vegetable stock, or chicken stock if not making it vegetarian
- 1 tbsp cornflour

Method

STEP 1

Heat the oil in a saucepan then add the vegetables and cook them over a medium-high heat for 10-15 mins to brown – if they burn at the edges, then all the better. Stir in the ketchup and dried mushrooms and cook together until everything becomes sticky, then splash in the vinegar. Stir in the stock and season with a pinch of salt, if you like. Bring to the boil, then simmer gently for 20 mins.

STEP 2

Using a hand blender, blitz to create a thin soup-like consistency, then pass through a sieve into another saucepan and bring to the simmer. Slake the cornflour with a splash of water, then pour into the liquid and continue to cook until thickened. Serve straightaway, chill, or freeze for reheating at a later date. Can be frozen for up to three months in an airtight container.

Ham & piccalilli salad

Prep: 15 mins No cook

Serves 4

Ingredients

- 4 tbsp piccalilli
- 3 tbsp natural yogurt
- 12 silverskin pickled onions, halved
- 130g pea shoots
- 180g pulled ham hock or shredded cooked ham
- ½ cucumber, halved and thickly sliced
- 100g fresh peas
- 40g mature cheddar, shaved
- crusty bread, to serve

Method

STEP 1

Mix the piccalilli, yogurt, onions and 4 tbsp water together to make a dressing. Season and set aside.

STEP 2

Toss the pea shoots, ham, cucumber and peas together. Pile onto a serving plate, then drizzle over the dressing. Top with the cheese and serve with crusty bread.

Lamb dopiaza with broccoli rice

Prep: 20 mins **Cook:** 1 hr and 30 mins

Serves 2

Ingredients

- 225g lamb leg steaks, trimmed of excess fat and cut into 2.5cm/ 1in chunks
- 50g full-fat natural bio yogurt, plus 4 tbsp to serve
- 1 tbsp medium curry powder
- 2 tsp cold-pressed rapeseed oil
- 2 medium onions, 1 thinly sliced, 1 cut into 5 wedges
- 2 garlic cloves, peeled and finely sliced

- 1 tbsp ginger , peeled and finely chopped
- 1 small red chilli , finely chopped (deseeded if you don't like it too hot)
- 200g tomatoes , roughly chopped
- 50g dried split red lentils , rinsed
- 1/2 small pack of coriander , roughly chopped, plus extra to garnish
- 100g pack baby leaf spinach

For the broccoli rice

- 100g wholegrain brown rice
- 100g small broccoli florets

Method

STEP 1

Put the lamb in a large bowl and season well with ground black pepper. Add the yogurt and 1/2 tbsp of the curry powder, and stir well to combine.

STEP 2

Heat half the oil in a large non-stick saucepan. Fry the onion wedges over a high heat for 4-5 mins or until lightly browned and just tender. Tip onto a plate, set aside and return the pan to the heat.

STEP 3

Add the remaining oil, the sliced onions, garlic, ginger and chilli, cover and cook for 10 mins or until very soft, stirring occasionally. Remove the lid, increase the heat and cook for 2-3 mins more or until the onions are tinged with brown – this will add lots of flavour, but make sure they don't get burnt.

STEP 4

Reduce the heat once more and stir in the tomatoes and remaining curry powder. Cook for 1 min, then stir the lamb and yogurt into the pan and cook over a medium-high heat for 4-5 mins, stirring regularly.

STEP 5

Pour 300ml cold water into the pan, stir in the lentils and coriander, cover with a lid and leave to cook over a low heat for 45 mins – the sauce should be simmering gently and you can add a splash of water if the curry gets a little dry. Remove the lid every 10-15 mins and stir the curry.

STEP 6

With half an hour of the curry cooking time remaining, cook the rice in plenty of boiling water for 25 mins or until just tender. Add the broccoli florets and cook for a further 3 mins. Drain well.

STEP 7

Remove the lid from the curry, add the reserved onion wedges and continue to simmer over a high heat for a further 15 mins or until the lamb is tender, stirring regularly. Just before serving, stir in the spinach, a handful at a time, and let it wilt. Serve with the yogurt, coriander and broccoli rice.

White velvet soup with smoky almonds

Prep: 10 mins **Cook:** 25 mins

Serves 2

Ingredients

- 2 tsp rapeseed oil
- 2 large garlic cloves, sliced
- 2 leeks, trimmed so they're mostly white in colour, washed well, then sliced (about 240g)
- 200g cauliflower, chopped
- 2 tsp vegetable bouillon powder
- 400g cannellini beans, rinsed
- fresh nutmeg, for grating
- 100ml whole milk
- 25g whole almonds, chopped
- ½ tsp smoked paprika
- 2 x 25g slices rye bread, to serve

Method

STEP 1

Heat the oil in a large pan. Add the garlic, leeks and cauliflower and cook for about 5 mins, stirring frequently, until starting to soften (but not colouring).

STEP 2

Stir in the vegetable bouillon and beans, pour in 600ml boiling water and add a few generous gratings of the nutmeg. Cover and leave to simmer for 15 mins until the leeks and cauliflower are tender. Add the milk and blitz with a hand blender until smooth and creamy.

STEP 3

Put the almonds in a dry pan and cook very gently for 1 min, or until toasted, then remove from the heat. Scatter the paprika over the almonds and mix well. Ladle the soup into bowls, top with the spicy nuts and serve with the rye bread.

Vegan bolognese

Prep: 20 mins **Cook:** 1 hr

Serves 3

Ingredients

- 15g dried porcini mushrooms
- 1 ½ tbsp olive oil
- ½ onion, finely chopped
- 1 carrot, finely chopped
- 1 celery stick, finely chopped
- 2 garlic cloves, sliced
- 2 thyme sprigs
- ½ tsp tomato purée
- 50ml vegan red wine (optional)
- 125g dried green lentils
- 400g can whole plum tomatoes
- 125g chestnut mushrooms, chopped
- 125g portobello mushrooms, sliced
- ½ tsp soy sauce
- ½ tsp Marmite
- 270g spaghetti
- handful fresh basil leaves

Method

STEP 1

Pour 400ml boiling water over the dried porcini and leave for 10 mins until hydrated. Meanwhile pour 1 tbsp oil into a large saucepan. Add the onion, carrot, celery and a pinch of salt. Cook gently, stirring for 10 mins until soft. Remove the porcini from the liquid, keeping the mushroomy stock and roughly chop. Set both aside.

STEP 2

Add the garlic and thyme to the pan. Cook for 1 min then stir in the tomato purée and cook for a min more. Pour in the red wine, if using, cook until nearly reduced, then add the lentils, reserved mushroom stock and tomatoes. Bring to the boil, then reduce the heat and leave to simmer with a lid on.

STEP 3

Meanwhile, heat a large frying pan. Add the remaining oil, then tip in the chestnut, portobello and rehydrated mushrooms. Fry until all the water has evaporated and the mushrooms are deep golden brown. Pour in the soy sauce. Give everything a good mix, then scrape the mushrooms into the lentil mixture.

STEP 4

Stir in the Marmite and continue to cook the ragu, stirring occasionally, over a low-medium heat for 30-45 mins until the lentils are cooked and the sauce is thick and reduced, adding extra water if necessary. Remove the thyme sprigs and season to taste.

STEP 5

Cook the spaghetti in a large pan of salted water for 1 min less than packet instructions. Drain the pasta, reserving a ladleful of pasta water, then toss the spaghetti in the sauce, using a little of the starchy liquid to loosen up the ragu slightly so that the pasta clings to the sauce. Serve topped with fresh basil and some black pepper.

Samosa pie

Prep: 5 mins **Cook:** 30 mins

Serves 4

Ingredients

- 2-3 tbsp vegetable oil
- 1 onion , chopped
- 500g lamb mince
- 2 garlic cloves , finely chopped
- 2 tbsp curry powder
- 1 large sweet potato (about 300g), peeled and grated
- 100g frozen peas
- handful coriander , roughly chopped
- juice 0.5 lemon
- 3-4 sheets filo pastry
- 1 tsp cumin seeds

Method

STEP 1

Heat oven to 180C/160C fan/gas 4. Heat 1 tbsp of the oil in a frying pan. Cook the onion and mince for about 5 mins until the meat is browned. Stir in the garlic, curry powder, sweet potato and 300ml water. Cook for 5-8 mins until the potato has softened. Stir in the peas, coriander and a squeeze of lemon juice, then season.

STEP 2

Spoon the mixture into a baking dish. Brush the sheets of filo with the remaining oil and scrunch over the top of the mince. Sprinkle with cumin seeds and bake for 10-15 mins or until the top is crisp.

Red pepper & bean tikka masala

Prep:10 mins **Cook:**20 mins

Serves 2

Ingredients

- 1 tbsp vegetable oil
- 1 onion , chopped
- 2 red peppers , deseeded and cut into strips
- 1 garlic clove , crushed
- thumb-sized piece of ginger , grated
- 1 red chilli , finely chopped
- ½ tbsp garam masala
- ½ tbsp curry powder
- 1 tbsp tomato purée
- 415g can baked beans
- ½ lemon , juiced
- rice and coriander, to serve

Method

STEP 1

Heat the oil in a saucepan over a medium heat, add the onion and red peppers with a pinch of salt and fry until softened, around 5 mins. Tip in the garlic, ginger and red chilli along with the spices and fry for a couple of mins longer.

STEP 2

Spoon in the tomato purée, stir, then tip in the baked beans along with 100ml water. Bubble for 5 mins, then squeeze in the lemon juice. Serve with the rice and scatter over the coriander leaves.

Spicy chicken & bean stew

Prep:15 mins **Cook:**1 hr and 20 mins

Serves 6

Ingredients

- 1¼ kg chicken thighs and drumsticks (approx. weight, we used a 1.23kg mixed pack)
- 1 tbsp olive oil
- 2 onions, sliced
- 1 garlic clove, crushed
- 2 red chillies, deseeded and chopped
- 250g frozen peppers, defrosted
- 400g can chopped tomatoes
- 420g can kidney beans in chilli sauce
- 2 x 400g cans butter beans, drained
- 400ml hot chicken stock
- small bunch coriander, chopped
- 150ml pot soured cream and crusty bread, to serve

Method

STEP 1

Pull the skin off the chicken and discard. Heat the oil in a large casserole dish, brown the chicken all over, then remove with a slotted spoon. Tip in the onions, garlic and chillies, then fry for 5 mins until starting to soften and turn golden.

STEP 2

Add the peppers, tomatoes, beans and hot stock. Put the chicken back on top, half-cover with a pan lid and cook for 50 mins, until the chicken is cooked through and tender.

STEP 3

Stir through the coriander and serve with soured cream and crusty bread.

Lentil & cauliflower curry

Prep: 10 mins **Cook:** 40 mins

Serves 4

Ingredients

- 1 tbsp olive oil
- 1 large onion, chopped
- 3 tbsp curry paste
- 1 tsp turmeric
- 1 tsp mustard seeds
- 200g red or yellow lentil
- 1l low-sodium vegetable or chicken stock (made with 2 cubes)
- 1 large cauliflower, broken into florets
- 1 large potato, diced
- 3 tbsp coconut yogurt
- small pack coriander, chopped

- juice 1 lemon
- 100g cooked brown rice

Method

STEP 1

Heat the oil in a large saucepan and cook the onion until soft, about 5 mins. Add the curry paste, spices and lentils, then stir to coat the lentils in the onions and paste. Pour over the stock and simmer for 20 mins, then add the cauliflower, potato and a little extra water if it looks a bit dry.

STEP 2

Simmer for about 12 mins until the cauliflower and potatoes are tender. Stir in the yogurt, coriander and lemon juice, and serve with the brown rice.

Mushroom baked eggs with squished tomatoes

Prep: 5 mins **Cook:** 30 mins

Serves 2

Ingredients

- 2 large flat mushrooms (about 85g each), stalks removed and chopped
- rapeseed oil , for brushing
- ½ garlic clove , grated (optional)
- a few thyme leaves
- 2 tomatoes , halved
- 2 large eggs
- 2 handfuls rocket

Method

STEP 1

Heat oven to 200C/180C fan/gas 6. Brush the mushrooms with a little oil and the garlic (if using). Place the mushrooms in two very lightly greased gratin dishes, bottom-side up, and season lightly with pepper. Top with the chopped stalks and thyme, cover with foil and bake for 20 mins.

STEP 2

Remove the foil, add the tomatoes to the dishes and break an egg carefully onto each of the mushrooms. Season and add a little more thyme, if you like. Return to the oven for 10-12 mins or until the eggs are set but the yolks are still runny. Top with the rocket and eat straight from the dishes.

Crispy cod fingers with wedges & dill slaw

Prep: 30 mins **Cook:** 40 mins

Serves 4

Ingredients

- 3 large sweet potatoes (700g), scrubbed and cut into wedges
- ½ tbsp sunflower oil , plus a little extra
- ¼ large red cabbage
- ½ medium red onion , finely sliced
- 6 large cornichons , quartered
- 3 tbsp Greek yogurt or mayonnaise
- 25g dill , finely chopped
- 4 skinned cod fillets (160g per fillet)
- 2 large eggs
- 100g fresh breadcrumbs

Method

STEP 1

Heat oven to 200C/180C fan/gas 6. In a bowl, toss the wedges with the oil, 1 tsp salt and 1/4 tsp pepper. Transfer to a baking sheet and roast for 25-30 mins, turning halfway through. The wedges should be crisp and golden brown.

STEP 2

Meanwhile, make the slaw. Remove the cabbage's white core and discard. Slice the leaves as finely as possible and put in a large mixing bowl with the onion and cornichons. In another bowl, combine the yogurt or mayonnaise with the dill and 2 tbsp of the cornichons' pickling liquid. Mix the dressing with the other slaw ingredients until everything is well coated, then set aside.

STEP 3

Heat grill to high. Slice each cod fillet into two or three fingers. Beat the eggs lightly in a shallow bowl and tip the breadcrumbs into a separate bowl with a good pinch of salt and pepper. Dip each cod finger in the egg and then in the breadcrumbs, and place on an oiled baking sheet. Grill for 6-7 mins or until cooked through and golden. Serve with the crispy wedges and a generous helping of the dill pickle slaw.

Sunshine smoothie

Prep: 5 mins no cook

Serves 3

Ingredients

- 500ml carrot juice, chilled
- 200g pineapple (fresh or canned)
- 2 bananas, broken into chunks
- small piece ginger, peeled
- 20g cashew nuts
- juice 1 lime

Method

STEP 1

Put the ingredients in a blender and whizz until smooth. Drink straight away or pour into a bottle to drink on the go. Will keep in the fridge for a day.

Caramelised onion & goat's cheese pizza

Prep: 20 mins **Cook:** 30 mins

Serves 2

Ingredients

For the base

- 125g wholemeal flour , plus a little for kneading if necessary
- ½ tsp instant yeast
- pinch of salt
- 1 tsp rapeseed oil , plus extra for greasing

For the topping

- 2 onions , halved and thinly sliced
- 2 tsp rapeseed oil
- 2 tsp balsamic vinegar
- 160g baby spinach leaves (not the very tiny ones), chopped
- 2 large garlic cloves , finely grated
- 50g soft goat's cheese
- 4 pitted Kalamata olives , quartered
- few soft thyme leaves
- 1 tsp sunflower seeds

Method

STEP 1

Heat oven to 220C/200C fan/gas 7. Tip the flour into a mixer with a dough hook, or a bowl. Add the yeast, salt, oil and just under 100ml warm water then mix to a soft dough. Knead in the food mixer for about 5 mins, but if making this by hand, tip onto a work surface and knead for about 10 mins. The dough is sticky, but try not to add too much extra flour. Leave in the bowl and cover with a tea towel while you make the topping. There is no need to let the dough prove for a specific time – just let it sit while you get on with the next step.

STEP 2

Tip the onions into a non-stick wok and add the oil, 4 tbsp water and balsamic vinegar. Cover with a saucepan lid that sits inside the pan to help the onions soften, then cook for 15 mins, stirring about 3 times and replacing the lid quickly so as not to lose too much moisture. After the time is up, the onions should be golden and all the liquid gone. Tip onto a plate. Add the spinach and garlic to the pan and stir-fry until the spinach has wilted.

STEP 3

Take the dough from the bowl and cut in half with an oiled knife, then press each piece into a 25-15 cm oval on a large greased baking sheet with oiled hands. Don't knead the dough first otherwise it will be too elastic and it will keep shrinking back.

STEP 4

Spread with the spinach followed by the onions, then dot with the cheese and scatter with the olives, thyme and sunflower seeds. Bake for 15 mins until golden and the base is cooked through.

Beef goulash soup

Prep: 15 mins **Cook:** 1 hr

Serves 2 - 3

Ingredients

- 1 tbsp rapeseed oil
- 1 large onion, halved and sliced
- 3 garlic cloves, sliced
- 200g extra lean stewing beef, finely diced
- 1 tsp caraway seeds
- 2 tsp smoked paprika
- 400g can chopped tomatoes
- 600ml beef stock
- 1 medium sweet potato, peeled and diced
- 1 green pepper, deseeded and diced

Supercharged topping

- 150g pot natural bio yogurt
- good handful parsley, chopped

Method

STEP 1

Heat the oil in a large pan, add the onion and garlic, and fry for 5 mins until starting to colour. Stir in the beef, increase the heat and fry, stirring, to brown it.

STEP 2

Add the caraway and paprika, stir well, then tip in the tomatoes and stock. Cover and leave to cook gently for 30 mins.

STEP 3

Stir in the sweet potato and green pepper, cover and cook for 20 mins more or until tender. Allow to cool a little, then serve topped with the yogurt and parsley (if the soup is too hot, it will kill the beneficial bacteria in the yogurt).

Prawn jalfrezi

Prep: 10 mins **Cook:** 22 mins

Serves 2

Ingredients

- 2 tsp rapeseed oil
- 2 medium onions, chopped
- thumb-sized piece ginger, finely chopped
- 2 garlic cloves, chopped
- 1 tsp ground coriander
- ½ tsp ground turmeric
- ½ tsp ground cumin
- ¼ tsp chilli flakes (or less if you don't like it too spicy)
- 400g can chopped tomato
- squeeze of clear honey
- 1 large green pepper, halved, deseeded and chopped
- small bunch coriander, stalks and leaves separated, chopped
- 140g large cooked peeled tiger prawns
- 250g pouch cooked brown rice
- minty yogurt or chutney, to serve (optional)

Method

STEP 1

Heat the oil in a non-stick pan and fry the onions, ginger and garlic for 8-10 mins, stirring frequently, until softened and starting to colour. Add the spices and chilli flakes, stir briefly, then pour in the tomatoes with half a can of water and the honey. Blitz everything in the pan with a hand blender until almost smooth (or use a food processor). Stir in the pepper and coriander stalks, cover the pan and leave to simmer for 10 mins. (The mixture will be very thick and splutter a little, so stir frequently.)

STEP 2

Stir in the prawns and scatter over the coriander leaves. Heat the rice following pack instructions. Serve both with a minty yogurt or chutney, if you like.

Vegan chocolate banana ice cream

Prep: 5 mins **Serves** 1

Ingredients

- 1 frozen banana
- 1 tsp cocoa powder

Method

STEP 1

In a blender, blitz the frozen banana with the cocoa powder until smooth. Eat straight away.

Lighter South Indian fish curry

Prep: 20 mins **Cook:** 20 mins

Serves 4

Ingredients

- 1 tbsp rapeseed oil
- ½ tsp cumin seeds
- 1 medium onion, halved lengthways and thinly sliced into wedges
- 3 garlic cloves, finely chopped
- 1 tbsp finely chopped ginger (about a 2.5cm/1in piece)
- 12 dried curry leaves
- 1 tsp black mustard seeds
- 2 small green chillies, halved lengthways, deseeded (or leave a few seeds in if you want a bit of heat)
- 1 tsp ground coriander
- ½ tsp garam masala
- ¼ tsp turmeric
- 400g can reduced-fat coconut milk
- ¼ tsp ground black pepper
- 500g skinned, firm white fish fillets, such as cod or haddock
- 100g fine green beans, trimmed and halved lengthways
- 1 ripe mango
- generous handful roughly chopped coriander, leaves only
- 200g basmati rice, cooked, to serve
- lime wedges, to serve

Method

STEP 1

Heat the oil in a large non-stick frying or sauté pan. Add the cumin seeds and fry for 1 min, then tip in the onion, garlic and ginger, and fry for 1 min more. Stir in the curry leaves and mustard seeds, and fry about 3-4 mins on a medium heat, stirring occasionally, until the onions are turning brown. Stir in the chillies, coriander, garam masala and turmeric, and fry for 30 secs.

STEP 2

Stir the coconut milk in the can, then pour half into the pan. It should start to bubble and thicken, so let it simmer until quite thick, about 3 mins, stirring occasionally. Pour in the rest of the coconut milk, add the pepper and a pinch of salt, and lower the heat.

STEP 3

Sit the fish in the coconut milk and press it down to half submerge it. Cover the pan and simmer gently for 4-5 mins (depending on the thickness of your fillets) until the fish is almost cooked. Do not stir or the fish will break up – just spoon some of the sauce over the top of the fish halfway through, then remove the pan from the heat and let the fish sit for another 3-4 mins to finish cooking slowly. When done, it should feel firm and no longer be opaque. If you want a thinner sauce, pour in a spoonful or two of water.

STEP 4

Meanwhile, steam the green beans for about 4 mins until just tender. De-stone the mango and slice the flesh into thin wedges (see tip below left), then scatter over the fish to warm through.

STEP 5

To serve, break the fish into big chunks by removing it to serving bowls with a slotted spoon, then pour the sauce over and around it. Serve with the beans, a scattering of coriander and the rice, with lime wedges on the side to squeeze over.

Mexican chicken stew

Prep: 20 mins **Cook:** 25 mins

Serves 4

Ingredients

- 1 tbsp vegetable oil
- 1 medium onion, finely chopped

- 3 garlic cloves, finely chopped
- ½ tsp dark brown sugar
- 1 tsp chipotle paste (we used Discovery)
- 400g can chopped tomatoes
- 4 skinless, boneless chicken breas
- 1 small red onion, sliced into rings
- a few coriander leaves
- corn tortillas, or rice to serve

Method

STEP 1

Heat the oil in a medium saucepan. Add the onion and cook for 5 mins or until softened and starting to turn golden, adding the garlic for the final min. Stir in the sugar, chipotle paste and tomatoes. Put the chicken into the pan, spoon over the sauce, and simmer gently for 20 mins until the chicken has cooked (add a splash of water if the sauce gets too dry).

STEP 2

Remove the chicken from the pan and shred with 2 forks, then stir back into the sauce. Scatter with a little red onion, the coriander, and serve with remaining red onion, tortillas or rice.

STEP 3

If you want to use a slow cooker, cook the onion and garlic as above, then put into your slow cooker with the sugar, chipotle, tomatoes and chicken. Cover and cook on High for 2 hours. Remove the chicken and shred then serve as above.

Healthy banana bread

Prep: 20 mins **Cook:** 1 hr and 15 mins

Cuts into 10 slices

Ingredients

- low-fat spread, for the tin, plus extra to serve
- 140g wholemeal flour
- 100g self-raising flour
- 1 tsp bicarbonate of soda
- 1 tsp baking powder
- 300g mashed banana from overripe black bananas
- 4 tbsp agave syrup
- 3 large eggs, beaten with a fork
- 150ml pot low-fat natural yogurt

- 25g chopped pecan or walnuts (optional)

Method

STEP 1

Heat oven to 160C/140C fan/gas 3. Grease and line a 2lb loaf tin with baking parchment (allow it to come 2cm above top of tin). Mix the flours, bicarb, baking powder and a pinch of salt in a large bowl.

STEP 2

Mix the bananas, syrup, eggs and yogurt. Quickly stir into dry ingredients, then gently scrape into the tin and scatter with nuts, if using. Bake for 1 hr 10 mins-1 hr 15 mins or until a skewer comes out clean.

STEP 3

Cool in tin on a wire rack. Eat warm or at room temperature, with low-fat spread.

Broccoli and kale green soup

Prep: 15 mins **Cook:** 20 mins

Serves 2

Ingredients

- 500ml stock , made by mixing 1 tbsp bouillon powder and boiling water in a jug
- 1 tbsp sunflower oil
- 2 garlic cloves , sliced
- thumb-sized piece ginger , sliced
- ½ tsp ground coriander
- 3cm/1in piece fresh turmeric root, peeled and grated, or 1/2 tsp ground turmeric
- pinch of pink Himalayan salt
- 200g courgettes , roughly sliced
- 85g broccoli
- 100g kale , chopped
- 1 lime , zested and juiced
- small pack parsley , roughly chopped, reserving a few whole leaves to serve

Method

STEP 1

Put the oil in a deep pan, add the garlic, ginger, coriander, turmeric and salt, fry on a medium heat for 2 mins, then add 3 tbsp water to give a bit more moisture to the spices.

STEP 2

Add the courgettes, making sure you mix well to coat the slices in all the spices, and continue cooking for 3 mins. Add 400ml stock and leave to simmer for 3 mins.

STEP 3

Add the broccoli, kale and lime juice with the rest of the stock. Leave to cook again for another 3-4 mins until all the vegetables are soft.

STEP 4

Take off the heat and add the chopped parsley. Pour everything into a blender and blend on high speed until smooth. It will be a beautiful green with bits of dark speckled through (which is the kale). Garnish with lime zest and parsley.

Easy creamy coleslaw

Prep: 20 mins No cook

Serves 4

Ingredients

- ½ white cabbage, shredded
- 2 carrots, grated
- 4 spring onions, chopped
- 2 tbsp sultanas
- 3 tbsp low-fat mayonnaise
- 1 tbsp wholegrain mustard

Method

STEP 1

Put the cabbage, carrots, spring onions and sultanas in a large bowl and stir to combine.

STEP 2

Mix the mayonnaise with the mustard in another small bowl and drizzle over the veg. Fold everything together to coat in the creamy sauce, then season to taste.

Spicy spaghetti with garlic mushrooms

Prep: 10 mins **Cook:** 15 mins

Serves 4

Ingredients

- 2 tbsp olive oil
- 250g pack chestnut mushroom, thickly sliced
- 1 garlic clove, thinly sliced
- small bunch parsley, leaves only
- 1 celery stick, finely chopped
- 1 onion, finely chopped
- 400g can chopped tomato
- 1/2 red chilli, deseeded and finely chopped, (or use drieds chilli flakes)
- 300g spaghetti

Method

STEP 1

Heat 1 tbsp oil in a pan, add the mushrooms, then fry over a high heat for 3 mins until golden and softened. Add the garlic, fry for 1 min more, then tip into a bowl with the parsley. Add the onion and celery to the pan with the rest of the oil, then fry for 5 mins until lightly coloured.

STEP 2

Stir in the tomatoes, chilli and a little salt, then bring to the boil. Reduce the heat and simmer, uncovered, for 10 mins until thickened. Meanwhile, boil the spaghetti, then drain. Toss with the sauce, top with the garlicky mushrooms, then serve.

Chakalaka (Soweto chilli)

Prep: 40 mins **Cook:** 30 mins

Serves 6 - 8

Ingredients

- 3 tbsp light olive oil , or vegetable oil
- 1 red or white onion , finely chopped
- 6 garlic cloves , crushed
- 1-2 green chillies , deseeded and chopped
- thumb-sized piece ginger , finely grated

- 2 tbsp milk, medium or hot curry powder
- 3 peppers (mix of red, green and yellow), finely chopped
- 5-6 large carrots, grated
- 2 tbsp tomato purée
- 5-6 large tomatoes or 400g can chopped tomatoes
- 2 tsp piri-piri spice blend
- 2 thyme sprigs, leaves only, or 2 tsp dried thyme
- spiced apple chutney, BBQ sauce, jerk sauce or piri-piri sauce to taste (optional)
- 400g can baked beans

To serve

- chopped coriander
- rice or mealie bread (South African cornbread)
- mixed green salad
- grilled meats

Method

STEP 1

Heat the oil in a casserole dish set over a medium heat. Add the onion and cook until soft and starting to caramelise.

STEP 2

Stir in the garlic, chillies and half the ginger. Cook for 1-2 mins, then add the curry powder and stir to make a curry paste. If the mixture is starting to catch, add a splash of water to stop it burning.

STEP 3

Stir in the peppers and cook for 2 mins more. Add the carrots and stir to make sure they are coated in the curry paste. Stir in the purée, tomatoes, piri-piri spice, thyme and apple chutney or sauce, if using.

STEP 4

Add the baked beans, then half-fill the can with water and add that too. Bring to the boil, reduce the heat and simmer for at least 10 mins until the vegetables are tender and the mixture has thickened.

STEP 5

Add the remaining ginger and season to taste. Sprinkle with coriander and serve hot or cold with rice or mealie bread, salad and grilled meats.

Cheat's chicken ramen

Prep: 10 mins **Cook:** 15 mins - 20 mins

Serves 4

Ingredients

- 1.2l good-quality chicken stock
- small pack coriander, stalks and leaves separated
- 1 red chilli (deseeded if you don't like it too hot), sliced
- 2 tbsp light soy sauce
- 100g grey oyster mushrooms, sliced
- 100g pack baby pak choi
- 2 skinless cooked chicken breasts, sliced
- 100g egg noodles
- 50g sliced bamboo shoots

Method

STEP 1

Set a large saucepan over a medium heat and pour in the stock. Finely chop the coriander stalks and add to the stock with most of the chilli. Bring to the boil and add 200ml water. Once boiled, reduce the heat and simmer for 5-10 mins to infuse the coriander and chilli.

STEP 2

Add the soy sauce and a grinding of black pepper, then the mushrooms, pak choi, chicken and noodles. Simmer for 2 mins until the noodles soften, before adding the bamboo shoots.

STEP 3

Serve in deep bowls topped with coriander leaves and the remaining chilli slices.

Summer carrot, tarragon & white bean soup

Prep: 10 mins **Cook:** 20 mins

Serves 4

Ingredients

- 1 tbsp rapeseed oil
- 2 large leeks , well washed, halved lengthways and finely sliced

- 700g carrots , chopped
- 1.4l hot reduced-salt vegetable bouillon (we used Marigold)
- 4 garlic cloves , finely grated
- 2 x 400g cans cannellini beans in water
- ⅔ small pack tarragon , leaves roughly chopped

Method

STEP 1

Heat the oil over a medium heat in a large pan and fry the leeks and carrots for 5 mins to soften.

STEP 2

Pour over the stock, stir in the garlic, the beans with their liquid, and three-quarters of the tarragon, then cover and simmer for 15 mins or until the veg is just tender. Stir in the remaining tarragon before serving.

Curried fishcake bites

Prep: 20 mins **Cook:** 15 mins

Makes 24 (12 of each flavour)

Ingredients

- 2 spring onions , trimmed
- 400g skinless cod loin , cubed
- ¼ pack fresh coriander
- 1 large egg
- 2 tsp Madras curry powder
- 1 tsp lemon juice
- 1 tbsp cornflour
- 1 tbsp ground almonds
- rapeseed oil , for frying

For the mango bites

- 12 chunks fresh ripe mango
- 3 thick slices of cucumber , quartered
- For the tomato bites
- 6 cherry tomatoes , halved
- 12 fresh coriander leaves

You will need

- 24 cocktail sticks

Method

STEP 1

Tip the spring onions into a food processor and pulse briefly to chop. Add all the remaining fishcake ingredients, except for the oil, and blitz to a paste. Shape into 24 mini cakes.

STEP 2

Heat a drizzle of the oil in a large non-stick frying pan. Fry half the fishcakes for 1-2 mins each side until firm and golden. Remove from the pan and repeat with the other fishcakes. Will keep in the fridge for up to two days.

STEP 3

To serve, thread the mango and cucumber onto 12 cocktail sticks, then the cherry tomato and a coriander leaf on the remaining sticks. Warm the fishcakes, if you like, at 180C/ 160C fan/gas 4 for 10 mins. Spear the mango version into the side of the fishcakes, then spear the cherry tomato version through the top of the remaining fishcakes.

Singapore chilli crab

Prep: 25 mins **Cook:** 5 mins

Serves 2

Ingredients

- 1 whole cooked crab (about 1kg)
- 2 tbsp flavourless oil
- 3 garlic cloves , very finely chopped
- thumb-sized piece ginger , very finely chopped
- 3 red chillies , 2 very finely chopped, 1 sliced
- 4 tbsp tomato ketchup
- 2 tbsp soy sauce
- handful coriander leaves, roughly chopped
- 2 spring onions , sliced
- rice or steamed bad buns, to serve

Method

STEP 1

The crab must be prepared before stir-frying (you can ask your fishmonger to do this). This involves removing the claws, the main shell, discarding the dead man's fingers, then cutting the body into four pieces, and cracking the claws and the legs so the sauce can get through to the meat.

STEP 2

Heat the oil in a large wok and sizzle the garlic, ginger and chopped chillies for 1 min or until fragrant. Add the ketchup, soy and 100ml water, and stir to combine. Throw in the crab, turn up the heat and stir-fry for 3-5 mins or until the crab is piping hot and coated in the sauce. Stir through most of the coriander, spring onions and sliced chilli.

STEP 3

Use tongs to arrange the crab on a serving dish, pour over the sauce from the pan and scatter over the remaining coriander, spring onions and sliced chilli. Serve with rice or bao buns, and a lot of napkins.

Lentil fritters

Prep: 15 mins **Cook:** 10 mins

Serves 2

Ingredients

- 300g leftover basic lentils
- handful of chopped coriander
- 1 chopped spring onion
- 50g gram flour
- 2 carrots
- 2 courgettes
- ½ tsp sesame seeds
- handful of coriander
- ½ tsp sesame oil
- juice of 1 lime
- 1 tbsp rapeseed oil

Method

STEP 1

Mix the leftover lentils with the chopped coriander, spring onion and gram flour, then set aside. Use a peeler to cut the carrots and courgettes into long ribbons, then toss the ribbons with the sesame seeds and coriander in sesame oil and the lime juice.

STEP 2

Heat the rapeseed oil in a frying pan. Spoon in four dollops of the lentil mixture and flatten into patties. Fry each side until golden and serve with the ribbon salad.

Stir-fried pork with ginger & honey

Prep: 15 mins **Cook:** 10 mins

Serves 2

Ingredients

- 2 nests medium egg noodles
- 2 tsp cornflour
- 2 tbsp soy sauce
- 1 tbsp honey
- 1 tbsp sunflower oil
- 250g/9oz pork tenderloin, cut into bite-sized pieces
- thumb-sized piece ginger, finely chopped
- 2 garlic cloves, finely chopped
- 1 green pepper, deseeded and sliced
- 100g mange tout
- 1 tsp sesame seed

Method

STEP 1

Bring a pan of salted water to the boil and cook the noodles following pack instructions. Meanwhile, mix the cornflour with 1 tbsp water, then stir in the soy sauce and honey, and set aside.

STEP 2

Heat the oil in a wok over a high heat. Add the pork and cook for 2 mins until browned all over. Add the ginger, garlic, pepper and mangetout, and cook for a further 2 mins. Reduce the heat, then add the soy and honey mixture, stirring and cooking until the sauce bubbles and thickens. Divide the drained noodles between 2 bowls. Top with the pork and vegetables, and finish with a sprinkling of sesame seeds.

Prawn tikka masala

Prep: 10 mins **Cook:** 30 mins

Serves 4

Ingredients

- 1 large onion , roughly chopped
- 1 thumb-sized piece ginger , peeled and grated
- 2 large garlic cloves
- 1 tbsp rapeseed oil
- 2-3 tbsp tikka curry paste
- 400g can chopped tomatoes
- 2 tbsp tomato purée
- ½ tbsp light brown soft sugar
- 3 cardamom pods , bashed
- 200g brown basmati rice
- 3 tbsp ground almonds
- 300g raw king prawns
- 1 tbsp double cream
- ½ bunch of coriander , roughly chopped
- naan breads , warmed, to serve (optional)

Method

STEP 1

Put the onion, ginger and garlic in a food processor and blitz to a smooth paste. Heat the oil in a large flameproof casserole dish or pan over a medium heat. Add the onion paste and fry for 8 mins or until lightly golden. Stir in the curry paste and fry for 1 min more. Add the tomatoes, tomato purée, sugar and cardamom pods. Bring to a simmer and cook, covered, for another 10 mins.

STEP 2

Cook the rice following pack instructions.

STEP 3

Scoop the cardamom out of the curry sauce and discard, then blitz with a hand blender, or in a clean food processor. Return to the pan, add the almonds and prawns, and cook for 5 mins. Season to taste and stir through the cream and coriander. Serve with the rice and naan breads, if you like.

Celery soup

Prep: 15 mins **Cook:** 40 mins

Serves 3 - 4

Ingredients

- 2 tbsp olive oil
- 300g celery, sliced, with tough strings removed
- 1 garlic clove, peeled
- 200g potatoes, peeled and cut into chunks
- 500ml vegetable stock
- 100ml milk
- crusty bread, to serve

Method

STEP 1

Heat the oil in a large saucepan over a medium heat, tip in the celery, garlic and potatoes and coat in the oil. Add a splash of water and a big pinch of salt and cook, stirring regularly for 15 mins, adding a little more water if the veg begins to stick.

STEP 2

Pour in the vegetable stock and bring to the boil, then turn the heat down and simmer for 20 mins further, until the potatoes are falling apart and the celery is soft. Use a stick blender to purée the soup, then pour in the milk and blitz again. Season to taste. Serve with crusty bread.

Beetroot & onion seed soup

Prep: 5 mins **Cook:** 5 mins

Serves 1

Ingredients

- 250g cooked beetroot
- 100g canned lentils
- 1 small apple
- 1 crushed garlic clove
- 1 tsp onion seeds (nigella), plus extra to serve
- 250ml vegetable stock

Method

STEP 1

Tip the beetroot, lentils, apple, garlic and onion seeds into a blender with the vegetable stock and some seasoning, and blitz until smooth. Heat until piping hot in the microwave or on the hob, then scatter over some extra onion seeds, if you like.

Lighter spaghetti & meatballs

Prep: 30 mins **Cook:** 35 mins

Serves 4

Ingredients

- 1 tsp rapeseed oil
- 280g spaghetti
- For the meatballs
- 200g green lentils (well drained weight from a 400g can)
- 250g lean minced pork (max 8% fat)
- ½ tsp finely chopped rosemary
- ½ tsp Dijon mustard
- 1 garlic clove , crushed

For the sauce

- 1 tbsp rapeseed oil
- 2 shallots , finely chopped
- 2 garlic cloves , finely chopped
- 500g cherry tomatoes , preferably on the vine, halved
- 2 tsp tomato purée
- pinch of chilli flakes
- 2 tbsp chopped oregano , plus a few chopped leaves to garnish

Method

STEP 1

Heat oven to 200C/180C fan/gas 6. Line a baking sheet with foil and brush with 1 tsp oil. Mash the lentils in a bowl with the back of a fork to break down a bit, but not completely. Stir in the pork, rosemary, mustard, garlic, some pepper to generously season, and mix well with the fork to distribute the lentils evenly. Divide the mixture into 4. Form each quarter into 5 small balls – to give you 20 in total – squeezing the mixture together well as you shape it. Lay the meatballs on the foil and roll them around in the oil to coat all over. Bake for 15 mins until cooked and lightly browned. Remove (leave the oven on) and set aside.

STEP 2

While the meatballs cook, heat 2 tsp of the oil for the sauce in a large non-stick frying pan. Tip in the shallots and garlic, and fry on a medium heat for 3-4 mins until softened and tinged brown. Pour in the remaining 1 tsp oil, lay the tomatoes in the pan so most of them are cut-side down (to help release the juices), raise the heat and fry them for 3-4 mins or until the tomatoes are starting to soften and release their juices. Don't stir, or they may lose their shape. Splash in 125-150ml water so it all bubbles, and gently mix in the tomato purée. Lower the heat and simmer for 2 mins to create a juicy, chunky sauce. Season with the chilli flakes, oregano, pepper and a pinch of salt, and give it a quick stir, adding a drop more water if needed – you want it thick enough to coat the meatballs.

STEP 3

Pour the sauce into a casserole dish, add the meatballs and spoon the sauce over them to coat. Cover with foil and bake for 10 mins while you cook the spaghetti.

STEP 4

Boil a large saucepan of water. Add the spaghetti, stir and bring back to the boil. Cook for 10-12 mins, or following pack instructions, until al dente. Drain well, season with pepper and serve with the meatballs, sauce and a light sprinkling of oregano.

Braised red cabbage

Prep: 10 mins **Cook:** 2 hrs and 10 mins

Serves 8

Ingredients

- 1 small red cabbage (about 900g)
- 1 sliced red onion
- 70g soft light brown sugar
- 70ml cider vinegar
- 150ml red wine
- a large knob of butter
- 1 cinnamon stick

Method

STEP 1

Quarter the red cabbage and remove the core, then finely shred. Tip into a large pan with the red onion, brown sugar, cider vinegar, red wine, butter and cinnamon stick and season well.

Bring to a simmer, then cover with a lid, lower the heat and cook for 1 1/2 hrs, stirring every so often. Remove the lid and continue cooking for 30 mins until tender. Will keep for two days, or can be frozen for two months. Reheat until piping hot.

Bean & barley soup

Prep: 5 mins **Cook:** 1 hr

Serves 4

Ingredients

- 2 tbsp vegetable oil
- 1 large onion , finely chopped
- 1 fennel bulb , quartered, cored and sliced
- 5 garlic cloves , crushed
- 400g can chickpea , drained and rinsed
- 2 x 400g cans chopped tomatoes
- 600ml vegetable stock
- 250g pearl barley
- 215g can butter beans , drained and rinsed
- 100g pack baby spinach leaves
- grated parmesan , to serve

Method

STEP 1

Heat the oil in a saucepan over a medium heat, add the onion, fennel and garlic, and cook until softened and just beginning to brown, about 10-12 mins.

STEP 2

Mash half the chickpeas and add to the pan with the tomatoes, stock and barley. Top up with a can of water and bring to the boil, then reduce the heat and simmer, covered, for 45 mins or until the barley is tender. Add another can of water if the liquid has significantly reduced.

STEP 3

Add the remaining chickpeas and the butter beans to the soup. After a few mins, stir in the spinach and cook until wilted, about 1 min. Season and serve scattered with Parmesan.

Curried cod

Prep: 10 mins **Cook:** 25 mins

Serves 4

Ingredients

- 1 tbsp oil
- 1 onion, chopped
- 2 tbsp medium curry powder
- thumb-sized piece ginger, peeled and finely grated
- 3 garlic cloves, crushed
- 2 x 400g cans chopped tomatoes
- 400g can chickpeas
- 4 cod fillets (about 125-150g each)
- zest 1 lemon, then cut into wedges
- handful coriander, roughly chopped

Method

STEP 1

Heat the oil in a large, lidded frying pan. Cook the onion over a high heat for a few mins, then stir in the curry powder, ginger and garlic. Cook for another 1-2 mins until fragrant, then stir in the tomatoes, chickpeas and some seasoning.

STEP 2

Cook for 8-10 mins until thickened slightly, then top with the cod. Cover and cook for another 5-10 mins until the fish is cooked through. Scatter over the lemon zest and coriander, then serve with the lemon wedges to squeeze over.

Spice-crusted aubergines & peppers with pilaf

Prep: 10 mins **Cook:** 30 mins

Serves 4

Ingredients

- 2 large aubergines, halved
- 2 tbsp extra virgin olive oil
- 2 red peppers, quartered
- 2 tsp ground cinnamon
- 2 tsp chilli flakes
- 2 tsp za'atar
- 4 tbsp pomegranate molasses
- 140g puy lentils

- 140g basmati rice
- seeds from 1 pomegranate
- small pack flat-leaf parsley, roughly chopped
- Greek or coconut yogurt, to serve

Method

STEP 1

Heat oven to 220C/200C fan/gas 7. Using a sharp knife, score a diamond pattern into the aubergines. Brush with 1 tbsp of the oil, season well and place on a baking tray, cut-side down. Cook in the oven for 15 mins. Add the peppers to the tray, turn the aubergines over and drizzle everything with the remaining oil. Sprinkle over the spices, 1 tbsp of the pomegranate molasses and a little salt. Roast in the oven for 15 mins more.

STEP 2

Boil the lentils in plenty of water until al dente. After they've been boiling for 5 mins, add the rice. Cook for 10 mins or until cooked through but with a bit of bite. Drain and return to the pan, covered with a lid to keep warm.

STEP 3

Stir the pomegranate seeds and parsley through the lentil rice. Divide between four plates or tip onto a large platter. Top with the roasted veg, a dollop of yogurt and the remaining pomegranate molasses drizzled over.

Creamy tomato soup

Prep: 30 mins **Cook:** 45 mins

Serves 6 adults and 6 kids

Ingredients

- 3 tbsp olive oil
- 2 onions, chopped
- 2 celery sticks, chopped
- 300g carrot, chopped
- 500g potato, diced
- 4 bay leaves
- 5 tbsp tomato purée
- 2 tbsp sugar
- 2 tbsp red or white wine vinegar
- 4 x 400g cans chopped tomatoes
- 500g passata
- 3 vegetable stock cubes
- 400ml whole milk

Method

STEP 1

Put the oil, onions, celery, carrots, potatoes and bay leaves in a big casserole dish, or two saucepans. Fry gently until the onions are softened – about 10-15 mins. Fill the kettle and boil it.

STEP 2

Stir in the tomato purée, sugar, vinegar, chopped tomatoes and passata, then crumble in the stock cubes. Add 1 litre boiling water and bring to a simmer. Cover and simmer for 15 mins until the potato is tender, then remove the bay leaves. Purée with a stick blender (or ladle into a blender in batches) until very smooth. Season to taste and add a pinch more sugar if it needs it. The soup can now be cooled and chilled for up to 2 days, or frozen for up to 3 months.

STEP 3

To serve, reheat the soup, stirring in the milk – try not to let it boil. Serve in small bowls for the children with cheesy sausage rolls then later in bowls for the adults as Hot Bloody Mary soup (see 'Goes well with' recipes, below).

Curried lentil, parsnip & apple soup

Prep: 20 mins **Cook:** 40 mins

Serves 6 - 8

Ingredients

- 2 tbsp sunflower oil
- 3 tbsp medium curry paste
- 2 medium onions , roughly chopped
- 500g parsnips (around 5 medium parsnips), peeled and cut into chunks
- 140g dried red lentils
- 2 Bramley apples (about 400g), peeled, cored and cut into chunks
- 1 ½l vegetable or chicken stock , made with 1 stock cube
- natural yogurt , to serve (optional)
- chopped coriander , to serve (optional)

Method

STEP 1

Heat the oil in a large saucepan. Fry the curry paste and onions together over a medium heat for 3 mins, stirring. Add the parsnips, lentils and apple pieces. Pour over the stock and bring to a simmer. Reduce the heat slightly and cook for 30 mins, stirring occasionally, until the parsnips are very soft and the lentils mushy.

STEP 2

Remove from the heat and blitz with a stick blender until smooth. (Or leave to cool for a few minutes, then blend in a food processor.) Adjust the seasoning to taste. Heat through gently, then ladle into deep bowls. Serve with natural yogurt and garnish with fresh coriander, if you like. (For freezing instructions see below left.)

Berry Bircher

Prep: 5 mins plus overnight chilling, no cook

Serves 2

Ingredients

- 70g porridge oats
- 2 tbsp golden linseeds
- 2 ripe bananas
- 140g frozen raspberries
- 175g natural bio yogurt

Method

STEP 1

Tip the oats and seeds into a bowl, and pour over 200ml boiling water and stir well. Add the bananas and three-quarters of the raspberries (chill the remainder), mash together, then cover and chill overnight.

STEP 2

The next day, layer the raspberry oats in two tumblers or bowls with the yogurt, top with the reserved raspberries and serve.

Spinach & chickpea curry

Prep: 5 mins **Cook:** 15 mins

Serves 4

Ingredients

- 2 tbsp mild curry paste
- 1 onion, chopped
- 400g can cherry tomatoes
- 2 x 400g cans chickpeas, drained and rinsed
- 250g bag baby leaf spinach
- squeeze lemon juice
- basmati rice, to serve

Method

STEP 1

Heat the curry paste in a large non-stick frying pan. Once it starts to split, add the onion and cook for 2 mins to soften. Tip in the tomatoes and bubble for 5 mins or until the sauce has reduced.

STEP 2

Add the chickpeas and some seasoning, then cook for 1 min more. Take off the heat, then tip in the spinach and allow the heat of the pan to wilt the leaves. Season, add the lemon juice, and serve with basmati rice.

Sweet potato & sprout hash with poached eggs

Prep: 15 mins **Cook:** 25 mins

Serves 3

Ingredients

- 2 large sweet potatoes , cut into chunks
- 2 tsp olive oil
- 2 red onions , thinly sliced
- 300g Brussels sprouts , thinly sliced
- grating of nutmeg
- 3 eggs

Method

STEP 1

Put the sweet potatoes in a bowl, cover with cling film and microwave on high for 5 mins until tender but still holding their shape. Uncover the bowl and leave to cool a little.

STEP 2

Meanwhile, heat the oil in a wide non-stick frying pan and add the onions. Cook for 5-8 mins until starting to caramelise. Add the sprouts and stir-fry over a high heat until softened. Push the sprouts and onions to one side of the pan and add the sweet potatoes, squashing them down in the pan with the back of a spatula. Leave undisturbed for 5 mins until starting to crisp on the underside. Season, add the nutmeg, mix in the sprouts and onions, and flip the potato over, trying not to break it up too much. Cook for a further 5 mins until really crispy.

STEP 3

Meanwhile, poach 3 eggs in a pan of barely simmering water. Serve the hash topped with poached eggs.

Spiced mushroom & lentil hotpot

Prep: 10 mins **Cook:** 35 mins

Serves 4

Ingredients

- 2 tbsp olive oil
- 1 medium onion, sliced
- 300g mini Portobello mushrooms or chestnut mushrooms, sliced
- 2 garlic cloves, crushed
- 1 ½ tsp ground cumin
- 1 tsp smoked paprika
- 2 x 400g cans green lentils, drained and rinsed (drained weight 240g)
- 1 tbsp soy sauce
- 1 tbsp balsamic vinegar
- 1 medium sweet potato, peeled and very thinly sliced
- 1 large potato, very thinly sliced
- 1 thyme sprig, leaves picked

Method

STEP 1

Heat oven to 200C/180C fan/gas 6. Heat half the oil in a medium saucepan. Fry the onion for 3 mins, then add the mushrooms. Cook for another 3 mins, then increase the heat and add the garlic, ground cumin and paprika, and cook for 1 min. Remove from the heat and add the lentils, soy sauce, balsamic vinegar and 100ml water. Season, then tip the mixture into a casserole dish.

STEP 2

Rinse the saucepan and return to the hob. Add a kettle full of boiled water and bring back to the boil over a high heat. Add the potato slices, cook for 3 mins, then drain. Arrange on top of the lentils, then brush with the remaining oil. Roast in the oven for 25 mins until the potatoes are golden, then scatter over the thyme before serving.

Mexican bean soup with crispy feta tortillas

Prep: 10 mins **Cook:** 15 mins

Serves 4

Ingredients

- 1 tbsp vegetable oil
- 1 onion , chopped
- 1 heaped tbsp chipotle paste
- 500g carton passata
- 500ml vegetable stock
- 400g can kidney beans , drained and rinsed
- 400g can black beans , drained and rinsed
- 200g feta
- 2 garlic cloves , crushed
- 4 large or 8 small flour tortillas
- small pack coriander , roughly chopped, to serve

Method

STEP 1

Heat the oil in a large pan and cook the onion over a medium heat for 10 mins to soften. Stir in the chipotle paste, passata, stock and all the beans. Season, bring to the boil, then gently simmer for 5 mins.

STEP 2

Meanwhile, in a bowl crumble the feta and mix with the garlic. Divide between the tortillas, spreading over one half of each, then sprinkle over a little pepper. Fold the uncovered side over and press down. Heat a dry frying pan and cook the tortillas on both sides for a couple of mins until the feta has melted and the tortillas are crisp.

STEP 3

Divide the soup between bowls, scatter with coriander and serve with the tortillas.

Rosemary chicken with oven-roasted ratatouille

Prep: 15 mins **Cook:** 40 mins

Serves 4

Ingredients

- 1 aubergine , cut into chunky pieces
- 2 courgettes , sliced into half-moons
- 3 mixed peppers , deseeded and roughly chopped
- 2 tsp finely chopped rosemary , plus 4 small sprigs
- 2 large garlic cloves , crushed
- 3 tbsp olive oil
- 4 skinless, boneless chicken breasts
- 250g cherry or baby plum tomato , halved

Method

STEP 1

Heat oven to 200C/180C fan/gas 6. In a large roasting tin, toss together the aubergine, courgettes and peppers with half the chopped rosemary, half the garlic, 2 tbsp oil and some seasoning. Spread out the vegetables in an even layer, then roast in the oven for 20 mins.

STEP 2

Meanwhile, mix remaining rosemary, garlic and oil together. Slash each of the chicken breasts 4-5 times with a sharp knife, brush over the flavoured oil, season and chill for 15 mins.

STEP 3

After veg have cooked for 20 mins, stir in the tomatoes. Make spaces in the roasting tin and nestle the chicken breasts amongst the vegetables. Place a rosemary sprig on top of each chicken breast. Return the tin to the oven for 18-20 mins, until the chicken is cooked through and the vegetables are lightly caramelised. Serve with some new potatoes, if you like.

Moroccan chicken with sweet potato mash

Prep: 10 mins **Cook:** 25 mins

Serves 4

Ingredients

- 1kg sweet potatoes , cubed
- 2 tsp ras-el-hanout , or a mix of ground cinnamon and cumin
- 4 skinless, boneless chicken breasts
- 2 tbsp olive oil
- 1 onion , thinly sliced
- 1 fat garlic clove , crushed
- 200ml chicken stock
- 2 tsp clear honey
- juice ½ lemon
- handful green olives , pitted or whole
- 20g pack coriander , leaves chopped

Method

STEP 1

Boil the potatoes in salted water for 15 mins or until tender. Mix the ras el hanout with seasoning, then sprinkle all over the chicken. Heat 1 tbsp oil in large frying pan, then brown the chicken for 3 mins on each side until golden.

STEP 2

Lift the chicken out of the pan. Add the onion and garlic and cook for 5 mins until softened. Add the stock, honey, lemon juice and olives, return the chicken to the pan, then simmer for 10 mins until the sauce is syrupy and the chicken cooked.

STEP 3

Mash the potatoes with 1 tbsp oil and season. Thickly slice each chicken breast and stir the coriander through the sauce. Serve the chicken and sauce over mash.

Butternut & cinnamon oats

Prep: 10 mins **Cook:** 10 mins plus overnight soaking

Serves 4

Ingredients

- 120g porridge oats
- 80g raisins
- 2 tsp ground cinnamon , plus a sprinkling to serve
- large chunk butternut squash , peeled and coarsely grated (approx 320g grated weight)
- 2 x 150ml pots bio yogurt
- 25g walnuts roughly broken
- milk , to serve (optional)

Method

STEP 1

Tip the oats, raisins and cinnamon into a large bowl and pour over 1 litre cold water. Cover the bowl and leave to soak overnight.

STEP 2

The next morning, tip the contents into a large saucepan and stir in the grated squash. Cook for about 8-10 mins over a medium heat, stirring frequently, until the oats are cooked and the squash is soft. Add a little more water if it's too thick.

STEP 3

Put half of the mixture in the fridge for the next day. Spoon the remainder into bowls, top each portion with 1 pot yogurt and half the nuts. Dust with cinnamon, then serve with a splash of milk.

Pizza sauce

Prep: 5 mins **Cook:** 50 mins

makes 4-6 pizzas

Ingredients

- 2 tbsp olive oil
- 1 small onion, finely chopped
- 1 fat garlic clove, crushed
- 2 x 400g cans chopped tomatoes
- 3 tbsp tomato purée
- 1 bay leaf
- 2 tbsp dried oregano
- 2 tsp brown sugar
- 1 small bunch basil, finely chopped

Method

STEP 1

Heat the oil in a saucepan over a low heat, then add the onion along with a generous pinch of salt. Fry gently for 12-15 mins or until the onion has softened and is turning translucent. Add the garlic and fry for a further min. Tip in the tomatoes and purée along with the bay, oregano and sugar. Bring to the boil and lower the heat. Simmer, uncovered, for 30-35 mins or until thickened and reduced. Season. For a really smooth sauce, blitz with a stick blender, otherwise leave as is.

STEP 2

Stir the basil into the sauce. The sauce will cover 4-6 large pizza bases. Keeps well in the fridge for 1 week or stored in a container in the freezer.

Ultimate veggie burger with pickled carrot slaw

Prep: 15 mins **Cook:** 20 mins plus chilling

Serves 4

Ingredients

- 2 tsp vegetable oil , plus extra for frying
- 1 small onion , diced
- 2 garlic cloves , chopped
- 2 large Portobello mushrooms , finely chopped
- 2 small sweet potatoes , peeled and diced
- 150g cooked quinoa
- 1 large beetroot , grated
- 1 egg , beaten
- 2 tbsp chopped coriander
- zest 2 limes
- 4 tbsp plain flour , plus extra for dusting

For the carrot slaw

- 1 large carrot , thinly shredded
- 2 tbsp rice wine vinegar
- 1 tsp golden caster sugar

To serve

- 2 tbsp mayonnaise
- 1 tbsp chilli sauce
- 4 burger buns , lightly toasted
- 2 handfuls rocket or spinach leaves

Method

STEP 1

In a medium frying pan, heat 2 tsp vegetable oil. Add the onion, garlic and mushrooms, season and fry until everything is soft, about 5 mins. Put the sweet potatoes in a microwaveable bowl, cover with cling film and microwave on high for 5-6 mins until soft. Mash the sweet potatoes, then add to the pan with the onion mix. Tip into a large mixing bowl and leave to cool.

STEP 2

Add the quinoa, beetroot, egg, coriander, lime zest, flour and some seasoning. Mix with your hands, then form into four large burgers. Sprinkle with flour and chill for 30 mins to firm up.

STEP 3

Put the carrots in a small bowl with the vinegar, sugar and 1 tsp salt. Cover and leave to pickle until ready to eat. Mix the mayonnaise with the chilli sauce.

STEP 4

Heat a frying pan and pour in a thin coating of oil. Fry the burgers on a medium-low heat to allow the centre to cook slowly. When browned, after about 7 mins, gently flip over and cook for the same time on the other side. Drain the pickled carrots and toast the buns.

STEP 5

Brush the buns with the chilli mayo. Layer on the spinach or rocket, burgers and the carrot slaw.

Gnocchi with roasted red pepper sauce

Prep: 2 mins **Cook:** 25 mins

Serves 4

Ingredients

- 500g pack gnocchi
- ½ batch roasted red pepper sauce (see 'Goes well with…' below)
- 125g ball mozzarella

- 2 handfuls breadcrumbs

Method

STEP 1

Heat the oven to 180C/ 160C fan/ gas 4. Cook a 500g pack gnocchi following pack instructions, then drain and tip into a casserole dish. Pour over ½ batch roasted red pepper sauce (see 'Goes well with…' below), then tear 125g ball mozzarella over the top and sprinkle over 2 handfuls breadcrumbs. Bake for 20 mins until golden and heated through.

Speedy Mediterranean gnocchi

Cook: 5 mins **Serves 2**

Ingredients

- 400g gnocchi
- 200g chargrilled vegetables (from the deli counter - I used chargrilled peppers, aubergines, artichokes and semi-dried tomatoes)
- 2 tbsp red pesto
- a handful of basil leaves
- parmesan or pecorino (or vegetarian alternative), to serve

Method

STEP 1

Boil a large pan of salted water. Add the gnocchi, cook for 2 mins or until it rises to the surface, then drain and tip back into the pan with a splash of reserved cooking water.

STEP 2

Add the chargrilled veg, chopped into pieces if large, red pesto and basil leaves. Serve with shavings of Parmesan or pecorino (or vegetarian alternative).

Creamy tomato, courgette & prawn pasta

Prep: 10 mins **Cook:** 25 mins

Serves 4

Ingredients

- 1 tbsp olive oil
- 2 fat garlic cloves , thinly sliced
- 2 large or 400g baby courgettes , sliced
- 400g orecchiette pasta, or any other small pasta shape
- 2 x 400g cans cherry tomatoes
- good pinch of sugar
- 200g raw prawn , peeled
- 100g half-fat crème fraîche
- small pack basil , leaves only, torn

Method

STEP 1

Heat the oil in a large pan, add the garlic and sizzle for a few mins, then add the courgettes and cook for a few mins more until starting to soften. Cook the pasta following pack instructions.

STEP 2

Add the tomatoes, sugar and seasoning to the pan, stir and simmer, uncovered, for about 10 mins while the pasta cooks.

STEP 3

Add the prawns to the sauce and bubble until they just turn pink. Drain the pasta and add to the sauce with the crème fraîche. Simmer for another 1-2 mins, then add the basil and serve.

Spelt & wild mushroom risotto

Prep: 15 mins **Cook:** 35 mins Plus 20 mins soaking

Serves 4

Ingredients

- 200g pearled spelt
- 25g dried porcini mushrooms
- ½ tbsp olive oil
- 1 onion , finely diced
- 2 garlic cloves , finely chopped
- 100g chestnut button mushroom , cut into quarters
- 100ml white wine
- 1l hot vegetable stock
- 1 tbsp low-fat crème fraîche
- bunch chives , finely chopped
- handful grated pecorino or parmesan to serve (optional)

Method

STEP 1

Cover the spelt with cold water and soak the dried mushrooms in 100ml boiling water in a separate bowl for 20 mins. Heat the olive oil in a large frying pan. Tip in the onion and garlic, cook for 2 mins, then add the chestnut mushrooms and cook for a further 2 mins. Drain the spelt and add along with the wine. Simmer until almost all the liquid evaporates, stirring often.

STEP 2

Drain the porcini mushrooms, add them to the pan and the soaking liquid to the vegetable stock. Stir in the stock 1 cup at a time and simmer, stirring often, until all liquid is absorbed and the spelt is just tender, about 20 mins in total. Stir in the crème fraîche and season with salt and pepper. Spoon onto plates and sprinkle over chives and cheese (if using).

Chickpea & coriander burgers

Prep: 15 mins **Cook:** 10 mins Plus chilling

Serves 4

Ingredients

- 400g can chickpeas, drained
- zest 1 lemon, plus juice ½
- 1 tsp ground cumin
- small bunch coriander, chopped
- 1 egg
- 100g fresh breadcrumbs
- 1 medium red onion, ½ diced, ½ sliced
- 1 tbsp olive oil
- 4 small wholemeal buns
- 1 large tomato, sliced, ½ cucumber, sliced and chilli sauce, to serve

Method

STEP 1

In a food processor, whizz the chickpeas, lemon zest, lemon juice, cumin, half the coriander, the egg and some seasoning. Scrape into a bowl and mix with 80g of the breadcrumbs and the diced onions. Form 4 burgers, press remaining breadcrumbs onto both sides and chill for at least 10 mins.

STEP 2

Heat the oil in a frying pan until hot. Fry the burgers for 4 mins each side, keeping the heat on medium so they don't burn. To serve, slice each bun and fill with a slice of tomato, a burger, a few red onion slices, some cucumber slices, a dollop of chilli sauce and the remaining coriander.

Korean clam broth - Jogaetang

Prep: 10 mins **Cook:** 10 mins

Serves 4

Ingredients

- 500g medium-sized clams , rinsed (see below)
- 1 tbsp gochujang chilli paste or white miso if you don't want it to be spicy
- 2 large garlic cloves , finely chopped
- 3 spring onions , whites finely sliced, greens roughly chopped
- 2 handfuls beansprouts
- 1 green chilli , cut into matchsticks
- toasted sesame oil , to serve
- cooked rice , to serve
- kimchi or pickled cucumber, to serve

Method

STEP 1

Drain the rinsed clams well and place them in a saucepan (with a lid) that fits them in a single layer. Pour over cold water to just cover (about 750ml should do it), then stir in the chilli paste, the garlic and the spring onion whites.

STEP 2

Cover with a lid, bring to the boil, then turn down the heat and simmer gently for 2-3 mins until the clams have all opened. Turn off the heat and stir through the beansprouts and chilli. Season with salt to taste, and decant into one large or two smaller bowls. Top with the spring onion greens and a drizzle of sesame oil, and enjoy with rice and something sharp like kimchi or pickled cucumber. You'll need soup spoons and a bowl for the empty shells.

Cajun prawn pizza

Prep: 10 mins **Cook:** 20 mins

Serves 2

Ingredients

For the base

- 200g wholemeal flour , plus a little for kneading if necessary
- 1 tsp instant yeast
- pinch of salt
- 2 tsp rapeseed oil , plus extra greasing

For the topping

- 1 tbsp rapeseed oil , plus extra for greasing
- 2 large sticks celery , finely chopped
- 1 yellow pepper or green pepper, de-seeded and diced
- 225g can chopped tomatoes
- 1 tsp smoked paprika
- 165g pack raw, peeled king prawns
- 2-3 tbsp chopped coriander
- ½ - 1 tsp Cajun spice mix
- 2 handfuls rocket , optional

Method

STEP 1

Heat oven to 220C/200C fan/gas 7. Tip the flour into a mixer with a dough hook, or a bowl. Add the yeast, salt, oil and 150ml warm water then mix well to a soft dough. Knead in the food mixer for about 5 mins, but if making this by hand, tip onto a work surface and knead for about 10 mins. The dough is sticky, but try not to add too much extra flour. Leave in the bowl and cover with a tea towel while you make the topping. There is no need to prove the dough for a specific time, just let it sit while you get on with the next step.

STEP 2

For the topping: heat the oil in a non-stick pan or wok. Add the celery and pepper and fry for 8 mins, stirring frequently, until softened. Tip in the tomatoes and paprika then cook for 2 mins more. Set aside to cool a little then stir in the prawns.

STEP 3

With an oiled knife, cut the dough in half and shape each piece into a 25cm round with lightly oiled hands on oiled baking sheets. Don't knead the dough first otherwise it will be too elastic and will shrink back. Spread each with half of the tomato and prawn mix then scatter with the coriander and sprinkle with the Cajun spice. Bake for 10 mins until golden. Serve with a green salad.

Spicy turkey sweet potatoes

Prep: 5 mins **Cook:** 45 mins

Serves 4

Ingredients

- 4 sweet potatoes
- 1 tbsp olive oil
- 1 onion, finely chopped
- 1 garlic clove, crushed
- 500g pack turkey thigh mince
- 500g carton passata
- 3 tbsp barbecue sauce
- ½ tsp cayenne pepper
- 4 tbsp soured cream
- ½ pack chives, finely snipped

Method

STEP 1

Heat oven to 200C/180C fan/gas 6. Prick the potatoes, place on a baking tray and bake for 45 mins or until really soft.

STEP 2

Meanwhile, heat the oil in a frying pan, add the onion and cook gently for 8 mins until softened. Stir in the garlic, then tip in the mince and stir to break up. Cook over a high heat until any liquid has evaporated and the mince is browned, about 10 mins. Pour in the passata, then fill the carton a quarter full of water and tip that in too. Add the barbecue sauce and cayenne, then lower the heat and simmer gently for 15 mins, adding a little extra water if needed. Taste and season.

STEP 3

When the potatoes are soft, split them down the centre and spoon the mince over the top. Add a dollop of soured cream and a sprinkling of chives.

Creamy mashed potatoes

Prep: 10 mins **Cook:** 15 mins

Serves 6

Ingredients

- 1½ kg floury potato, such as King Edward or Maris Piper, cut into even chunks
- 125ml semi-skimmed milk
- 1 tbsp butter
- 4 tbsp crème fraîche

Method

STEP 1

Bring a large saucepan of water to the boil. Add the potatoes and boil for about 15 mins or until tender. Transfer to a colander and drain well, then return to the pan and set over a very low heat for 2 mins to dry completely.

STEP 2

Heat the milk and butter in a small pan, then pour over the potatoes. Remove from the heat, then mash potatoes using an electric hand whisk or potato masher. Tip in the créme fraîche and beat with a wooden spoon until smooth and creamy. Season with pepper and a pinch of salt.

Tomato & thyme cod

Prep: 5 mins **Cook:** 15 mins

Serves 4

Ingredients

- 1 tbsp olive oil
- 1 onion, chopped
- 400g can chopped tomatoes
- 1 heaped tsp light soft brown sugar
- few sprigs thyme, leaves stripped
- 1 tbsp soy sauce
- 4 cod fillets, or another white flaky fish, such as pollock

Method

STEP 1

Heat 1 tbsp olive oil in a frying pan, add 1 chopped onion, then fry for 5-8 mins until lightly browned.

STEP 2

Stir in a 400g can chopped tomatoes, 1 heaped tsp light soft brown sugar, the leaves from a few sprigs of thyme and 1 tbsp soy sauce, then bring to the boil.

STEP 3

Simmer 5 mins, then slip 4 cod fillets into the sauce.

STEP 4

Cover and gently cook for 8-10 mins until the cod flakes easily. Serve with baked or steamed potatoes.

Peppered pinto beans

Prep: 5 mins **Cook:** 15 mins

Serves 10

Ingredients

- 1 tbsp plain flour
- 30g butter
- 300ml beef stock
- 50ml cider vinegar
- 1 tbsp Worcestershire sauce
- 2 tbsp honey
- 2 tsp dark muscovado sugar
- 2 bay leaves
- 1 tsp black peppercorns, crushed
- 3 x 400g cans pinto beans

Method

STEP 1

Heat the flour and butter in a large frying pan, mixing to make a roux. Keep cooking until it's biscuity brown, stirring continuously. Add the stock, vinegar, Worcestershire sauce, honey, sugar, bay and pepper, then season with salt. Bring to the boil, bubble for 2-3 mins, then add the beans and cook for 10 mins more. Can be made 1-2 days ahead; store in the fridge and reheat before serving.

Baked fish with tomatoes, basil & crispy crumbs

Prep: 5 mins **Cook:** 25 mins

Serves 4

Ingredients

- 2 x 400g cans cherry tomatoes
- 1 tbsp balsamic vinegar
- 3 tbsp basil pesto
- 2 tbsp breadcrumbs
- 4 skinless firm white fish fillets (about 140g each)
- 320g pack green bean
- 320g pack thin-stemmed broccoli

Method

STEP 1

Heat oven to 200C/180C fan/gas 6. Tip the tomatoes into a roasting tin, and stir in the vinegar and 1 tbsp of the pesto. Season, mix, then bake in the oven for 10 mins.

STEP 2

Mix together the remaining pesto and the breadcrumbs, then press onto each fish fillet. Add to the roasting tin and return to the oven for 12-15 mins until the fish flakes easily and the topping is slightly crisp.

STEP 3

Meanwhile, boil the green beans and broccoli, then drain. Serve the bake scattered with the vegetables.

Thai-style steamed fish

Prep: 10 mins - 15 mins **Cook:** 15 mins

Serves 2

Ingredients

- 2 trout fillets, each weighing about 140g/5oz
- a small knob of fresh root ginger, peeled and chopped
- 1 small garlic clove, chopped

- 1 small red chilli (not bird's eye), seeded and finely chopped
- grated zest and juice of 1 lime
- 3 baby pak choi, each quartered **lengthways**
- 2 tbsp soy sauce

Method

STEP 1

Nestle the fish fillets side by side on a large square of foil and scatter the ginger, garlic, chilli and lime zest over them. Drizzle the lime juice on top and then scatter the pieces of pak choi around and on top of the fish. Pour the soy sauce over the pak choi and loosely seal the foil to make a package, making sure you leave space at the top for the steam to circulate as the fish cooks.

STEP 2

Steam for 15 minutes. (If you haven't got a steamer, put the parcel on a heatproof plate over a pan of gently simmering water, cover with a lid and steam.)

Meatball & tomato soup

Prep: 5 mins **Cook:** 15 mins

Serves 4

Ingredients

- 1½ tbsp rapeseed oil
- 1 onion, finely chopped
- 2 red peppers, deseeded and sliced
- 1 garlic clove, crushed
- ½ tsp chilli flakes
- 2 x 400g cans chopped tomatoes
- 100g giant couscous
- 500ml hot vegetable stock
- 12 pork meatballs
- 150g baby spinach
- ½ small bunch of basil
- grated parmesan, to serve (optional)

Method

STEP 1

Heat the oil in a saucepan. Fry the onion and peppers for 7 mins, then stir through the garlic and chilli flakes and cook for 1 min. Add the tomatoes, giant couscous and veg stock and bring to a simmer.

STEP 2

Season to taste, then add the meatballs and spinach. Simmer for 5-7 mins or until cooked through. Ladle into bowls and top with the basil and some parmesan, if you like.

Better-than-baked beans with spicy wedges

Prep: 10 mins **Cook:** 35 mins

Serves 2

Ingredients

- 1 tsp oil
- 1 onion , halved and thinly sliced
- 2 rashers streaky bacon , cut into large-ish pieces
- 1 tsp sugar , brown if you have it

For the wedges

- 1 tbsp white flour (plain or self-raising)
- 0.5 tsp cayenne pepper , paprika or mild chilli powder
- 1 tsp dried mixed herb (optional)

- 400g can chopped tomato
- 200ml stock from a cube
- 410g can cannellini bean , butter or haricot beans in water

- 2 baking potatoes , each cut into 8 wedges
- 2 tsp oil

Method

STEP 1

Heat oven to 200C/fan 180C/gas 6. For the wedges, mix the flour, cayenne and herbs (if using), add some salt and pepper, then toss with the potatoes and oil until well coated. Tip into a roasting tin, then bake for about 35 mins until crisp and cooked through.

STEP 2

Meanwhile, heat the oil in a non-stick pan, then gently fry the onion and bacon together for 5-10 mins until the onions are softened and just starting to turn golden. Stir in the sugar, tomatoes, stock and seasoning to taste, then simmer the sauce for 5 mins. Add the beans, then simmer for another 5 mins until the sauce has thickened. Serve with the wedges.

Ham & potato hash with baked beans & healthy 'fried' eggs

Prep: 10 mins **Cook:** 25 mins - 30 mins

Serves 4

Ingredients

- 600g potato, diced
- 1 Cal cooking spray, for frying
- 2 leeks, trimmed, washed and sliced
- 175g lean ham, weighed after trimming and discarding any fat, chopped
- 2 tbsp wholegrain mustard
- 5 eggs
- 2 x 415g cans reduced sugar & salt baked beans

Method

STEP 1

Bring a large pan of salted water to the boil. Add the potatoes and boil for 5 mins until just tender. Drain well and leave in the colander to steam-dry.

STEP 2

Meanwhile, spray an ovenproof pan with cooking spray. Add the leeks with a splash of water and fry until very soft and squishy. Add a few more sprays of the oil, tip in the potatoes along with the ham, and fry to crisp up a little. Heat oven to 200C/180C fan/gas 6.

STEP 3

Stir in the mustard, 1 egg and a good amount of seasoning with a fork break up some of the potatoes roughly as you do. Flatten down the mixture, spray the top with oil, and bake in the oven for 15-20 mins until the top is crisp.

STEP 4

When the hash is nearly ready, heat 200ml water in a non-stick frying pan with a lid (or use a baking sheet as a lid). When it is steaming (but before it simmers), crack in the remaining 4 eggs and cover with a lid. Cook for 2-4 mins until the eggs are done to your liking. Meanwhile, heat the beans.

STEP 5

Lift an egg onto each plate, add a big scoop of hash and spoon on some beans.

Indian butternut squash curry

Prep: 10 mins **Cook:** 40 mins

Serves 4

Ingredients

- 200g brown basmati rice
- 1 tbsp olive oil
- 1 butternut squash, diced
- 1 red onion, diced
- 2 tbsp mild curry paste
- 300ml vegetable stock
- 4 large tomatoes, roughly chopped
- 400g can chickpeas, rinsed and drained
- 3 tbsp fat-free Greek yogurt
- small handful coriander, chopped

Method

STEP 1

Cook the rice in boiling salted water, as per pack instructions. Meanwhile, heat the oil in a large frying pan and cook the butternut squash for 2-3 mins until lightly browned. Add the onion and the curry paste and fry for 3-4 mins more.

STEP 2

Pour over the stock, then cover and simmer for 15-20 mins, or until the squash is tender. Add the tomatoes and chickpeas, then gently cook for 3-4 mins, until the tomatoes slightly soften.

STEP 3

Take off the heat and stir through the yogurt and coriander. Serve with the rice and some wholemeal chapattis if you like.

Curried chicken pie

Prep: 20 mins **Cook:** 25 mins

Serves 4

Ingredients

- 2 tbsp cold pressed rapeseed oil
- 500g chicken breasts , cut into chunks
- 4 spring onions , sliced
- 3 garlic cloves , grated
- thumb-sized piece ginger , grated
- 1 tbsp curry powder
- 1 large head broccoli , cut into florets, top of stalk thinly sliced
- 1 tsp soy sauce
- 250ml low-fat coconut milk , plus a splash
- 250ml chicken stock
- 1 heaped tsp cornflour mixed with 1 tbsp hot water
- 4 large handfuls kale
- 4 sheets filo pastry
- ½ tbsp nigella seeds

Method

STEP 1

Heat oven to 220C/200C fan/gas 7. Pour 1 tbsp oil into a flameproof casserole dish. Add the chicken, season and fry for 4-5 mins on a medium heat, turning, until lightly browned. Remove with tongs and set aside.

STEP 2

Pour another ½ tbsp oil into the casserole dish and add the spring onions. Fry gently for a couple of mins, then stir in the garlic, ginger and curry powder. Cook for 1 min, then tip the chicken back into the pan, along with the broccoli, soy sauce, coconut milk, chicken stock and cornflour mixture. Bring to the boil, then stir in the kale. Once the kale has wilted, take the dish off the heat.

STEP 3

Mix the remaining oil with the splash of coconut milk. Unravel the pastry. Brush each sheet lightly with the oil mixture, then scrunch up and sit on top of the pie mixture. Scatter over the nigella seeds, then cook in the oven for 12 mins, or until the pastry is a deep golden brown. Leave to stand for a couple of mins before serving.

Instant berry banana slush

Prep: 5 mins no cook

Serves 2

Ingredients

- 2 ripe bananas
- 200g frozen berry mix (blackberries, raspberries and currants)

Method

STEP 1

Slice the bananas into a bowl and add the frozen berry mix. Blitz with a stick blender to make a slushy ice and serve straight away in two glasses with spoons.

Apple & clementine Bircher

Prep: 10 mins plus overnight chilling, no cook

Serves 4

Ingredients

- 200g porridge oats
- ½ tsp ground cinnamon
- 500ml apple juice
- 4 apples, grated (we used Braeburn)
- 2 clementines, segmented
- 1 tbsp flaked almonds, toasted
- 2 tbsp pomegranate seeds

Method

STEP 1

The night before, mix the oats with the cinnamon in a large bowl. Stir in the apple juice and grated apple, cover with cling film and leave overnight in the fridge.

STEP 2

In the morning, stir through the clementine segments, divide between four bowls, then scatter over the almonds and pomegranate seeds.

Wild garlic & nettle soup

Prep: 15 mins **Cook:** 35 mins

Serves 4 - 6

Ingredients

- 1 tbsp rapeseed oil , plus extra for drizzling
- 25g butter
- 1 onion , finely diced
- 1 leek , finely diced
- 2 celery sticks, thinly sliced
- 1 carrot , finely diced
- 1 small potato , peeled and diced
- 1.2l good-quality vegetable stock
- 300g young nettle leaves
- 200g wild garlic leaves (keep any flowers if you have them)
- 3 tbsp milk

Method

STEP 1

Heat the oil and butter in a large saucepan. Add the onion, leek, celery, carrot, potato and a good pinch of salt, and stir until everything is well coated. Cover and sweat gently for 15-20 mins, stirring every so often to make sure that the vegetables don't catch on the bottom of the pan.

STEP 2

Pour in the stock and simmer for 10 mins. Add the nettles in several batches, stirring, then add the wild garlic leaves and simmer for 2 mins.

STEP 3

Remove from the heat and blend using a stick blender or tip into a blender. Return to the heat and stir through the milk, then taste for seasoning. Ladle into bowls and drizzle over a little extra oil, then top with a few wild garlic flowers, if you have them.

Cranberry & raspberry smoothie

Prep: 10 mins **Serves** 4 - 6

Ingredients

- 200ml cranberry juice
- 175g frozen raspberry , defrosted
- 100ml milk
- 200ml natural yogurt
- 1 tbsp caster sugar , or to taste
- mint sprigs, to serve

Method

STEP 1

Place all the ingredients into a blender and pulse until smooth. Pour into glasses and serve topped with fresh mint.

Indian-spiced shepherd's pie

Prep: 15 mins **Cook:** 50 mins

Serves 6

Ingredients

- 500g pack lean minced lamb
- 1 onion , chopped
- 2 carrots , diced
- 2 tbsp garam masala
- 200ml hot stock (lamb, beef or chicken)
- 200g frozen peas
- 800g potatoes , diced
- 1 tsp turmeric
- small bunch coriander , roughly chopped
- juice half lemon , plus wedges to serve

Method

STEP 1

In a large non-stick frying pan, cook the lamb, onion and carrots, stirring often, until the lamb is browned and veg is starting to soften, about 8 mins. Add the garam masala and some seasoning and cook for a further 2 mins until fragrant. Pour in the stock, bring to the boil, tip in the peas and cook for a further 2 mins until the peas are cooked and most of the liquid has evaporated.

STEP 2

Meanwhile, cook potatoes in a large pan of salted water until just tender, about 8 mins. Drain well, return to the pan and gently stir in turmeric and coriander – try not to break up the potatoes too much.

STEP 3

Heat oven to 200C/180C fan/gas 6. Transfer the mince to a baking dish and top with the turmeric potatoes. Squeeze over the lemon juice, then bake for 30-35 mins until potatoes are golden. Serve immediately with extra lemon wedges on the side.

Sticky lemon chicken

Prep: 15 mins **Cook:** 15 mins

Serves 4

Ingredients

- 4 chicken breast fillets with skin, about 150g/5oz each
- 1 large lemon
- 2 tsp fresh thyme leaves or a generous sprinkling of dried
- 1½ tbsp clear honey

Method

STEP 1

Preheat the grill to high and lightly oil a shallow heatproof dish. Put the chicken in the dish, skin side down, and season with salt and pepper. Grill for 5 minutes. While the chicken is grilling, cut four thin slices from the lemon.

STEP 2

Turn the chicken fillets over and put a slice of lemon on top of each one. Sprinkle over the thyme and a little more seasoning, then drizzle with the honey. Squeeze over the juice from the remaining lemon and spoon round 2 tbsp water. Return to the grill for 10 minutes more, until the chicken is golden and cooked all the way through. Serve the chicken and the sticky juices with rice or potatoes and a green veg – broccoli or leeks are good.

Chickpea soup with chunky gremolata

Prep: 15 mins **Cook:** 30 mins

Serves 4

Ingredients

- 2 tbsp cold-pressed rapeseed oil
- 3 onions , chopped (about 340g)
- 3 x 400g cans chickpeas , don't drain off the liquid
- 3 large cloves garlic , finely grated
- 1 red chilli , seeded and chopped
- 2 tsp ground coriander
- 1 tsp cumin seeds
- 4 tsp vegetable bouillon powder
- 1 aubergine , finely cubed (350g)
- 2 tbsp tahini
- 210g can chickpeas , drained
- 100g cherry tomatoes , cut into quarters
- 1 lemon , zested and half juiced
- 15g parsley , finely chopped
- 3 tbsp chopped mint leaves
- smoked paprika , for dusting

Method

STEP 1

Heat 1 tbsp oil in a large pan and fry the onions for 10 mins to soften. Tip the 3 cans of chickpeas into the pan and stir in 2 of the grated garlic cloves, the chilli, coriander and cumin along with the bouillon powder, aubergine and 1½ cans of water. Cover and simmer for 15-20 mins until the aubergine is tender, then remove from the heat, add the tahini and blitz with a hand blender until smooth.

STEP 2

Meanwhile, make the gremolata. Tip the small can of chickpeas into a bowl add the tomatoes, lemon zest and juice, parsley and mint with the remaining oil and garlic.

STEP 3

If you're following our Healthy Diet Plan, spoon half the soup into two bowls or large flasks and top with or pack up half the gremolata and a sprinkling of paprika. Cool and chill the remaining soup for another day on the plan. Reheat the soup in a pan or microwave to serve.

Bagels for brunch

Prep: 30 mins **Cook:** 30 mins Plus 1 hr rising

Makes 10 bagels

Ingredients

- 7g sachet dried yeast
- 4 tbsp sugar
- 2 tsp salt
- 450g bread flour
- poppy, fennel and/or sesame seeds to sprinkle on top (optional)

Method

STEP 1

Tip the yeast and 1 tbsp sugar into a large bowl, and pour over 100ml warm water. Leave for 10 mins until the mixture becomes frothy.

STEP 2

Pour 200ml warm water into the bowl, then stir in the salt and half the flour. Keep adding the remaining flour (you may not have to use it all) and mixing with your hands until you have a soft, but not sticky dough. Then knead for 10 mins until the dough feels smooth and elastic. Shape into a ball and put in a clean, lightly oiled bowl. Cover loosely with cling film and leave in a warm place until doubled in size, about 1hr.

STEP 3

Heat oven to 220C/fan 200C/gas 7. On a lightly floured surface, divide the dough into 10 pieces, each about 85g. Shape each piece into a flattish ball, then take a wooden spoon and use the handle to make a hole in the middle of each ball. Slip the spoon into the hole, then twirl the bagel around the spoon to make a hole about 3cm wide. Cover the bagel loosely with cling film while you shape the remaining dough.

STEP 4

Meanwhile, bring a large pan of water to the boil and tip in the remaining sugar. Slip the bagels into the boiling water - no more than four at a time. Cook for 1-2 mins, turning over in the water until the bagels have puffed slightly and a skin has formed. Remove with a slotted spoon and drain away any excess water. Sprinkle over your choice of topping and place on a baking tray lined with parchment. Bake in the oven for 25 mins until browned and crisp - the bases should sound hollow when tapped. Leave to cool on a wire rack, then serve with your favourite filling.

Instant frozen berry yogurt

Prep: 2 mins No cook

Serves 4

Ingredients

- 250g frozen mixed berry
- 250g 0%-fat Greek yogurt
- 1 tbsp honey or agave syrup

Method

STEP 1

Blend berries, yogurt and honey or agave syrup in a food processor for 20 seconds, until it comes together to a smooth ice-cream texture. Scoop into bowls and serve.

Inside-out chicken Kiev

Prep: 5 mins **Cook:** 20 mins

Serves 4

Ingredients

- 4 skinless, boneless chicken breasts
- 25g garlic butter, softened
- 25g crispy breadcrumbs

Method

STEP 1

Place the chicken on a baking tray, rub with a little of the butter, season and cook under the grill for 15 mins, turning once until cooked through.

STEP 2

Mix together the remaining garlic butter and breadcrumbs. Remove the chicken from the grill and top each breast with a smear of the breadcrumbed butter. Return to the grill and cook 3-5 mins until the breadcrumbs are golden and the butter melted. Serve any buttery juices, alongside new potatoes and peas or broad beans.

Creamy cod chowder stew

Prep: 10 mins **Cook:** 20 mins

Serves 2

Ingredients

- 200g floury potatoes, cubed
- 200g parsnips, cubed
- 140g skinless cod fillet
- 140g skinless undyed smoked haddock fillets
- 500ml semi-skimmed milk
- ¼ small pack parsley, leaves finely chopped, stalks reserved
- 6 spring onions, whites and greens separated, both finely chopped
- 2 tbsp plain flour
- zest and juice 1 lemon
- 2 tbsp chopped parsley
- crusty wholemeal bread, to serve

Method

STEP 1

Bring a saucepan of salted water to the boil, add the potato and parsnips, and boil until almost tender – about 4 mins. Drain well.

STEP 2

Meanwhile, put the fish in a pan where they will fit snugly but not on top of each other. Cover with the milk, poke in the parsley stalks and bring the milk to a gentle simmer. Cover the pan, turn off the heat and leave to sit in the milk for 5 mins. Lift the fish out and break into large chunks. Discard the parsley stalks but keep the milk.

STEP 3

Put the spring onion whites, milk and flour in a saucepan together. Bring to a simmer, whisking continuously, until the sauce has thickened and become smooth. Turn the heat down, add the drained potatoes and parsnips, the lemon zest and half the juice, and cook gently for 5 mins, stirring occasionally. Stir in the spring onion greens, fish and parsley, and taste for seasoning – it will need plenty of pepper, some salt and maybe more lemon juice from the leftover half. Divide between two shallow bowls, serve with chunks of crusty bread and enjoy.

Singapore noodles

Prep: 15 mins **Cook:** 30 mins Plus marinating

Serves 4

Ingredients

- 3 tbsp teriyaki sauce
- ½ tsp Chinese five-spice powder
- 2 tsp medium Madras curry powder
- 300g/11oz pork tenderloin, trimmed of any fat
- 140g medium egg noodle
- 1 tbsp sunflower oil
- 2 x 300g packs fresh mixed stir-fry vegetables
- 100g cooked prawn, thawed if frozen

Method

STEP 1

Mix the teriyaki sauce, five-spice and curry powders. Add half to the pork, turning to coat, and leave to marinate for 15 mins.

STEP 2

Heat oven to 200C/180C fan/ gas 6. Remove pork from the marinade and put on a small baking tray lined with foil. Roast for 15-20 mins.

STEP 3

Meanwhile, cook the noodles following pack instructions, but reduce the cooking time by 1 min. Refresh in cold water and drain very well.

STEP 4

Transfer the pork to a chopping board and rest for 5 mins. Set a large non-stick frying pan or wok over a medium-high heat. Add the oil and stir-fry the veg for 3-4 mins. Cut the pork in half lengthways, then thinly slice. Tip into the pan, with the prawns, noodles and remaining marinade. Toss together for 2-3 mins until hot.

Chipotle chicken & slaw

Prep: 25 mins **Cook:** 40 mins

Serves 4

Ingredients

- 1 tbsp rapeseed oil
- 2 tbsp chipotle paste
- 1½ tbsp honey
- 8 chicken drumsticks
- 1 lime, zested and juiced
- 1 small avocado, stoned
- 2 tbsp fat-free Greek yogurt
- 125g each red and white cabbage, both shredded
- 1 large carrot, cut into matchsticks
- 3 spring onions, sliced
- 4 corn on the cobs, steamed, to serve (optional)

Method

STEP 1

Heat the oven to 200C/180C fan/gas 6. Whisk the oil, chipotle paste and honey together in a large bowl. Add the chicken and toss to coat, then spread out on a non-stick baking tray. Roast for 30 mins, turning halfway through.

STEP 2

Put the lime zest and juice, avocado flesh, yogurt and a good pinch of salt into a blender and blitz until completely smooth. Put the sauce in a large bowl with the cabbage, carrot and spring onion and toss to combine.

STEP 3

Serve the drumsticks with the slaw and steamed corn, if you like.

Super-quick fish curry

Prep: 5 mins **Cook:** 10 mins

Serves 4

Ingredients

- 1 tbsp vegetable oil
- 1 large onion, chopped
- 1 garlic clove, chopped
- 1-2 tbsp Madras curry paste (we used Patak's)
- 400g can tomato
- 200ml vegetable stock
- sustainable white fish fillets, skinned and cut into big chunks
- rice or naan bread

Method

STEP 1

Heat the oil in a deep pan and gently fry the onion and garlic for about 5 mins until soft. Add the curry paste and stir-fry for 1-2 mins, then tip in the tomatoes and stock.

STEP 2

Bring to a simmer, then add the fish. Gently cook for 4-5 mins until the fish flakes easily. Serve immediately with rice or naan

Pitta pocket

Prep: 2 mins **Serves 1**

Ingredients

- ½ wholemeal pitta bread
- 25g cooked skinless chicken breast
- ¼ cucumber , cut into chunks
- 4 cherry tomatoes , halved

Method

STEP 1

Fill the pitta half with the chicken breast, cucumber and cherry tomatoes.

Jerk cod & creamed corn

Prep: 12 mins **Cook:** 25 mins

Serves 2

Ingredients

- 2 thick cod fillets (about 120g each)
- 1 tbsp olive oil
- 2 tsp jerk seasoning
- bunch spring onions
- 326g can sweetcorn, drained
- 2 tbsp single cream
- 20g parmesan, finely grated
- ½-1 small red chilli, deseeded and finely chopped
- ½ small bunch coriander, finely chopped
- lime wedges, to serve (optional)

Method

STEP 1

Heat the oven to 200C/180C fan/gas 6. Put the cod on a baking sheet and rub with half the oil, the jerk seasoning and some salt and pepper. Cook for 12-15 mins until cooked through and flaking.

STEP 2

Meanwhile, heat a griddle pan or non-stick frying pan over a high heat. Rub the remaining oil over the whole spring onions. Add to the pan and cook for 8-10 mins or until charred and beginning to soften. Keep warm on a plate.

STEP 3

Put the corn in a saucepan with the cream and warm through for 2 mins. Using a stick blender, roughly blitz the corn to a semi-smooth consistency. Stir though the parmesan, chilli and half the coriander, then season to taste.

STEP 4

Serve the cod with the charred spring onions, creamed corn and lime wedges for squeezing over, and scatter over the remaining coriander.

Ruby cranberry sauce

Prep: 5 mins **Cook:** 5 mins

Serves 8

Ingredients

- 100g light soft brown sugar
- 1 large orange, zested and juiced
- 250g pack cranberries (fresh or frozen)
- 1 tbsp ruby port

Method

STEP 1

Tip all the ingredients into a saucepan. Bring to a simmer and cook for 5 mins (or a little longer if the berries are frozen). Cool, then chill for up to four days or freeze for two months. Serve at room temperature.

Supergreen soup with yogurt & pine nuts

Prep: 5 mins **Cook:** 25 mins

Serves 2

Ingredients

- 2 tsp olive oil
- 1 onion , chopped
- 2 garlic cloves , crushed
- 1 potato (approx 250g), cut into small cubes
- 600ml vegetable stock
- 120g bag mixed watercress, rocket and spinach salad
- 150g pot natural yogurt
- 20g pine nuts , toasted
- chilli oil , to serve (optional)

Method

STEP 1

Heat the oil in a medium saucepan over a low-medium heat. Add the onion and a pinch of salt, then cook slowly, stirring occasionally, for 10 mins until softened but not coloured. Add the garlic and cook for 1 min more.

STEP 2

Tip in the potato followed by the veg stock. Simmer for 10-12 mins until the potato is soft enough that a cutlery knife will slide in easily. Add the bag of salad and let it wilt for 1 min, then blitz the soup in a blender until it's completely smooth.

STEP 3

Serve with a dollop of yogurt, some toasted pine nuts and a drizzle of chilli oil, if you like.

Butternut soup with crispy sage & apple croutons

Prep: 20 mins **Cook:** 30 mins

Serves 4

Ingredients

- 1 tbsp olive oil
- 1 large onion , chopped
- 1 garlic clove , chopped
- 1 butternut squash , about 1kg, peeled, deseeded and chopped
- 3 tbsp madeira or dry Sherry
- 500ml gluten-free vegetable stock , plus a little extra if necessary
- 1 tsp chopped sage , plus 20 small leaves, cleaned and dried
- sunflower oil , for frying

For the apple croutons

- 1 tbsp olive oil
- 1 large eating apple , peeled, cored and diced
- a few pinches of golden caster sugar

Method

STEP 1

Heat the oil in a large pan, add the onion and fry for 5 mins. Add the garlic and squash, and cook for 5 mins more. Pour in the Madeira and stock, stir in the chopped sage, then cover and simmer for 20 mins until the squash is tender.

STEP 2

Blitz with a hand blender or in a food processor until completely smooth. Allow to cool in the pan, then chill until ready to serve. Will keep for 2 days or freeze for 3 months. To make the crispy sage, heat some oil (a depth of about 2cm) in a small pan, then drop in the sage leaves until they are crisp – you will need to do this in batches. Drain on kitchen paper. Will keep for several hours.

STEP 3

Just before serving, reheat the soup in a pan. The texture should be quite thick and velvety, but thin it with a little stock if it is too thick.

STEP 4

For the apple croutons, heat the oil in a large pan, add the apple and fry until starting to soften. Sprinkle with the sugar and stir until lightly caramelised.

STEP 5

To serve, ladle the soup into small bowls and top with the apple, sage and a grinding of black pepper.

Healthy carrot soup

Prep: 5 mins **Cook:** 5 mins

Serves 1

Ingredients

- 3 large carrots
- 1 tbsp grated ginger
- 1 tsp turmeric
- a pinch of cayenne pepper , plus extra to serve
- 20g wholemeal bread
- 1 tbsp soured cream , plus extra to serve
- 200ml vegetable stock

Method

STEP 1

Peel and chop the carrots and put in a blender with the ginger, turmeric, cayenne pepper, wholemeal bread, soured cream and vegetable stock. Blitz until smooth. Heat until piping hot. Swirl through some extra soured cream, or a sprinkling of cayenne, if you like.

Chinese-style pork fillet with fried rice

Prep: 15 mins **Cook:** 25 mins Plus marinating

Serves 4

Ingredients

- 420g pack pork fillet, trimmed and sliced into medallions
- 1 tbsp soy sauce
- 1 tbsp Chinese five-spice
- 2 tbsp honey
- 1 tbsp cornflour
- 1 egg, beaten
- 225g cooked rice
- 200g frozen pea, defrosted
- 2 spring onions, sliced

Method

STEP 1

Mix the pork medallions with the soy sauce and five-spice; leave to marinate for 5 mins. Heat a large non-stick pan, then fry the pork for 2-3 mins on each side until cooked through. Pour in 150ml boiling water with the honey and bubble for 2 mins. Mix the cornflour with a little water, stir into the sauce and cook until it thickens and is glossy.

STEP 2

Meanwhile, make the fried rice. Pour the egg into a non-stick frying pan to make an omelette, cooking for 2 mins on each side. Remove, roll up, and cut into thin strips. Add the rice to the pan with the peas and stir-fry for 3-5 mins until piping hot, then gently stir through the omelette with the spring onions and seasoning and cook for 1 min. Serve with the pork and a dash more soy sauce.

Courgette & quinoa-stuffed peppers

Prep: 10 mins **Cook:** 20 mins

Serves 4

Ingredients

- 4 red peppers
- 1 courgette , quartered lengthways and thinly sliced
- 2 x 250g packs ready-to-eat quinoa
- 85g feta cheese , finely crumbled
- handful parsley , roughly chopped

Method

STEP 1

Heat oven to 200C/180C fan/gas 6. Cut each pepper in half through the stem, and remove the seeds. Put the peppers, cut-side up, on a baking sheet, drizzle with 1 tbsp olive oil and season well. Roast for 15 mins.

STEP 2

Meanwhile, heat 1 tsp olive oil in a small frying pan, add the courgette and cook until soft. Remove from the heat, then stir through the quinoa, feta and parsley. Season with pepper.

STEP 3

Divide the quinoa mixture between the pepper halves, then return to the oven for 5 mins to heat through. Serve with a green salad, if you like.

Carrot biryani

Prep: 10 mins **Cook:** 15 mins

Serves 4

Ingredients

- 2 tbsp olive oil
- 1 onion, sliced
- 1 green chilli, chopped (deseeded if you don't like it very hot)
- 1 garlic clove, peeled
- 1 tbsp garam marsala
- 1 tsp turmeric
- 3 carrots, grated
- 2 x 200g pouch brown basmati rice
- 150g frozen peas
- 50g roasted cashews
- coriander and yogurt, to serve

Method

STEP 1

Heat the oil in a large frying pan, tip in the onion with a big pinch of salt and fry until softened, around 5 mins, then add the chilli and crush in the garlic and cook for 1 min more. Stir in the spices with a splash of water and cook for a couple of mins before adding the carrots and stirring well to coat in all of the spices and flavours.

STEP 2

Tip in the rice, peas and cashews, then use the back of your spoon to break up any clumps of rice and combine with the rest of the ingredients, cover and cook over a high heat for 5 mins (it's nice if a bit of rice catches on the base to give a bit of texture to the dish). Scatter over the coriander with spoonfuls of yogurt, then serve straight from the pan.

Spicy fish stew

Prep: 10 mins **Cook:** 40 mins

Serves 4

Ingredients

- 1 tbsp rapeseed oil
- 2 onions , thinly sliced
- 3 spring onions , chopped
- 3 garlic cloves , chopped
- 1 red chilli , seeded and thinly sliced
- few thyme sprigs
- 2 x 400g cans chopped tomatoes
- 400ml vegetable bouillon made with 2 tsp vegetable bouillon powder
- 2 green peppers , seeded and cut into pieces
- 160g brown basmati rice
- 400g can and 210g can red kidney beans , drained
- handful fresh coriander , chopped, plus a few sprigs extra
- handful flat-leaf parsley , chopped
- 550g pack frozen wild salmon , skinned and cut into large pieces
- 1 lime , zested

Method

STEP 1

Heat the oil in a large non-stick pan and fry the onions for 8-10 mins until softened and golden. Add the spring onions, garlic, chilli and thyme. Cook, stirring, for 1 min. Pour in the tomatoes and bouillon, then stir in the peppers. Cover and leave to simmer for 15 mins.

STEP 2

Meanwhile, cook the rice according to pack instructions. Stir in the beans with the coriander and parsley, then leave to cook gently for another 10 mins until the peppers are tender. Add the salmon and lime zest and cook for 4-5 mins until cooked through.

STEP 3

Ladle half of the stew into two bowls and scatter with the coriander sprigs. Cool the remaining stew, then cover and chill to eat on another night. Gently reheat in a saucepan until bubbling.

Crushed pea & mint dip with carrot sticks

Prep: 5 mins **Serves** 1

Ingredients

- 70g defrosted frozen peas
- 1 tbsp ricotta
- juice of ½ lemon
- chopped mint
- 1 carrot, cut into sticks for dipping

Method

STEP 1

In the small bowl of a food processor, blitz the peas with the ricotta, lemon juice, mint and some black pepper. Serve with the carrot sticks.

Prawn & rice noodle stir-fry

Prep: 10 mins **Cook:** 15 mins

Serves 4

Ingredients

- 200g rice noodles
- 1 tbsp vegetable oil
- 1 leek, sliced
- 200g fine green beans
- 300g beansprouts
- 1 garlic clove, crushed
- 300g peeled raw king prawns
- 1-2 tbsp soy sauce

To serve

- 2 tsp toasted sesame seeds
- pickled ginger

Method

STEP 1

Pour boiling water over the rice noodles in a large heatproof bowl and leave for 3-5 mins to soften. Meanwhile, in a large wok or frying pan, heat the oil, add the leek and stir-fry over a high heat until starting to soften. Add the green beans and beansprouts, then cook for another

3 mins. Add the garlic and prawns, and cook until the prawns are starting to turn pink. Splash in the soy sauce and heat until everything is cooked through.

STEP 2

Tip the contents of the wok onto a large serving dish, drain the rice noodles, add to the serving dish, then toss everything together. Top with the toasted sesame seeds and pickled ginger to serve.

Slow cooker spiced apples with barley

Prep: 15 mins **Cook:** 2 hrs

Serves 4

Ingredients

- ½ cup barley
- 2 eating apples
- ½ tsp cinnamon
- a grating of fresh nutmeg
- finely grated zest 1 large orange
- 4 tbsp natural yogurt

Method

STEP 1

Heat the slow cooker if necessary. Put the barley and 750ml boiling water into the slow cooker. Peel and core the apples so you have a hole the size of a pound coin in each one. Cut each apple in half.

STEP 2

Stand the apples skin side down on the barley. Mix the cinnamon, nutmeg and orange zest, and sprinkle them over the apples.

STEP 3

Cook on Low for 2 hours. Serve with natural yogurt.

Breakfast burrito

Prep: 5 mins **Cook:** 10 mins

Serves 1

Ingredients

- 1 tsp chipotle paste
- 1 egg
- 1 tsp rapeseed oil
- 50g kale
- 7 cherry tomatoes, halved
- ½ small avocado, sliced
- 1 wholemeal tortilla wrap, warmed

Method

STEP 1

Whisk the chipotle paste with the egg and some seasoning in a jug. Heat the oil in a large frying pan, add the kale and tomatoes.

STEP 2

Cook until the kale is wilted and the tomatoes have softened, then push everything to the side of the pan. Pour the beaten egg into the cleared half of the pan and scramble. Layer everything into the centre of your wrap, topping with the avocado, then wrap up and eat immediately.

Pea & new potato curry

Prep: 15 mins **Cook:** 1 hr and 10 mins

Serves 4

Ingredients

- 1 tbsp vegetable oil
- 2 onions, sliced
- 3 red chillies, deseeded and finely sliced
- thumb-sized piece ginger, roughly chopped
- 2 tsp cumin seed
- 1 tsp Madras curry powder
- ½ tsp turmeric
- 750g new potato, halved
- juice 1 lime
- 500ml pot natural yogurt
- small bunch coriander, stalks and leaves finely chopped
- 200-300ml vegetable stock, or pea stock (to make your own, see step 1)
- 300g podded fresh pea (or use frozen)
- lime wedges, to serve
- 2 naan bread, to serve

Method

STEP 1

To make your own pea stock: put leftover pea pods in a large saucepan with half bunch each mint, thyme and parsley. Add enough water to cover, and some salt and black peppercorns. Gently bring to the boil and simmer for 35 mins, then strain. Chill for up to 5 days or freeze for up to a month.

STEP 2

Heat the oil in a large, deep frying pan. Add the onions and cook over a low heat for 10-15 mins until soft. Throw in the chillies, ginger and spices, and cook for a few mins. Stir in the potatoes and lime juice, coating in the spice mix.

STEP 3

Add the yogurt, coriander stalks and the stock. Simmer slowly for 35-40 mins until the potatoes are soft and the sauce has reduced. Stir through the peas and cook for another 5 mins. Sprinkle over the coriander leaves, and serve with lime wedges and warm naan bread.

Low-fat Spanish omelette

Prep: 10 mins **Cook:** 15 mins

Serves 1

Ingredients

- 180g sweet potato, peeled and cut into 2cm chunks
- 5ml olive oil
- 55g onion, sliced
- 140g red pepper, diced
- 1 garlic clove, grated
- 5 slices turkey bacon, sliced
- 1 rosemary sprig (optional)
- 5 eggs (1 whole egg and 4 egg whites)
- 2 handfuls green salad leaves
- 150g 0% fat Greek yogurt

Method

STEP 1

Heat oven to 180C/160C fan/gas 4. Heat the sweet potato chunks in the microwave for 3 mins, leave to rest for 2 mins, then heat again for a further 2 mins, by which time they should be cooked through and soft.

STEP 2

Meanwhile, heat the oil in a nonstick ovenproof frying pan over a medium-high heat. Add the onion, pepper, turkey, garlic and rosemary (if using), and cook for 2-3 mins. When the potatoes are ready, add them to the pan as well.

STEP 3

Beat the egg and egg whites together, then pour into the frying pan. Use a spatula to move the eggs around, scraping it up from the base, for 1-2 mins or until there is a good proportion of cooked egg in the pan and the ingredients are well mixed. Put the pan in the oven and heat until the egg is cooked through. Slide the omelette from the pan and enjoy with a side salad and a good dollop of yogurt.

Low-fat turkey bolognese

Prep: 10 mins **Cook:** 45 mins

Serves 4 - 6

Ingredients

- 400g lean turkey mince (choose breast instead of thigh mince if you can, as it has less fat)
- 2 tsp vegetable oil
- 1 large onion, chopped
- 1 large carrot, chopped
- 3 celery sticks, chopped
- 250g pack brown mushroom, finely chopped
- pinch of sugar
- 1 tbsp tomato purée
- 2 x 400g cans chopped tomato with garlic & herbs
- 400ml chicken stock, made from 1 low-sodium stock cube
- cooked wholemeal pasta and fresh basil leaves (optional), to serve

Method

STEP 1

Heat a large non-stick frying pan and dry-fry the turkey mince until browned. Tip onto a plate and set aside.

STEP 2

Add the oil and gently cook the onion, carrot and celery until softened, about 10 mins (add a splash of water if it starts to stick). Add the mushrooms and cook for a few mins, then add the sugar and tomato purée, and cook for 1 min more, stirring to stop it from sticking.

STEP 3

Add the tomatoes, turkey and stock with some seasoning. Simmer for at least 20 mins (or longer) until thickened. Serve with the pasta and fresh basil, if you have it.

Low-fat chicken biryani

Prep: 25 mins **Cook:** 1 hr and 35 mins Plus marinating

Serves 5

Ingredients

- 3 garlic cloves , finely grated
- 2 tsp finely grated ginger
- ¼ tsp ground cinnamon
- 1 tsp turmeric
- 5 tbsp natural yogurt
- 600g boneless, skinless chicken breast , cut into 4-5cm pieces
- 2 tbsp semi-skimmed milk
- good pinch saffron
- 4 medium onions
- 4 tbsp rapeseed oil
- ½ tsp hot chilli powder
- 1 cinnamon stick , broken in half
- 5 green cardamom pods , lightly bashed to split
- 3 cloves
- 1 tsp cumin seed
- 280g basmati rice
- 700ml chicken stock
- 1 tsp garam masala
- handful chopped coriander leaves

Method

STEP 1

In a mixing bowl, stir together the garlic, ginger, cinnamon, turmeric and yogurt with some pepper and ¼ tsp salt. Tip in the chicken pieces and stir to coat (see step 1, above). Cover and marinate in the fridge for about 1 hr or longer if you have time. Warm the milk to tepid, stir in the saffron and set aside.

STEP 2

Heat oven to 200C/180C fan/gas 6. Slice each onion in half lengthways, reserve half and cut the other half into thin slices. Pour 1½ tbsp of the oil onto a baking tray, scatter over the sliced onion, toss to coat, then spread out in a thin, even layer (step 2). Roast for 40-45 mins, stirring halfway, until golden.

STEP 3

When the chicken has marinated, thinly slice the reserved onion. Heat 1 tbsp oil in a large sauté or frying pan. Fry the onion for 4-5 mins until golden. Stir in the chicken, a spoonful at a time, frying until it is no longer opaque, before adding the next spoonful (this helps to prevent the yogurt from curdling). Once the last of the chicken has been added, stir-fry for a further 5 mins until everything looks juicy. Scrape any sticky bits off the bottom of the pan, stir in the chilli powder, then pour in 100ml water, cover and simmer on a low heat for 15 mins. Remove and set aside.

STEP 4

Cook the rice while the chicken simmers. Heat another 1 tbsp oil in a large sauté pan, then drop in the cinnamon stick, cardamom, cloves and cumin seeds. Fry briefly until their aroma is released. Tip in the rice (step 3) and fry for 1 min, stirring constantly. Stir in the stock and bring to the boil. Lower the heat and simmer, covered, for about 8 mins or until all the stock has been absorbed. Remove from the heat and leave with the lid on for a few mins, so the rice can fluff up. Stir the garam masala into the remaining 1½ tsp oil and set aside. When the onions are roasted, remove and reduce oven to 180C/160C fan/gas 4.

STEP 5

Spoon half the chicken and its juices into an ovenproof dish, about 25 x 18 x 6cm, then scatter over a third of the roasted onions. Remove the whole spices from the rice, then layer half of the rice over the chicken and onions. Drizzle over the spiced oil. Spoon over the rest of the chicken and a third more onions. Top with the remaining rice (step 4) and drizzle over the saffron-infused milk. Scatter over the rest of the onions, cover tightly with foil and heat through in the oven for about 25 mins. Serve scattered with the mint and coriander.

Low-fat moussaka

Prep: 15 mins **Cook:** 40 mins

Serves 4

Ingredients

- 200g frozen sliced peppers
- 3 garlic cloves , crushed
- 200g extra-lean minced beef
- 100g red lentils
- 2 tsp dried oregano , plus extra for sprinkling
- 500ml carton passata
- 1 aubergine , sliced into 1.5cm rounds
- 4 tomatoes , sliced into 1cm rounds
- 2 tsp olive oil
- 25g parmesan , finely grated
- 170g pot 0% fat Greek yogurt
- freshly grated nutmeg

Method

STEP 1

Cook the peppers gently in a large non-stick pan for about 5 mins – the water from them should stop them sticking. Add the garlic and cook for 1 min more, then add the beef, breaking up with a fork, and cook until brown. Tip in the lentils, half the oregano, the passata and a splash of water. Simmer for 15-20 mins until the lentils are tender, adding more water if you need to.

STEP 2

Meanwhile, heat the grill to Medium. Arrange the aubergine and tomato slices on a non-stick baking tray and brush with the oil. Sprinkle with the remaining oregano and some seasoning, then grill for 1-2 mins each side until lightly charred – you may need to do this in batches.

STEP 3

Mix half the Parmesan with the yogurt and some seasoning. Divide the beef mixture between 4 small ovenproof dishes and top with the sliced aubergine and tomato. Spoon over the yogurt topping and sprinkle with the extra oregano, Parmesan and nutmeg. Grill for 3-4 mins until bubbling. Serve with a salad, if you like.

Mushroom stroganoff

Prep: 10 mins **Cook:** 20 mins

Serves 2

Ingredients

- 2 tsp olive oil
- 1 onion, finely chopped
- 1 tbsp paprika
- 2 garlic cloves, crushed
- 300g mixed mushrooms, chopped
- 150ml low-sodium beef or vegetable stock
- 1 tbsp Worcestershire sauce, or vegetarian alternative
- 3 tbsp half-fat soured cream
- small bunch of parsley, roughly chopped
- 250g pouch cooked wild rice

Method

STEP 1

Heat the olive oil in a large non-stick frying pan and soften the onion for about 5 mins.

STEP 2

Add the paprika and garlic, then cook for 1 min more. Add the mushrooms and cook on a high heat, stirring often, for about 5 mins.

STEP 3

Pour in the stock and Worcestershire sauce. Bring to the boil, bubble for 5 mins until the sauce thickens, then turn off the heat and stir through the soured cream and most of the parsley. Make sure the pan is not on the heat or the sauce may split.

STEP 4

Heat the wild rice following pack instructions, then stir through the remaining chopped parsley and serve with the stroganoff.

20-minute seafood pasta

Total time 20 mins Ready in 20 mins

Serves 4

Ingredients

- 1 tbsp olive oil
- 1 onion, chopped
- 1 garlic clove, chopped
- 1 tsp paprika

- 400g can chopped tomatoes
- 1l chicken stock (from a cube is fine)
- 300g spaghetti, roughly broken
- 240g frozen seafood mix, defrosted
- handful of parsley leaves, chopped, and lemon wedges, to serve

Method

STEP 1

Heat the oil in a wok or large frying pan, then cook the onion and garlic over a medium heat for 5 mins until soft. Add the paprika, tomatoes and stock, then bring to the boil.

STEP 2

Turn down the heat to a simmer, stir in the pasta and cook for 7 mins, stirring occasionally to stop the pasta from sticking. Stir in the seafood, cook for 3 mins more until it's all heated through and the pasta is cooked, then season to taste. Sprinkle with the parsley and serve with lemon wedges.

Low-fat cherry cheesecake

Prep: 1 hr **Cook:** 30 mins Plus overnight chilling

Cuts into 8 slices

Ingredients

- 25g butter , melted
- 140g amaretti biscuit , crushed
- 3 sheets leaf gelatine
- zest and juice 1 orange
- 2 x 250g tubs quark
- 250g tub ricotta
- 2 tsp vanilla extract
- 100g icing sugar

For the topping

- 400g fresh cherry , stoned
- 5 tbsp cherry jam
- 1 tbsp cornflour

Method

STEP 1

Line the sides of a 20cm round loose-bottomed cake tin with baking parchment. Stir the butter into twothirds of the biscuit crumbs, and reserve the rest. Sprinkle the buttery crumbs over the base of the tin and press down. Soak the gelatine in cold water for 5-10 mins until soft.

STEP 2

Warm the orange juice in a small pan or the microwave until almost boiling. Squeeze the gelatine of excess water, then stir into the juice to dissolve.

STEP 3

Beat the quark, ricotta, vanilla and icing sugar together with an electric whisk until really smooth. Then, with the beaters still running, pour in the juice mixture and beat to combine. Pour the cheesecake mixture over the crumbs and smooth the top. Cover with cling film and chill overnight.

STEP 4

To make the topping, put the cherries in a pan with the orange zest and 100ml water. Cook, covered, for 15 mins until the cherries are softened. Put one-third of the cherries in a bowl and mash with a potato masher to give you a chunky compote. Return to the pan, add the jam, cornflour and 2 tbsp water, and mix to combine. Cook until thickened and saucy – if the sauce is too dry, add a splash more water. Cool to room temperature.

STEP 5

Just before serving, carefully remove the cheesecake from the tin and peel off the parchment. Scatter over the remaining biscuit crumbs and some cherry sauce. Serve in slices with the remaining cherry sauce alongside.

Chilli prawn linguine

Prep: 5 mins **Cook:** 20 mins - 25 mins

Serves 6

Ingredients

- 280g linguine pasta
- 200g sugar snap peas, trimmed
- 2 tbsp olive oil
- 2 large garlic cloves, finely chopped
- 1 large red chilli, deseeded and finely chopped

- 24 raw king prawns, peeled
- 12 cherry tomatoes, halved
- a handful of fresh basil leaves
- mixed salad leaves and crusty white bread, to serve
- For the lime dressing
- 2 tbsp virtually fat-free fromage frais
- grated zest and juice of 2 limes
- 2 tsp golden caster sugar

Method

STEP 1

To make the dressing, mix 2 tbsp virtually fat-free fromage frais, the grated zest and juice of 2 limes and 2 tsp golden caster sugar in a small bowl and season with salt and pepper. Set aside.

STEP 2

Cook 280g linguine pasta according to the packet instructions. Add 200g trimmed sugar snap peas for the last minute or so of cooking time.

STEP 3

Meanwhile, heat 2 tbsp olive oil in a wok or big frying pan, toss in 2 finely chopped large garlic cloves and 1 deseeded and finely chopped large red chilli and cook over a fairly gentle heat for about 30 seconds without letting the garlic brown.

STEP 4

Tip in 24 peeled raw king prawns and cook over a high heat, stirring frequently, for about 3 minutes until they turn pink.

STEP 5

Add 12 halved cherry tomatoes and cook, stirring occasionally, for 3 minutes until they just start to soften.

STEP 6

Drain the linguine pasta and sugar snap peas well, then toss into the prawn mixture.

STEP 7

Tear in a handful of basil leaves, stir, and season with salt and pepper.

STEP 8

Serve with mixed salad leaves drizzled with the lime dressing, and warm crusty white bread.

Spinach, sweet potato & lentil dhal

Prep: 10 mins **Cook:** 35 mins

Serves 4

Ingredients

- 1 tbsp sesame oil
- 1 red onion, finely chopped
- 1 garlic clove, crushed
- thumb-sized piece ginger, peeled and finely chopped
- 1 red chilli, finely chopped
- 1 ½ tsp ground turmeric
- 1 ½ tsp ground cumin
- 2 sweet potatoes (about 400g/14oz), cut into even chunks
- 250g red split lentils
- 600ml vegetable stock
- 80g bag of spinach
- 4 spring onions, sliced on the diagonal, to serve
- ½ small pack of Thai basil, leaves torn, to serve

Method

STEP 1

Heat 1 tbsp sesame oil in a wide-based pan with a tight-fitting lid.

STEP 2

Add 1 finely chopped red onion and cook over a low heat for 10 mins, stirring occasionally, until softened.

STEP 3

Add 1 crushed garlic clove, a finely chopped thumb-sized piece of ginger and 1 finely chopped red chilli, cook for 1 min, then add 1 ½ tsp ground turmeric and 1 ½ tsp ground cumin and cook for 1 min more.

STEP 4

Turn up the heat to medium, add 2 sweet potatoes, cut into even chunks, and stir everything together so the potato is coated in the spice mixture.

STEP 5

Tip in 250g red split lentils, 600ml vegetable stock and some seasoning.

STEP 6

Bring the liquid to the boil, then reduce the heat, cover and cook for 20 mins until the lentils are tender and the potato is just holding its shape.

STEP 7

Taste and adjust the seasoning, then gently stir in the 80g spinach. Once wilted, top with the 4 diagonally sliced spring onions and ½ small pack torn basil leaves to serve.

STEP 8

Alternatively, allow to cool completely, then divide between airtight containers and store in the fridge for a healthy lunchbox.

West Indian spiced aubergine curry

Prep: 30 mins **Cook:** 15 mins

Serves 2

Ingredients

- 1 tsp ground cumin
- 1 tsp ground coriander
- ½ tsp ground turmeric
- 1 large aubergine
- 2 tbsp tomato purée
- ½ green chilli, finely chopped
- 1cm piece ginger, peeled and finely chopped
- 2 tsp caster sugar
- ½-1 tbsp rapeseed oil
- 3 spring onions, chopped
- ½ bunch of coriander, shredded
- cooked rice, natural yogurt, roti and lime wedges, to serve

Method

STEP 1

Mix the dry spices and 1 tsp salt together in a bowl and set aside.

STEP 2

Slice the aubergine into 1cm rounds, then score both sides of each round with the tip of a sharp knife. Rub with the spice mix until well coated (you should use all of the mix), then transfer to a board. Put 150ml water in the empty spice bowl with the tomato purée, chilli, ginger and sugar. Set aside.

STEP 3

Heat the oil in a large non-stick frying pan over a medium heat and arrange the aubergine in the pan, overlapping the rounds if needed. Fry for 5 mins on each side, or until golden. Add the liquid mix from the bowl, bring to a simmer, cover and cook for 15-20 mins, turning the aubergine occasionally until it's cooked through. If it seems dry, you may need to add up to 100ml more water to make it saucier. Season.

STEP 4

Scatter over the spring onions and coriander, and serve with rice, yogurt, roti and lime wedges for squeezing over.

Rice pudding

Prep: 5 mins **Cook:** 2 hrs

Serves 4

Ingredients

- 100g pudding rice
- butter, for the dish
- 50g sugar
- 700ml semi-skimmed milk
- pinch of grated nutmeg or strip lemon zest
- 1 bay leaf, or strip lemon zest

Method

STEP 1

Heat the oven to 150C/130C fan/gas 2. Wash and drain the rice. Butter a 850ml baking dish, then tip in the rice and sugar and stir through the milk. Sprinkle in the nutmeg and top with the bay leaf or lemon zest.

STEP 2

Cook for 2 hrs or until the pudding wobbles ever so slightly when shaken.

Burnt aubergine veggie chilli

Prep: 25 mins **Cook:** 2 hrs

Serves 4

Ingredients

- 1 aubergine
- 1 tbsp olive oil or rapeseed oil
- 1 red onion, diced
- 2 carrots, finely diced
- 70g puy lentils or green lentils, rinsed
- 30g red lentils, rinsed
- 400g can kidney beans
- 3 tbsp dark soy sauce
- 400g can chopped tomatoes
- 20g dark chocolate, finely chopped
- ¼ tsp chilli powder
- 2 tsp dried oregano
- 2 tsp ground cumin
- 2 tsp sweet smoked paprika
- 1 tsp coriander
- 1 tsp cinnamon
- 800ml vegetable stock
- ½ lime, juiced

To serve

- brown rice
- tortilla chips, mashed avocado, yogurt or soured cream, grated cheddar, roughly chopped coriander (optional)

Method

STEP 1

If you have a gas hob, put the aubergine directly onto a lit ring to char completely, turning occasionally with kitchen tongs, until burnt all over. Alternatively, use a barbecue or heat the grill to its highest setting and cook, turning occasionally, until completely blackened (the grill won't give you the same smoky flavour). Set aside to cool on a plate, then peel off the charred skin and remove the stem. Roughly chop the flesh and set aside.

STEP 2

In a large pan, heat the oil, add the onion and carrots with a pinch of salt, and fry over a low-medium heat for 15-20 mins until the carrots have softened.

STEP 3

Add the aubergine, both types of lentils, the kidney beans with the liquid from the can, soy sauce, tomatoes, chocolate, chilli powder, oregano and the spices. Stir to combine, then pour in the stock. Bring to the boil, then turn down the heat to very low. Cover with a lid and cook for 1 1/2 hrs, checking and stirring every 15-20 mins to prevent it from burning.

STEP 4

Remove the lid and let the mixture simmer over a low-medium heat, stirring occasionally, for about 15 mins until you get a thick sauce. Stir in the lime juice and taste for seasoning – add more salt if needed. Serve hot over rice with whichever accompaniments you want!

Spiced lentil & butternut squash soup

Prep: 10 mins **Cook:** 40 mins

Serves 4-6

Ingredients

- 2 tbsp olive oil
- 2 onions, finely chopped
- 2 garlic cloves, crushed
- ¼ tsp hot chilli powder
- 1 tbsp ras el hanout
- 1 butternut squash, peeled and cut into 2cm pieces
- 100g red lentils
- 1l hot vegetable stock
- 1 small bunch coriander, leaves chopped, plus extra to serve
- dukkah (see tip) and natural yogurt, to serve

Method

STEP 1

Heat the oil in a large flameproof casserole dish or saucepan over a medium-high heat. Fry the onions with a pinch of salt for 7 mins, or until softened and just caramelised. Add the garlic, chilli and ras el hanout, and cook for 1 min more.

STEP 2

Stir in the squash and lentils. Pour over the stock and season to taste. Bring to the boil, then reduce the heat to a simmer and cook, covered, for 25 mins or until the squash is soft. Blitz the soup with a stick blender until smooth, then season to taste. To freeze, leave to cool completely and transfer to large freezerproof bags.

STEP 3

Stir in the coriander leaves and ladle the soup into bowls. Serve topped with the dukkah, yogurt and extra coriander leaves.

Lentil soup

Prep: 10 mins **Cook:** 1 hr

Serves 4

Ingredients

- 2l vegetable or ham stock
- 150g red lentils
- 6 carrots, finely chopped
- 2 medium leeks, sliced (about 300g)
- small handful of chopped parsley, to serve

Method

STEP 1

Heat the stock in a large pan and add the lentils. Bring to the boil and allow the lentils to soften for a few minutes.

STEP 2

Add the carrots and leeks and season (don't add salt if you use ham stock as it will make it too salty). Bring to the boil, then reduce the heat, cover and simmer for 45-60 mins until the lentils have broken down. Scatter over the parsley and serve with buttered bread, if you like.

Tandoori chicken

Prep: 30 mins **Cook:** 15 mins

Serves 8

Ingredients

- juice 2 lemons
- 4 tsp paprika
- 2 red onions, finely chopped
- 16 skinless chicken thighs
- vegetable oil, for brushing
- For the marinade
- 300ml Greek yogurt
- large piece ginger, grated
- 4 garlic cloves, crushed
- ¾ tsp garam masala
- ¾ tsp ground cumin
- ½ tsp chilli powder
- ¼ tsp turmeric

Method

STEP 1

Mix the lemon juice with the paprika and red onions in a large shallow dish. Slash each chicken thigh three times, then turn them in the juice and set aside for 10 mins.

STEP 2

Mix all of the marinade ingredients together and pour over the chicken. Give everything a good mix, then cover and chill for at least 1 hr. This can be done up to a day in advance.

STEP 3

Heat the grill. Lift the chicken pieces onto a rack over a baking tray. Brush over a little oil and grill for 8 mins on each side or until lightly charred and completely cooked through.

Mexican penne with avocado

Prep: 10 mins **Cook:** 20 mins

Serves 2

Ingredients

- 100g wholemeal penne
- 1 tsp rapeseed oil
- 1 large onion, sliced, plus 1 tbsp finely chopped
- 1 orange pepper, deseeded and cut into chunks
- 2 garlic cloves, grated
- 2 tsp mild chilli powder
- 1 tsp ground coriander
- ½ tsp cumin seeds
- 400g can chopped tomatoes
- 196g can sweetcorn in water
- 1 tsp vegetable bouillon powder

- 1 avocado, stoned and chopped
- 1/2 lime, zest and juice
- handful coriander, chopped, plus extra to serve

Method

STEP 1

Cook the pasta in salted water for 10-12 mins until al dente. Meanwhile, heat the oil in a medium pan. Add the sliced onion and pepper and fry, stirring frequently for 10 mins until golden. Stir in the garlic and spices, then tip in the tomatoes, half a can of water, the corn and bouillon. Cover and simmer for 15 mins.

STEP 2

Meanwhile, toss the avocado with the lime juice and zest, and the finely chopped onion.

STEP 3

Drain the penne and toss into the sauce with the coriander. Spoon the pasta into bowls, top with the avocado and scatter over the coriander leaves.

Double bean & roasted pepper chilli

Prep: 30 mins **Cook:** 1 hr and 15 mins

Serves 8

Ingredients

- 2 onions, chopped
- 2 celery sticks, finely chopped
- 2 yellow or orange peppers, finely chopped
- 2 tbsp sunflower oil or rapeseed oil
- 2 x 460g jars roasted red peppers
- 2 tsp chipotle paste
- 2 tbsp red wine vinegar
- 1 tbsp cocoa powder
- 1 tbsp dried oregano
- 1 tbsp sweet smoked paprika
- 2 tbsp ground cumin
- 1 tsp ground cinnamon
- 2 x 400g cans chopped tomatoes
- 400g can refried beans
- 3 x 400g cans kidney beans, drained and rinsed
- 2 x 400g cans black beans, drained and rinsed

Method

STEP 1

Put the onions, celery and chopped peppers with the oil in your largest flameproof casserole dish or heavy-based saucepan, and fry gently over a low heat until soft but not coloured.

STEP 2

Drain both jars of peppers over a bowl to catch the juices. Put a quarter of the peppers into a food processor with the chipotle paste, vinegar, cocoa, dried spices and herbs. Whizz to a purée, then stir into the softened veg and cook for a few mins.

STEP 3

Add the tomatoes and refried beans with 1 can water and the reserved pepper juice. Simmer for 1 hr until thickened, smoky and the tomato chunks have broken down to a smoother sauce.

STEP 4

At this stage you can cool and chill the sauce if making ahead. Otherwise add the kidney and black beans, and the remaining roasted peppers, cut into bite-sized pieces, then reheat. (This makes a large batch, so once the sauce is ready it might be easier to split it between two pans when you add the beans and peppers.) Once bubbling and the beans are hot, season to taste and serve.

Slow-cooker chicken curry

Prep: 10 mins **Cook:** 6 hrs Plus overnight chilling

Serves 2

Ingredients

- 1 large onion, roughly chopped
- 3 tbsp mild curry paste
- 400g can chopped tomatoes
- 2 tsp vegetable bouillon powder
- 1 tbsp finely chopped ginger
- 1 yellow pepper, deseeded and chopped
- 2 skinless chicken legs, fat removed
- 30g pack fresh coriander, leaves chopped
- cooked brown rice, to serve

Method

STEP 1

Put 1 roughly chopped large onion, 3 tbsp mild curry paste, a 400g can chopped tomatoes, 2 tsp vegetable bouillon powder, 1 tbsp finely chopped ginger and 1 chopped yellow pepper into the slow cooker pot with a third of a can of water and stir well.

STEP 2

Add 2 skinless chicken legs, fat removed, and push them under all the other ingredients so that they are completely submerged. Cover with the lid and chill in the fridge overnight.

STEP 3

The next day, cook on Low for 6 hrs until the chicken and vegetables are really tender.

STEP 4

Stir in the the chopped leaves of 30g coriander just before serving over brown rice.

Vegetarian bolognese

Prep: 10 mins **Cook:** 1 hr

Serves 4

Ingredients

- 2 tbsp olive oil
- 1 medium onion, finely chopped
- 2 carrots, very finely chopped
- 2 celery sticks, very finely chopped
- 1 garlic clove, crushed
- 350g frozen Quorn mince
- 1 bay leaf
- 500ml passata
- 1 good-quality vegetable stock cube
- 100ml milk
- small bunch basil, chopped
- 600g cooked spaghetti or other pasta shape (about 250g dried)
- vegetarian hard cheese, to serve
- Method

STEP 1

Heat the oil in a saucepan and gently fry the onion, carrots and celery until the onion is starting to soften. Stir in the garlic and the Quorn (there's no need to defrost it) and fry for a couple of mins. Add the bay leaf, passata, vegetable stock cube and 200ml water, then bring everything to the boil.

STEP 2

Turn down the heat and simmer for 30 mins or until all the pieces of veg are tender and disappearing into the tomato sauce. Add the milk, then cover with a lid and cook for 10 mins. Season to taste. If the sauce is a bit thin, keep bubbling until it thickens. Stir through the basil. Serve with the spaghetti and grate the cheese over the top, if you like. Can be frozen into portions and reheated.

Quinoa chilli with avocado & coriander

Prep: 10 mins **Cook:** 45 mins

Serves 2

Ingredients

- 1 tbsp rapeseed oil
- 1 large onion , sliced
- 2 large garlic cloves , chopped
- 1 green pepper , chopped
- ½-1 tsp smoked paprika
- ½-1 tsp chilli powder
- 2 tsp cumin
- 2 tsp coriander
- 400g can chopped tomatoes
- ½ tsp dried oregano
- 2 tsp vegetable bouillon powder (check the label if you're vegan)
- 80g quinoa , rinsed under cold water
- 400g can black beans , drained and rinsed
- generous handful of coriander , chopped
- 2 tbsp bio yogurt or coconut yogurt (optional)
- 1 small avocado , stoned, peeled and sliced

Method

STEP 1

Heat the oil in a non-stick frying pan and fry the onion and garlic for 8 mins. Add the pepper and spices to taste and fry for 1 min more.

STEP 2

Tip in the tomatoes and a can of water, stir in the oregano, bouillon and quinoa, bring to the boil, then cover and simmer for 20 mins.

STEP 3

Stir in the black beans and cook, uncovered, for 5 mins more. Add most of the coriander, then serve topped with the yogurt (if using), the remaining coriander and the avocado slices

Printed in Great Britain
by Amazon